Fourth Edition

WRITING

RESEARCH PAPERS

A NORTON GUIDE

MELISSA WALKER Emory University

W · W · NORTON & COMPANY · NEW YORK · LONDON

The text of this book is composed in Meridien.
Composition by ComCom, a division of Haddon Craftsmen, Inc.
Manufacturing by R.R. Donnelley & Sons Company.
Cover design by Trudi Gershenov.

Library of Congress Cataloging-in-Publication Data

Walker, Melissa.
Writing research papers : a Norton guide / Melissa Walker.—4th ed.
p.   cm.
Includes bibliographical references and index.
ISBN 0-393-97108-2 (spiral pbk.)
1. Report writing.   2. Research.   I. Title.
LB2369.W25   1996
808'.02—dc20   96-29447

W. W. Norton & Company, Inc., 500 Fifth Avenue, New York, N.Y. 10110
http://www.wwnorton.com

W. W. Norton & Company Ltd., 10 Coptic Street, London WC1A 1PU

3 4 5 6 7 8 9 0

CONTENTS

PREFACE TO THE FOURTH EDITION

Writing Research Papers: A Norton Guide provides all the necessary guidance and information students need to produce satisfactory college research papers. It gives instruction in basic research skills: narrowing a topic, using library sources, recording information, and organizing material. It offers guidance in the process of writing and documenting a research paper: writing rough drafts, revising, preparing a bibliography, integrating sources, and producing a final copy. But it goes beyond teaching students how to write research papers; it attempts to teach students the spirit and value of independent learning, and to help them appreciate that learning to do independent research is an exciting part of their college experience. To further these aims, I have made several changes in preparing the Fourth Edition.

Emphasis on the Process of Research

In addition to explaining the research process in detail, *Writing Research Papers: A Norton Guide* takes readers on a guided tour of entire research projects, following five students as they develop interests, focus ideas, search sources, take notes, and draft, revise, edit, and design final papers. New to the Fourth Edition is Cherwanda Williams, a psychology major at Emory University, who investigates the possible relationship between depression and eating disorders. Cherwanda uses print and electronic sources in her search, including electronic databases, e-mail, and the World Wide Web. Her final paper is included in chapter 13, "Writing Research Papers in the Social Sciences Using APA Style," and reflects the latest APA documentation guidelines.

New Coverage of the Internet and Other Electronic Sources

The Fourth Edition provides all the information students need to do traditional research and offers comprehensive guidance for using the latest electronic research tools. In addition to updated information about online and CD-ROM databases, computer-generated indexes, and online catalogs, I include common-sense advice on using the Internet as a research tool. Although many students regularly use e-mail, browse the Web, and participate in mailing lists, few have used Internet sources for serious research. Chapter 5, "Using the Internet and Searching Beyond the Library," has been expanded to include both advice on contacting and interviewing people and help with searching the various features of the Internet—e-mail, mailing lists and newsgroups, gopher sites, and the World Wide Web—as well as evaluating critically the material found there. Throughout the text, students follow Cherwanda Williams, author of the new paper in chapter 13, as she uses the World Wide Web and e-mail in her research; her final paper includes citations of these electronic sources.

Expanded Coverage on Writing with Computers

While retaining the extensive material on how to take notes, organize material, and draft a paper by hand, the Fourth Edition assumes that students will at the very least prepare final papers on word processors. I have expanded coverage of using computers for prewriting, notetaking, drafting, and designing and presenting final papers.

Up-to-date Coverage of Documentation Styles

The advice and sample citations in chapter 10 and the corresponding student papers in chapters 8, 11, and 12 have been updated to reflect the *MLA Handbook for Writers of Research Papers* (1995). Similarly, the advice and sample citations in chapter 13, and the bibliography to Cherwanda Williams's paper on depression and eating disorders, correspond to the documentation guidelines set forth in the *Publication Manual of the American Psychological Association* (1994). Both MLA and APA now offer guidelines for citing electronic sources, and in this edition I have provided sample citations for documenting e-mail correspondence, Listserv discussion, the World Wide Web, online databases, and other electronic sources.

Finally, chapter 14 provides guidance and sample citations for documenting papers according to *Scientific Style and Format: The CBE Manual for Authors, Editors, and Publishers* (1994).

Quick-Reference Features

Writing Research Papers: A Norton Guide contains several features designed to make it a more useful reference tool:

- Checklists provide clear summaries of important information, ranging from using computers as research and writing tools to evaluating sources.
- Shaded pages in the MLA and APA chapters make examples easier to spot.
- Student projects—examples of the research process in action—are set off in boxes within chapters.
- Appendix B, "An Annotated List of Selected Reference Works," provides a comprehensive overview of print and electronic research tools.

Acknowledgments

To my colleagues, friends, and students who have shared their ideas and helped me see more clearly, I am grateful. For his help with the revision of chapter 13, I thank Professor Stephen Nowicki at Emory University. Much credit goes to the students in his psychology class who allowed me to follow their research projects in order to better understand their experiences. One of those students, Cherwanda Williams, made an invaluable contribution to this edition by writing the paper on depression and eating disorders. Not only did Cherwanda write an excellent paper on a topic of interest to most students, but she made a special effort to ensure that her paper illustrates everything students need to know to produce accurately documented and satisfactory papers in the social sciences.

I am deeply grateful to Alan Cattier of Emory University for teaching me how to use the Internet for serious research. His mastery of electronic sources and his skill as a teacher have helped me understand how students can search the Internet to find reliable information that would be difficult to find elsewhere.

I very much appreciate the work of the reference librarians at Emory University who have helped me through all editions of this book. For their contribution to the Fourth Edition I am especially indebted to Bill Anderson, David Vidor, and Elaine Wagner.

I am grateful to Joseph Gibaldi at the Modern Language Association for clarifying details about citing sources using the MLA style, Leslie Cameron of the American Psychological Association for helping ensure that the citations in chapter 13 conform to the latest revisions of the APA style, and to Edward Huth of the Council of Biology Editors for his guidance in writing the citations for the CBE style.

For thoughtfully reviewing the Third Edition in preparation for the Fourth, I thank Allen Bradshaw, Mesa Community College; Paul Resnick, Illinois Central College; Richard Sax, Madonna University; Kip Strasma, Illinois Central College; and Kristin Woolever, Northeastern University.

For her careful attention to details and excellent editing, I am especially grateful to Carol Hollar-Zwick of W. W. Norton. Others at Norton who have contributed in important ways to this book are Kate Lovelady, Marian Johnson, Diane O'Connor, Kristin Sheerin, Allen Clawson, and Kurt Wildermuth. For their valuable contributions to previous editions, I thank Sue Brekka, Jim Gibson, John Mardirosian, Libby Miles, and Lib Triplett. For his seminal role in the creation of this book, I will forever be grateful to the late Barry Wade.

UNDERSTANDING
WHAT RESEARCH IS

1

An Introduction to Research

You may think of research as something you do in laboratories and libraries, usually as a requirement for a college course. But think for a minute. When you or your parents or friends are in the market for a new car, what do you do? You probably read consumer guides, visit car dealers, and talk to other people about their cars. When you look for a job, you may study the want ads, check bulletin boards, and ask around among your friends. Choosing a college or academic major or graduate school, deciding on a career, settling on a place to live, buying a house—all these activities require research.

While the word *research* has come to mean a serious, systematic activity, one requiring hard work, dedication, and perseverance, it once referred to a man's effort to win a woman in love or marriage, rarely a systematic business. The common element, however, in a lover's suit and a scholarly inquiry is found in the first two letters of the word. The prefix *re-* has the general sense of "back" or "again" and suggests repetition. The struggle to obtain what is personally desirable, socially good, or intellectually true is usually a matter of searching again and again.

To try again and again to understand other people, the natural world, and social and political structures is a significant step toward living consciously and deliberately. Researching has probably already played an important part in determining what you think and what you do. The skill with which you conduct research in the future can have a significant impact on the quality of your life, influencing how you perceive the world and what choices you make.

Exploring

Before setting out to investigate a subject systematically, it is helpful to recall that you are a natural investigator. You have been conducting informal research all your life. As an infant you conducted research primarily through your hands and mouth, often grasping, dropping, and grasping the same object again and again, until one day you were able to hold it and make it your own. As a two-year-old you probably discovered the nature of a dog by feeling it; perhaps you learned an unforgettable lesson about canine behavior by examining its teeth or pulling its tail.

As soon as you could talk, you discovered that there are shortcuts to knowledge, and so you began to ask questions: Does that dog bite? Is the stove hot? What is that thing? You probably never stopped asking questions, although the nature of those questions may have changed: What is inflation? How does a camera work? What did Martin Luther King Jr. accomplish? What are genes?

By the time you enroll in college, your success as a student depends on how much responsibility you take for your own learning, particularly on how you try to answer questions. Following through on questions can help develop habits that will make learning a part of your daily life, not just as a student, but in the years to come. Questions have a way of leading both to answers and to other questions, and the search for answers can help you keep alive—or recapture—the curiosity that comes so naturally to a child.

As an adult—particularly as a student and researcher—it is important that you learn to discriminate, to choose which questions seem the most important. It is not a good idea to look up every word you do not recognize in a difficult text, to ask professors to clarify every statement that you do not understand in a long lecture, or to go to the library for information on every subject about which you would like to know more. Rather, it is more productive to look up those definitions that you need to understand an author's main ideas, to ask a professor for clarification when independent study of the text still leaves you baffled, and to select topics of particular interest to explore in the library.

The issue is not *whether* you will need to conduct research, but *how well* you want to do it. The success you will have in finding information is dependent on both your attitude and your skills.

The first step in good research is gathering the available facts. Whether you are trying to discover the best way to go from one place to another on public transportation or a politician's stand on particular issues, you want to begin with the facts. If you consult a published bus schedule or a campaign brochure, you may only have just begun. To verify the reliability of the bus schedule and the campaign brochure, you may need to talk with people who actually ride a particular bus route in the first case and to consult a senator's voting record in the second. Does the bus actually run on time? Are the candidate's campaign promises reflected in his or her voting record?

Getting at the truth of what has actually happened is perhaps one of the most challenging of human efforts, and often the more we know about a subject the more we are aware of the difficulty of achieving absolute knowledge. Consider the physician who is asked to bring relief to a patient suffering from the most common of human ailments: a headache. To really help, the doctor must consider the possible causes of pain: Is there stress in the patient's life or some chemical imbalance in the patient's body? Has the patient had too much to drink or eaten food containing monosodium glutamate or other substances that cause headaches? There is no way to be certain what has happened in the body to cause pain, but a careful physician will consider the evidence for each of the possibilities and make a judgment about the best treatment and the best way to prevent future headaches. In daily life, people frequently have to gather evidence, reach conclusions, and take action without having reached absolute certainty; but conclusions are more likely to be valid if they are based on evidence that has been carefully collected.

Once the evidence has been gathered, the researcher must learn to understand and evaluate it. The first step in this process is learning when to trust and when to doubt the validity of sources. A book on the wonders of marine life by a skin-diving instructor probably does not contain the most reliable information about sharks; a study of cholesterol funded by the egg industry would not have the same authority as one conducted by objective researchers. A general biologist who personally opposes the development of procedures for creating test tube babies may overemphasize the dangers, while another who has a grant to do genetic research may understate the risks of such procedures.

But the unreliability of sources, or at least the fact that they present material from a particular perspective alone, is not always obvious, and you may sometimes need to investigate the author to make that judgment. Learning to identify a person's special interests and prejudices can help you determine if that person is likely to slant a presentation of facts to lead to a particular interpretation. Of course you will not always be able to judge the authority of a text or a person's oral statements, but you can ask yourself what assumptions are behind what you read or hear. It is a good idea to suspend judgment and to get a balanced view of any subject before you reach conclusions, before you take a stand on controversial ethical issues,

CHECKLIST 1

Evaluating Sources

Before deciding to use any source, consider the following questions:

1. Is the source up-to-date?
2. What are the author's credentials?
3. In the case of a journal or newspaper, is it known to be slanted to support a particular point of view?
4. Does the author have a special interest in the topic that might affect the reliability of the source?
5. Is the source adequately documented so that readers can determine what authorities the author uses as supporting evidence?
6. In the case of controversial subjects, does the source give a balanced view, acknowledging both sides of the argument?
7. Is the language vague or nonspecific? Is it discriminatory? Are percentages misleading?
8. Is the book published by a respected publishing house?
9. How was the book reviewed?
10. Is the author of a Web page or other Internet source reliable? When was a source first posted and last edited? Is it up-to-date?

(See pp. 78–82 for more information.)

assume a political position, adopt a theory of human personality, or accept a set of standards for judging a work of art or literature.

There may be issues in these areas about which you keep an open mind all of your life and about which you never feel that you have reached final conclusions. There will be many times, however, both in school and in everyday life, when you will ask questions that have definite answers, when it will be reasonably clear what processes are at work and what events produce certain results. You will be able to study and determine how the heart functions to pump blood through the body, how the sun is used to heat water, what diseases have been linked to cigarette smoking, how a computer stores information, and how certain tax laws favor the rich.

As a student researcher, you will mainly be concerned with discovering for yourself what other people have already studied more exhaustively than you will be able to do, and one of your tasks will be to distinguish between what is known and what is still open to further research. At times you may want to conduct original research to test the conclusions of others (as in interviews, polls, and surveys), and occasionally you may wish to design an original research project (such as correlating the eating and exercise habits of a group of students with their academic achievements). Though most of the time you will be researching what is known, your research report will still be original: You will be the one to make sense of the facts and to arrive at your own conclusions.

Reporting

When you do research, you ask questions and look for answers; you find some answers and identify questions that you cannot answer; and usually, even when you are doing informal research, you make some kind of record of what you find. You record an address, write down a memorable quotation, jot down figures, or take notes from what you read. When you conduct a systematic and sustained research project, you may not be sure of what you have learned until you organize and try to make sense of what you have found. Writing a formal research paper is a way of making connections and reaching conclusions. By outlining your findings, writing a first draft, revising, documenting your sources, and producing a polished final paper, not only will you try to make sense of your research, but you will also try to communicate what you have found as clearly as possible to others.

The requirements for writing research papers depend on the purpose of a given assignment. The kind of topic (assigned or selected), the time allotted for researching it, the number and kinds of sources consulted, the methods used to record information—these may vary from one research project to another. The purpose of a particular assignment will dictate the organization, the length, and the style of documentation of a final paper.

In all cases, however, you want to report your research in a paper that is organized, clear, readable, and interesting. The real value of a research report depends on what you as a researcher have discovered and how well you tell others about it. The outline, title, list of sources, and notes are details that can help you record and communicate the conclusions of your research so that how you arrived at those conclusions will be perfectly clear to your reader. A good research paper will reflect your best effort to make what you have discovered understandable to others.

An Introduction to Resources

An unusually large number of resources for satisfying your curiosity are available to you in college. You probably have more sources of information and more experiences than you have time to use. Even in a small college community there are more people with experiences different from yours than you will be able to talk to, and there are more books even in a small college library than you can read in a lifetime. Learning to find and tap the resources around you is an important skill both in formal education and in everyday life.

The research resource that most people think of first is the library, and it is the place on a college campus where you will find the largest concentration of sources. But there may be other academic resources for you to explore, such as the bookstore, the computer center, or a museum. Beyond every college is a town or city with public establishments, businesses, and even shops and restaurants that may serve as resources for learning. Finally, the people you already know—family members, classmates, teachers, friends, and acquaintances—as well as those you can arrange to meet—other professors, experts from the community, specialists in one field or another—will prove to be living sources of information and opinion.

The Library

A college library is an inexhaustible and ever-changing storehouse of information. New books, periodicals, databases, and other sources of information are constantly being added to the collection. An academic library benefits from the knowledge of many people on the college campus, since faculty members from all disciplines keep up with the latest books, magazines, journals, and other information sources so that they can select the best ones for the library.

Of course not all college libraries are the same; each reflects the institution it is part of—the courses in the curriculum and the interests of the faculty and students. A school of technology will certainly have much more information on technological and scientific subjects than will a general liberal arts college, while a university with a business school will provide a full range of books and periodicals on economics and the various aspects of business. Libraries use computers to catalog their collections, to provide access to databases, and to read indexes stored in mainframes or on compact discs. Many libraries have computer terminals for students to use for e-mail and to access the World Wide Web and other Internet sources.

Learning to use a library's computer-based information retrieval systems is a requirement for effective use of library sources.

You will discover the valuable resources of your own library only by spending time there, so take a few minutes to explore: find the periodicals, the reference books, the stacks, the circulation desk. You can easily find your favorite magazines, but if you look further you may discover many other journals and newspapers that you will enjoy reading. You can probably find books by your favorite authors that you have never read, as well as books containing information that is new to you on a subject you know well. Locate the computer terminals that you may use for finding articles in periodicals or books in the collection.

Other Academic Resources

While the main college library is the most obvious research resource on the college campus, there are many others. Some institutions have more than one library, and most have other resources for independent learning. To find them you might begin by asking the following questions: Is the library collection all in one place, or is it spread out in several locations? How many libraries are there? Is there a museum? an art gallery? Does your institution publish a newspaper? a magazine? an academic journal? Is there a computer center? a theater? a lecture series? Some of these questions can be answered by studying your catalog or by talking with other students. Others may require some investigation.

For example, what does your college bookstore have to offer? To answer this you may want to go there and spend some time. Browsing among the shelves and skimming texts can help you choose your courses more carefully and learn something about the many courses you will not be able to take; and, when you are trying to decide on a major, you will want to survey carefully the texts used in the discipline that interests you. Finally, when you choose a research topic, you may want to find out if your topic is being studied in a course on your campus; you may want to examine the assigned books and in some cases consult the course instructor.

The Internet

If you already have the skills needed to navigate the Internet, then you probably know that a lot of valuable information is available within this complex system of storing and delivering information—many thousands of databases and constantly changing World Wide Web sites that, literally, connect you to the world. Doing a search of Web sites on rain forests, for example, calls up pages from Australia, Malaysia, England, Japan, and

Brazil, among other places around the globe. The resources of the Internet are so vast and varied that you have to be very selective about the ones you use for academic research. For the most reliable information, look for Web sites put up by universities, reputable nonprofit organizations, or government institutions.

If you are not experienced in finding information on the Internet, a research project is an excellent opportunity to find out what's possible. Begin by discovering what is available on your campus. Are there computer terminals with Internet access in the library, a computer lab, or elsewhere? Are there Internet courses you can take? Where are they offered and when? Learn what's out there, and then decide whether you want to use it and, if so, how.

The Community

Your college is part of a larger community—whether a small town, a huge metropolis, or something in between. Often there is an exchange arrangement between the services of a college and those of the greater community. You may be able to use the public library, borrow materials from public organizations, or attend meetings or lectures at other institutions. Each community has its own individuality: its traditions, civic organizations, political climate, cultural and social identity, businesses, and public services. It is a good idea for you to know something about the greater community in which your college is located and to find out which of its institutions are available for your use. Again you will want to ask questions: Is there a theater? a museum? an art gallery? (In large cities, you will want to ask how many such places there are and whether there are specialized ones.) What cultural events are there? What is the ethnic makeup of the population? Are there many people from other countries? Are there consulates to serve them? What about public libraries, other academic institutions, social services, historical associations, religious organizations, institutes, and foundations? What is the economic base of the community—its trade, manufacturing, and management organizations? What kinds of shops and restaurants are there?

If there are commercial bookstores in your community, you may want to begin there. When you visit such a store, you will usually find books that reflect the interests of a town or a particular neighborhood. It is a good idea to learn how the books are classified before you begin to explore the shelves. If you plan to spend any time browsing in a bookstore, you will probably be able to discover for yourself how the books are organized. If not, people who work in bookstores usually will help, and they typically like to talk about the books they sell. Remember also to look for used-book stores and those that specialize in certain types of books, since these stores can often help you find hard-to-get or unusual materials for your research.

People

Learning what people have to teach us may be more difficult than learning the content of a book or the holdings of a library. People we meet do not provide us with a table of contents, an index, or a card catalog, nor can we punch a button to receive a printout of their interests. Rather, we have to ask questions: What kind of work do you do? What are your hobbies? Have you traveled very much? Where have you lived? Simply by chatting with your classmates, you may discover that some are citizens of other countries, some have intriguing hobbies, and others have special skills. Making such discoveries often requires that you listen carefully to what other people have to say and that you resist talking too much about yourself.

Research as a Vocation

Many professional researchers are busy answering questions that are not likely to affect the quality of life on earth:

1. Will Americans buy potato chips made with a fat substitute?
2. Will red covers sell more books at Christmas than blue ones?
3. Do people spend more money in hamburger restaurants with orange-and-yellow decorations than in those decorated with cool colors?
4. How many Americans will buy environmentally friendly products that cost more?
5. Do shoppers buy more in stores that smell like cookies baking?

Though these questions may seem trivial, they are important to people concerned with marketing strategies.

There are people in many fields whose full-time job is to address the stubborn questions that continue to plague human beings. By considering these questions, we get a sense of the huge challenges facing researchers and the extent to which research is necessary to the quality of life and even the survival of life on the planet. Consider the following challenges:

1. Confronting the AIDS epidemic
2. Searching for renewable energy sources
3. Building sustainable societies
4. Understanding the environmental consequences of fossil fuels
5. Comprehending the consequences of illiteracy
6. Deterring nuclear proliferation
7. Stopping deforestation
8. Controlling population growth
9. Preventing heart disease
10. Feeding the hungry

Each of these pressing concerns is engaging the energies of people around the globe, and the chances are that at some point your life will be affected very personally by the extent to which they succeed or fail in these areas.

LISA LEE

Lisa intends to major in biology and perhaps go to graduate school in environmental studies or forestry. Growing up in a rural area of northern California, Lisa had teachers and friends who were concerned about the misuse of forests in her own state. It was not until she came to college, however, that she learned that many people are concerned about the fate of forests all over the world. After attending a lecture on life in the rain forests of Central America, Lisa brainstorms on the subject of rain forests (p. 18), reads a book the lecturer recommended, Adrian Forsyth and Ken Miyata's *Tropical Nature*, and becomes fascinated by the amazing ways plants and animals have adapted to their environment. Lisa's research project may be the first step leading to her vocation.

Activities

A. Suppose a hospital is considering building a fitness and preventive medicine facility. What kinds of questions might marketing researchers ask to determine if such a center is feasible?

B. If you were planning to open a bookstore in a suburban shopping mall, what would you need to know about the people who live nearby?

C. Choose one of the ten challenges listed on p. 10 and make a list of questions that you think researchers are attempting to answer. For example, for decades people have explored the factors affecting heart disease and have in fact reached certain conclusions, but questions remain: Does the benefit of using alcohol to lower the risk of heart disease outweigh the possible ill effects? How high should a person's cholesterol be before cholesterol-lowering drugs are prescribed?

CHOOSING A TOPIC   2

Doing independent research is a valuable way to enrich your study of the courses you take in college. What you learn in class or from assigned textbooks will probably be more enjoyable and meaningful if you also explore aspects of the subject on your own. Once you learn research techniques, you will be able to go to the library or to appropriate experts to learn more about the topics in your courses that particularly interest you. Some courses include assignments specifically designed to teach you how to do research and to write a paper based on what you have found. The first step in that process is to find a topic—a specific aspect of a general subject—or to adapt an assigned topic to the resources available to you.

The choice of a research topic, like the choice of a friend, is not usually made after a systematic investigation; rather, it is the consequence of circumstances and actions involving both conscious effort and luck. The professional writer deciding on a subject for a new book, the graduate student choosing a thesis, and the college student selecting a topic for a limited research project all have the same general set of resources: where they live and where they have been; the people they know and those they have known; what books they have read and what they have done. The particular details of people's lives determine their existing interests as well as what new subjects they are able to learn about.

Five Important Activities

Whether your instructor assigns a topic or asks you to select your own, there is a process you need to go through to adapt a topic to your own interests and abilities. The early stages of any research project should include the following five activities:

1. Budgeting time
2. Following and developing interests
3. Letting ideas brew
4. Asking the right questions
5. Making a commitment

Budgeting Time

Throughout your project, you will need to budget your time. While this is not always easy, since you may not know how long particular activities will take, it is important that you plan from the beginning how to use the time you have. Begin by making lists. If you have four weeks set aside for a research project, then decide what you hope to accomplish each week. Your first decision will be to decide how many hours or days you can allot for choosing a topic. Remember that if you exceed your budget at one stage, you will have less time for other tasks; and you may need to revise your budget every few days. It is also a good idea to coordinate your research project with your other responsibilities. For example, do not schedule the final writing of your paper the day before you have a major test for another course.

Following Interests

Once you stop and think, you will probably find that there are many subjects you would like to explore. One way to begin to choose a subject for research is to recall what interests you already have, to think about what you already know, and to consider how to build on what you know.

In choosing a subject for research, you will want first to think about what you already know and what you have to build on. The next step is to consider those subjects that you think you want to learn about.

A carefully chosen research topic can contribute to your educational goals whether you are exploring possibilities for a course of study and a career or you know for certain what you plan to do with your life. Imagine that you are trying to decide between two majors: biology and psychology. Conducting research in one of these two areas might help you make that decision. If you are still considering a number of different possibilities among subjects you don't know much about, a research assignment is an opportunity to investigate a new discipline.

You may already know of several subjects that you have an interest in and would like to research. There may also be subjects suggested in your classes, by your instructor, or in this book about which you are curious enough to want to learn more. Before you commit yourself, it is wise to take time to consider the possibilities. You may want to make three lists:

1. A list of subjects that you already know something about—perhaps you have played the piano, read science fiction, or raced bicycles. Perhaps you are an expert on cars, movies, rock and roll, or computers. You may be able to use what you already know as a context for new knowledge—for example, a student who is interested in computers and in music would be prepared to study the development of electronic synthesizers.
2. A list of new subjects that you would like to explore—perhaps you would like to learn more about alcoholism, drug rehabilitation, or weight reduction programs; you are considering studying psychology and would like to know something about Sigmund Freud, B. F. Skinner, or Carol Gilligan; you would like to be more physically fit and to learn about speed walking, nutrition, and yoga.
3. A list of those items on the first two lists that are appropriate for your assignment.

Letting Ideas Brew

By now you probably have many ideas, and it will be good if you can take the time to think about each of them. Discuss your ideas—even seemingly trivial or fleeting ones—with as many people as possible: friends, family, faculty, or others who may know something about the subject that interests you. Other people—your teachers or the reference librarian—may discourage you from pursuing some ideas because of the difficulty of finding materials or simply because a subject is not compatible with the goals of a given class. Once you have arrived at a subject that is acceptable to your instructor, give yourself time to determine whether it is one you want to pursue for three weeks, a month, six weeks, or in some cases more. Live with your ideas for a while; let them brew.

LISA LEE

In preparation for choosing a research paper topic, Lisa's instructor asks the students to think of a large subject they already know something about and to break it into subheadings by making a branching diagram like the one below:

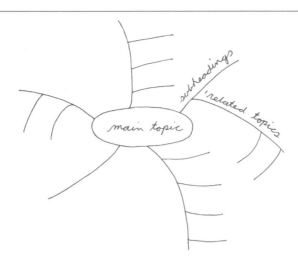

Since she has taken a course in ecology and is already interested in the environment, Lisa readily breaks down that large subject using a branching diagram:

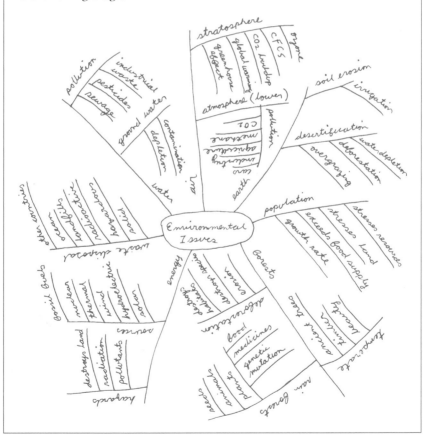

(Branching is the right-brain alternative to outlining. An outline is a list of points usually arranged under headings and subheadings, and it can show exactly the sequence of development that an essay will follow. [For more on this see pp. 146–55.] But unless you already know how your essay will develop its points, you can't very well list them in sequential order. What you can do, however, is put them on branches radiating from a single idea, and make the branches sprout more ideas. You can thus generate a picture of the ideas in your mind—a pattern of connections to look at.)

Asking Questions

Next you will want to explore possibilities by asking questions: You may ask your classmates, your instructors, or other people what they can tell you about the possibilities you are considering. You may want to look up several items on your list in encyclopedias or other general reference books. If you decide in advance how much time you can give to exploring possibilities, you will find it easier to draw the line at the appropriate point and say, "I must decide now."

Often the final decision about a topic can be made simply by jotting down questions to which you would like to know the answers. Each of the questions below could lead to interesting research:

1. What is there to know about the planet Jupiter and its moons?
2. How did the civil rights movement change life in Selma, Alabama?
3. What agricultural practices harm the environment? How can they be changed?
4. What can a potential employer or creditor find out about a person's financial or medical history?
5. What legal recourse do people have when they are sexually harassed by an employer?
6. How does the Canadian health care system work?
7. How do diet, exercise, and/or stress affect the risk of heart disease?
8. What is the incidence of mental disorders among the homeless?
9. How influential are right-wing militia groups in the United States?
10. How is capitalism changing life in Russia?

This technique is particularly helpful if you have identified a general subject area and broken it into a number of particular topics. The questions above, for example, result from breaking down general subject areas like space exploration, civil rights, or the environment. The best topic sometimes emerges when you study such questions and think about how they might be answered.

It will be easy to choose your topic if there is one thing in particular you want to know more about. Look at the list of questions you have made about possible topics and see if there is one that you would most like to be able to answer. When several questions interest you, ask yourself which is the most important, the most relevant to your studies, the most challenging, or the most suited to your resources.

LISA LEE

Once Lisa has decided that she wants to focus on some aspect of tropical rain forests, she further narrows her topic by making the following list of questions:

1. What kinds of rain forests are there?
2. Where are they located on the globe?
3. Who is destroying them?
4. Why are they being destroyed?
5. Will the trees grow back?
6. Can the cleared land be used for farms? for grazing?
7. What happens to such land after a few years?
8. What do the animals do when the trees they live in are destroyed?
9. How will the loss of animal life affect regrowth?
10. In what ways are animals and plants interdependent?

Lisa is not yet sure how she will focus her topic, but the list of questions reflects her growing interest in animal/plant interaction.

Making a Commitment

After you have selected a subject, done a little background reading, and talked to your instructor and others about it, you will probably be ready to make a commitment. Remember that you will live with a research topic for several weeks, and so you should stop and ask yourself if you have a sincere interest in the subject. If the answer is yes, then proceed with the conviction that you will not change your mind. You are now ready to begin your research by focusing on a limited, manageable topic.

Brainstorming

During the period when you are collecting ideas for research topics, keep a small notebook or note cards with you at all times so that when interesting topics come up in class or in conversation, you can write them down and later add them to your file of possibilities. A word processor can be very helpful for storing and ordering ideas.

LISA LEE

After attending the lecture about rain forests, Lisa comes back to her room, turns on her computer, and opens a brainstorming file. She has already narrowed her topic with a list of questions; now she brainstorms on the subject of rain forests before discussing possible topics with her English teacher. The following list is the result:

```
Forests endangered
Rapid deforestation in Costa Rica
Massive loss of forests in Brazil
Animals in peril from forest fires
Many species will be lost
Plants with possible medicinal value are lost every day
Why animals are important to health of the forest
Loss of one species threatens others
Animals and plants need each other
Forest dynamics
The fate of forests without birds and mammals
Pollinators and seed dispersers
```

Following Lisa's progress, you will see that the kernel of her research project is present in this original brainstorming list, even though she did not know it at the time.

Exploring a Broad Subject

Some research projects focus on the achievements of individual people. If you are going to study a prominent person, for example, you will want to consider some particular aspect of his or her life. While it is a good idea to inform yourself of the general outline of a person's life, your paper need not include a summary of his or her life. Anyone can find a summary of the lives of famous people in an encyclopedia or other reference work. A meaningful research project will combine material from different sources in an original way.

LINDA ORTON

Linda is enrolled in an English composition class in which she is asked to write a short research paper of approximately one thousand words, or four typed pages. The assignment is to explore a particular aspect of the work of a person on the following list:

Rachel Carson	Colin Powell
Angela Davis	Janet Reno
Bill Gates	Eleanor Roosevelt
Jane Goodall	Gloria Steinem
Charles Lindbergh	Oliver Stone
Senator Joseph McCarthy	Barbra Streisand
Ralph Nader	Ted Turner

Linda begins by checking the index to the *Encyclopedia Americana,* where she finds articles on most of the people on this list. She turns first to the article on Eleanor Roosevelt and identifies the following aspects of her life as possible topics for research:

1. Activities during World War I
2. Work in women's organizations in the 1920s
3. Career as an educator: The Todhunter School
4. Radio program
5. The furniture factory at Hyde Park
6. Syndicated newspaper column, "My Day"
7. War work: World War II
8. Role in the formation of the United Nations
9. The United Nations Declaration of Human Rights
10. Fighting for the underprivileged and racial minorities
11. Contribution to Adlai Stevenson's campaign

Each of these topics, suggested by a general encyclopedia article, is appropriate for student research. There are other aspects of Eleanor Roosevelt's life—her childhood, her struggles with her mother-in-law, and her personal suffering—that may be interesting but that Linda will not be able to research as thoroughly as her role in public life. It is, after all, people's accomplishments and their roles in society that are reported in newspapers; studied by scholars; witnessed by observers; and, finally, recorded and analyzed in periodicals, books, and films. The events of private lives are often obscure, rarely recorded accurately, and seldom accessible to researchers.

Once you start reading about an individual's life and accomplishments, you may, like Linda, find several possible topics, but of course you will soon have to focus on one such as those below:

1. Rachel Carson's influence on the banning of DDT
2. Angela Davis and the struggle for economic equality
3. Bill Gates and the future of computer technology
4. Jane Goodall's study of social rejection among chimpanzees
5. The politics of Charles Lindbergh
6. The anticommunist crusade of Senator Joseph McCarthy
7. Ralph Nader's work to improve auto safety
8. Colin Powell's role in the Persian Gulf War
9. Gloria Steinem and the National Women's Political Caucus
10. Oliver Stone's use or misuse of history
11. The political activism of Barbra Streisand
12. Ted Turner and the rise of cable television

Focusing a Subject

Once you have committed yourself to a subject, you will want to take some time to explore possible ways to focus your study: talking to people about it, doing some background reading, and thinking about what aspects of the subject most appeal to you. Again, decide on how much time you can afford to spend before you begin concentrated research.

It can be helpful to see how other students break down large subjects and finally focus on a particular topic. Consider the progress of two students who start with general subjects and arrive at manageable, limited topics.

MICHAEL GOLD

When Michael was growing up in New York, his father regularly took him to the movies on Saturday afternoons, and at a very early age, Michael became interested in old movies, especially those of the fifties and sixties. During their high school years, he and his sister frequently rented videos to watch on weekends. By the time he enrolls in college, Michael has watched hundreds of movies, some of them several times. Studying his college catalog, he is surprised to discover that academic courses are offered in film history, film appreciation, and film theory. When Michael is asked to choose a topic for a research project as part of his freshman English course, he immediately thinks that he would like to learn more about the history of film. Michael first goes to the library and consults the *Encyclopedia Americana*. He looks up "film" and "movies" and finally finds an article entitled "Motion Picture." (It would have been quicker to use the index, but Michael enjoys browsing in encyclopedias.) After reading the article, he concludes that one way to approach the subject is to break it down into different types of movies. Michael then visits his college bookstore and examines the textbooks that are used for film courses. Skimming through one book, David Cook's *History of Narrative Film*, he soon discovers that there is much more to learn about film than he had thought. At lunch one day, he talks with a student who is taking a film course. He asks her a few questions about the course and discovers that she is studying films that have influenced film making. By asking more specific questions, Michael learns the titles of important films he has never seen and of those that have attracted a cult following of fans who see them over and over again.

Based on what he already knew about movies and what he has learned from a little preliminary research, Michael begins to jot down ideas. The subject is so broad that he finds it helpful to divide it into rough categories. In a few minutes, he has produced this:

```
                    TYPES OF FILM
Comedy              Fantasy             Spy
Western             Gangster            History
Spectacle           Horror              Musical
Social realism      Thriller            War
Political propaganda Detective
```

```
                        TYPES BY NATIONALITY
    American        German        Swedish        Soviet
    French          Italian       Japanese


                           OTHER TYPES
    Feature films   Documentaries         Animated films
    Shorts          Blockbusters


                          LANDMARK FILMS
    The Great Train Robbery (1903) Citizen Kane (1941)
    The Birth of a Nation (1915)   Rebel Without a Cause (1956)
    The Battleship Potemkin (1925) 2001: A Space Odyssey (1968)
    The Jazz Singer (1927)


              TECHNIQUES AND SKILLS OF FILM MAKING
    Editing               Dubbing
    Processing            Special effects
    Adapting music        Scriptwriting
    Sound                 Adapting scripts from other media


                        OTHER APPROACHES
    Great actors          Equipment
    Great directors       Industry vs. art
    The star system       The economics of film production


                        FILM AND SOCIETY
    Censorship            Political propaganda
    Cult films            Social values on film
    Violence and film
```

Michael looks at the lists he has made, somewhat amazed at the possible approaches to a subject that he thought he knew something about. He considers researching a particular film genre, such as the Western or the musical, but after some background reading in Cook's *History of Narrative Film*, he realizes that the Western has really spanned almost the entire history of film and the musical began with the first talking movies. Not quite sure how to limit such broad subjects, Michael considers other possibilities. In doing so, he checks the topics that interest him and consolidates them in another list:

```
American films
Social realism
Social values
Great actors
Feature films
Cult films
Rebel Without a Cause
```

A little baffled about how to limit his topic, Michael puts his list aside and decides to come back to it later. The next day, he considers the list again and begins to see that all of the topics that he has checked are related. *Rebel Without a Cause* is a landmark American feature-length film; it is a film of social realism that is an indictment of certain social values. Its star, James Dean, is considered by some to be one of the most charismatic actors of the twentieth century, and, what is more, he became a cult figure. Michael takes a clean sheet of paper and writes the following questions:

```
How does a film like Rebel come to be made?
How can we account for its success?
What influence did it have?
Was James Dean's charisma responsible for its impact?
```

LISA LEE

Delighted when her English teacher approves her proposal to write a research paper on some aspect of life in tropical forests, Lisa heads for the library and checks out five general books on the subject. She spends several hours a day reading about topics that particularly interest her, developing a general understanding of tropical forests and of the complex economic and political forces that affect their future. She decides to focus on the scientific aspects of her subject. Using her word processor, she adds the following possible topics to the list she began earlier:

```
Chemical defenses in insects and frogs
Defense mechanisms in plants
Gap ecology
```

```
Life in the canopy
Medicinal use of plants
Nutrient cycling
Reproduction systems of tropical frogs
Seed dispersal
Soil nutrients
Treefalls
```

Lisa is also taking a course in botany, and so she makes an appointment with her biology teacher to discuss which of these topics seem most appropriate. Together they brainstorm, and it soon becomes clear that she is particularly interested in the ways that animals and plants interact. She first considers defense mechanisms, the ways that plants defend themselves from being eaten by insects and other creatures, a subject which is studied by scientists interested in the chemical composition of the poisons that plants produce.

More interesting to Lisa, however, is the way seeds are dispersed throughout the forest and what conditions make it possible for a seed to germinate and grow. Consulting her library books again, she learns that seeds of most tropical trees are in fact dispersed by animals. At last she arrives at a tentative title for her research paper: How Animals Disperse Seeds in a Tropical Forest. Lisa's topic will become much more focused and structured as she discovers what scientists already know about the topic and what they are attempting to find out.

Like Michael Gold, Lisa has identified a subject that really interests her. Like Michael, she has much to learn. Both will do research that leads to unexpected discoveries.

Adapting the Assigned Topic

College teachers frequently ask their students to research some aspect of a general subject. A psychology teacher, for example, may assign a term paper on some aspect of developmental psychology, an economics teacher on deficit spending, a physics teacher on applied technology, and an English teacher on twentieth-century fiction. Students who are assigned such general topics face the challenge of narrowing the broad subject area to a manageable topic.

CHERWANDA WILLIAMS

Cherwanda is taking a psychology course, and on the first day of class her professor assigns a research paper on some aspect of abnormal psychology. The paper is due on the last day of class, but the instructor encourages students to choose a topic right away so that they can spread out their research over the term. Not wanting to put herself under unnecessary pressure at the end of the term, Cherwanda takes the professor's advice and begins immediately to plan her paper—she knows from past experience that she does not do her best work at the last minute.

Cherwanda begins by browsing through the table of contents and the index of her textbook. Although she finds much that interests her, she is particularly drawn to the sections that discuss mood and eating disorders. Cherwanda suspects that her friend Sarah, who lives down the hall from her, is depressed. Sarah has trouble sleeping, feels sad much of the time, and says she can't concentrate. She is also obsessed with her weight. Although her friend claims to be dieting and wants to be thin, Cherwanda sees empty cookie boxes in the trash when she visits Sarah's room. She suspects that Sarah binge eats and then vomits to keep from gaining weight. As she reads about mood disorders, she becomes convinced that her friend is depressed. Could the depression be causing the obsession with her weight and with food? Cherwanda decides to do some research to find out if there is a connection between depression and eating disorders. This is the beginning of her research paper.

CARLA MEDINA

Carla is taking an English course in which she is required to write two research papers, each focusing on a controversial literary work. The first assignment is to combine research findings with her own analysis of a work. The second is to conduct extensive research on an actual controversy, to take a position about the source and significance of the controversy, and finally to write a paper using her research findings to support her position. The professor provides the class with the following list:

Baldwin, James, <u>Another Country</u> (1962)
Baudelaire, Charles, <u>The Flowers of Evil</u> (1857)
Beckett, Samuel, <u>Waiting for Godot</u> (1955)
Brontë, Emily, <u>Wuthering Heights</u> (1848)
Chopin, Kate, <u>The Awakening</u> (1899)
Clemens, Samuel (Mark Twain), <u>Adventures of Huckleberry Finn</u> (1885)
Coupland, Doug, <u>Generation X: Tales for an Accelerated Culture</u> (1991)
Eliot, T. S., <u>The Waste Land</u> (1922)
Flaubert, Gustave, <u>Madame Bovary</u> (1856)
Hemingway, Ernest, <u>The Sun Also Rises</u> (1926); <u>A Farewell to Arms</u> (1929)
Ginsberg, Allen, <u>Howl</u> (1956)
Golding, William, <u>Lord of the Flies</u> (1954)
Hall, Radclyffe, <u>The Well of Loneliness</u> (1928)
Hurston, Zora Neale, <u>Their Eyes Were Watching God</u> (1937)
Jackson, Shirley Anne, "The Lottery" (1948)
Joyce, James, <u>Dubliners</u> (1914)
Lawrence, D. H., <u>Lady Chatterley's Lover</u> (1928)
Nabokov, Vladimir, <u>Lolita</u> (1955)
Rushdie, Salman, <u>The Satanic Verses</u> (1988)
Salinger, J. D., <u>The Catcher in the Rye</u> (1951)
Stowe, Harriet Beecher, <u>Uncle Tom's Cabin</u> (1853)
Styron, William, <u>The Confessions of Nat Turner</u> (1967)
Walker, Alice, <u>The Color Purple</u> (1982)
Zola, Émile, <u>Nana</u> (1880)

Carla chooses to write her first paper on the work from this list that most interests her: Alice Walker's novel *The Color Purple*. Her second paper will be on Mark Twain's *Adventures of Huckleberry Finn*.

Activities

A. The items in the list below each include a general subject followed by a specific topic. Identify other topics related to each subject:
   1. "All-Time Best Sellers" → "Public Response to *Gone with the Wind* and *Scarlett"*

2. "Interpretations of Dreams" → "Dream Lore among the Xhosa People"
3. "African-American Religion" → "Malcolm X and the Rise of the Nation of Islam"
4. "Twentieth-Century Painting" → "Frieda Kahlo's Depiction of Women's Experience"
5. "American Literature of the 1920s" → "Fitzgerald's Use of Popular Culture in *The Great Gatsby*"
6. "Innovations in Business Technology" → "Uses of the Computer in Restaurants"
7. "Baseball Greats" → "Choosing a League's Most Valuable Player"
8. "History of Jazz" → "John Coltrane and the Be-bop Era"
9. "Neotropical Rain Forest Mammals" → "Feeding Habits of Howler Monkeys"
10. "Marketing Strategies" → "The Use of Color in Selling Food"
11. "Ethical Problems in Medicine" → "The Right of Physicians to Assist in Suicides"
12. "The AIDS Crisis" → "The Responsibility of the Federal Government for Funding AIDS Research"
13. "Environmental Policy" → "Keeping Forests a Renewable Resource"
14. "Wildlife Management" → "The Role of the Hunter in Wildlife Management"
15. "Photography as an Art" → "The Photographic Achievement of Mary Ellen Mark"
16. "Racism in America" → "The Internment of Japanese-Americans during World War II"
17. "The Struggle for a Sustainable World" → "Protecting the Ozone Layer"
18. "The Early Space Race" → "Sputnik: The Aftermath in American Education"
19. "Chinese Traditional Medicine" → "Acupuncture in the Operating Room"
20. "Hispanic-American Literature" → "Going Home: The Poetry of Gary Soto"

B. Study the list of reference works in appendix B. Then go to the library and find one of the specialized encyclopedias or dictionaries such as the *Encyclopedia of American History,* the *McGraw-Hill Encyclopedia of Science and Technology, Grzimek's Animal Life Encyclopedia,* or the *International Encyclopedia of Social Sciences.* Browse through it looking for material that interests you. Then make a list of general subject areas and another of specific topics that would be appropriate for student research.

C. Choose a general topic frequently treated in the media—drug abuse, endangered species, health insurance, tobacco companies—and search the World Wide Web for sites about different aspects of that topic. Look at the list of twenty topics above and search the Internet for sites that mention at least three of them.

D. For each of the following subjects, make a list of questions to which the answers are not readily available: space exploration, health risks of plastic surgery, venomous animals, the great apes, secret societies, assassinations of public figures, unsolved murders, the activities of the Central Intelligence Agency, crack use in small towns, and high-risk sports.

E. Make a list of questions you have about subjects that interest you, and search the World Wide Web for ideas about research you might do to answer these questions.

F. Select a book from your own collection—perhaps a textbook—or one from the library on a subject that interests you. Study the index, and make a list of the topics that would be appropriate for student research.

IDENTIFYING LIBRARY SOURCES

3

An academic library has many resources for informal learning as well as for formal research. A knowledge of the material and services available in your own college library is essential to your success as a student. When you can easily use your library, you will be able to supplement required reading, pass an hour of leisure browsing among books and periodicals, or pursue independent research. This chapter will introduce you to the main resources of an academic library, and it will indicate the kinds of material available in different sections of the library. There are more resources described in this chapter than you will use for a given research project, but you should know that there is library material to help you answer most research questions. The next chapter gives instructions for using the various library resources, including specific information about collecting and recording references for a research project as well as advice on evaluating the reliability of your sources (pp. 78–82). You may want to read these chapters in your academic library so that you can find the parts of the library as you read about them.

Libraries and Librarians

Some large universities may have several libraries: one library for general use, plus more specialized ones for the schools of law, medicine, or agriculture, for example, or a central library with several branches. But most universities have one main library for the general collection. Although most of your library work will take place in the main library, you will probably be allowed to use other campus libraries as well.

Libraries may have sections of rooms, individual rooms, or even separate floors designated for material on specific subjects and for different kinds of material. If you are not familiar with the layout of your library, you may want to take an informal tour to locate and become familiar with each department. (See the activities at the end of this chapter.) Some libraries will provide you with a map or a formal tour. In any case, you will probably be more at ease in a library after you explore it on your own.

The people who work in libraries have various kinds of skills. Some are part-time student workers who only check out or reshelve books. Others are highly trained, sometimes specialized, librarians whose responsibilities may include selecting and ordering new books, cataloging books,

---

✓ CHECKLIST 2

Getting to Know Your Library

If your library provides organized orientation sessions to familiarize students with library resources, by all means attend one of these and ask questions about library procedures you do not understand. Before you actually begin a research project, however, you may want to know the following:

1. Where the circulation and reference desks are located.
2. Where reference books and circulating books are shelved.
3. Where periodicals are shelved and how they are indexed.
4. Where to find the card catalog and/or the computer catalog and when to use each.
5. Whether all your library's material is cataloged online.
6. Whether only recently acquired materials are cataloged online.
7. What information is available on CD-ROMs.
8. What is available through computer terminals and how to use these and other online source materials.
9. Whether your library provides access to the Internet.
10. Whether your library houses government documents.
11. How to make an appointment with a reference librarian for assistance in planning a search.
12. How to get help using government documents, CD-ROMs, or other computerized indexes.

or managing the circulation department. Librarians who are mainly responsible for providing personal services to the patrons of the library are usually called reference librarians. It is important that you learn to identify the different members of the library staff. The person who checks out your books is probably a student worker; someone in an office behind the circulation desk may manage the circulation of books as well as the reserve room; a reference librarian will have a desk or office near the reference section.

The Reference Section

Any member of the library staff can answer general questions—where the card or computer catalog is, whether there are CD-ROMs available, or where the recent issues of newspapers are stored—but when you have questions about a specific research topic, you should ask a reference librarian. Some reference librarians are specialists in reference materials on particular subjects—science, social science, or literature, for example—and in a large library, there will probably be several reference librarians, along with other staff people whose job is to help you find what you need. Once you have located someone who is willing to help you, you should be as specific and clear as possible about what you want to know. Perhaps you are looking for some recent articles for the general reader on World Wide Web navigators. You find a reference librarian and ask where the *Readers' Guide to Periodical Literature* is located. The librarian may point to the appropriate shelf or suggest that you use one of the CD-ROM indexes of InfoTrac (a computerized collection of databases on current topics). If, however, you had explained from the beginning that you wanted to find information on Web software technology, the librarian could have led you to *Applied Science and Technology Index,* which cites articles in specialized journals of technology rather than in popular magazines. You should always tell a reference librarian exactly what you are looking for rather than ask for reference works that you think may have the information.

Remember that reference librarians can help you do your work, but they do not do it for you. Think of them as consultants, people with whom you can discuss your research and who will then make suggestions. It is usually best to have a short conversation with a librarian to explain your research project, what you have already found, and what you hope to find.

MICHAEL GOLD

Michael goes to the reference desk, notes the librarian's name on a sign at the front of the desk, and explains that he is doing a research project on the movie *Rebel Without a Cause* and that he has found information in a few books and several magazines. He then asks for help finding articles in film journals. The librarian suggests that Michael consult the *International Index to Film Periodicals* and that he look under the name of the director as well as the title of the film. Within a few minutes of doing so, Michael has made a long list of articles, some of which he finds in his library and two of which are extremely useful for his project.

A SAMPLE REFERENCE IN THE *International Index to Film Periodicals,* 1979 EDITION

```
REBEL WITHOUT A CAUSE (US, Nicholas Ray, 1955)
Thomson,D.: Rebel without a cause.
Take One VII/4,Mar 79,p. 15-16,illus. (Review).
A reappraisal of the movie and its director, Nicholas
Ray.
```

Before you ask a reference librarian for help, make sure that you have done what you can to find material. Read this chapter carefully, study the annotated list of references at the end of this book, and find out if there is a guide to your library. Once you have done these things, feel free to ask questions. When you find someone who is willing to help you, it is a good idea to come back to the same person for any further questions. Since librarians usually work shifts, you may want to ask when a particular person will be available.

The reference area of the library contains books that cannot be checked out, books such as dictionaries, bibliographies (lists of books and articles), encyclopedias, indexes, and other catalogs of information. Many reference books are intended to provide small pieces of information as quickly as possible—the spelling of a word, the publication date of a book, the birthplace of a famous person. Others, such as encyclopedias, give an overview of large topics; and still others, such as indexes and bibliographies, help you find information in periodicals and other books. For a description of specific reference works, see Appendix B.

In the reference section of many libraries, you will find computers that are linked to the World Wide Web and other Internet sources, some linked to local area networks, and still others that read CD-ROMs directly.

General Encyclopedias

Several encyclopedias, including the *Encyclopaedia Britannica,* are available online or on CD-ROMs. Many universities subscribe to online encyclopedias for their students; you may be able to access these sources from computers outside the library or perhaps even from your own room.

Encyclopedias are familiar to most students, but you may need to be reminded that the major encyclopedias in English differ from one another in significant ways.

Academic American Encyclopedia is the newest multivolume encyclopedia intended for students. The articles are brief and most entries are current. A good source for accurate facts, but not for in-depth coverage, this encyclopedia is particularly strong in scientific and technical subjects. There is a general index for the twenty-one bound volumes, and the entire work is available in electronic versions.

Collier's Encyclopedia has an accessible style and balanced coverage emphasizing the kinds of things taught in American colleges. It is factually reliable and up-to-date. A general, comprehensive index makes it easy for you to find what you are looking for, and an annotated bibliography suggests further reading. Both index and bibliography are in the final volume.

The *Encyclopedia Americana,* aimed at a similar readership (age fifteen and up), is approximately 30 percent longer and features twice as many articles. The *Americana* is particularly strong in the history, culture, and geography of the United States and Canada; 40 percent of its entries are biographies, and it includes brief articles on particular works of literature, music, and art. It is generally up-to-date on urgent topics such as political upheavals, but because the revision is spread out over a period of years, some articles are not current. An effective general index is easy to use, and

LISA LEE

An article under the heading "jungle and rain forest" in the *Academic American Encyclopedia* is of great help to Lisa as she focuses and refines her topic. Not only does it provide a clear, brief overview of the subject, but it also includes useful bibliographic information. A portion of the article is reprinted on the following pages.

tients are made aware of both the personal and collective (archetypal) meanings inherent in their symptoms and difficulties. Under favorable conditions they may enter into the individuation process: a lengthy series of psychological transformations culminating in the integration of opposite tendencies and functions and the achievement of personal wholeness.

GEORGE ATWOOD

Bibliography: Bennet, E. A., *What Jung Really Said* (1971; repr. 1983); Brome, Vincent, *Jung* (1978); Jacobi, Jolande, *The Psychology of C. G. Jung*, 7th ed. (1968); Jung, Carl G., *The Collected Works of Carl G. Jung*, 20 vols. (1953–75), and *The Essential Jung*, ed. by A. Storr (1983); Moreno, Antonio, *Jung, Gods and Modern Man* (1970); Nagy, Marilyn, *Philosophical Issues in the Psychology of C. G. Jung* (1991); Stern, Paul, *C. G. Jung: The Haunted Prophet* (1976); Wehr, Gerhard, *Jung: A Biography* (1987; repr. 1989).

Jungfrau [yung'-frow]

The Jungfrau is a famous peak in the Bernese Alps, on the border of the Bern and Valais cantons of Switzerland. Noted for its graceful contours and the dazzling whiteness of its snow cover (Jungfrau in German means "virgin"), it rises to a height of 4,158 m (13,642 ft). ALETSCH GLACIER lies on its south side, which was first ascended in 1927. The eastern side was climbed in 1811. Tourists and winter sports enthusiasts can ascend by rail to the Jungfraujoch, a mountain saddle at 3,454 m (11,332 ft), which is also the site of a scientific research observatory.

Jungle, The

The Jungle (1906), a novel by Upton SINCLAIR, is a particularly graphic example of "muckraking" fiction (see MUCKRAKERS). The book centers on the life of a Lithuanian immigrant, Jurgis Rudkus, who finds work in the Chicago stockyards. As the story proceeds, the unsanitary, exploitative conditions of the stockyards are fully documented. Working in such a barbaric environment, Rudkus becomes completely demoralized and,

seeking a remedy, turns to socialism. The novel caused a public outcry when published and is believed to have been instrumental in the passage of the Pure Food and Drug Act of 1906. Corrective labor regulation, however, did not come for another 30 years.

CHARLOTTE D. SOLOMON

Jungle Book, The

The Jungle Book (1894) is a group of stories by the English writer Rudyard KIPLING. They relate the history of an Indian boy, Mowgli, who strays from his village and is reared by a family of wolves. Mowgli's intelligence and manual dexterity make him valuable to the animals, who defend him from the perils of the wilderness. Mowgli learns the complex "Law of the Jungle" and in turn imparts human qualities to the animals. Although ostensibly a work for children, *The Jungle Book* has found many appreciative adult readers, some of whom have regarded it as an allegory of colonial government. Kipling repeated his success with *The Second Jungle Book* (1895).

jungle and rain forest

Jungle and *rain forest* are terms that are often used synonymously but with little precision. The more meaningful and restrictive of these terms is *rain forest*, which refers to the climax or primary forest in regions with high rainfall (greater than 1.8 m/70 in per year), chiefly but not exclusively found in the tropics. Rain forests are significant for their valuable timber resources, and in the tropics they afford sites for commercial crops such as rubber, tea, coffee, bananas, and sugarcane. They also include some of the last remaining areas of the Earth that are both unexploited economically and inadequately known scientifically.

The term *jungle* originally referred to the tangled, brushy vegetation of lowlands in India, but it has come to be used for any type of tropical forest or woodland. The word is more

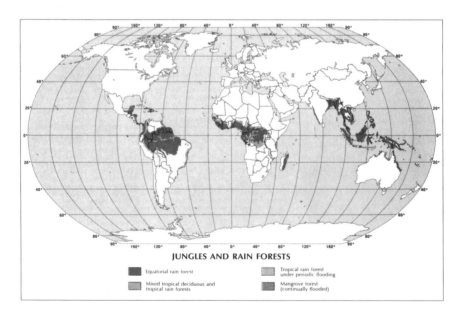

JUNGLES AND RAIN FORESTS

Equatorial rain forest

Mixed tropical deciduous and tropical rain forests

Tropical rain forest under periodic flooding

Mangrove forest (continually flooded)

Animals of a South American rain forest include: black-capped capuchins (1), Cebus appella, and howler monkeys (2), Alovatta seniculus; the three-toed sloth (3), Bradypus tricactylus; and the opossum (4), Didelphis marsupialis. The tamandua (5), Tamandua tetradactyla, is related to the great anteater (6), Myrmelophaga tridactyla. Other inhabitants are the brown coatimundi (7), Nasua narica; the capybara (8), Hydrochoerus hydrochaeris, and the paca (9), Cuniculus paca; and the red brocket deer (10), Mazama americana. A jaguar (11), Panthera onca, strikes its prey, a tapir (12), Tapirus terrestris. Birds include: the scarlet macaw (13), Ara macao; the scarlet ibis (14), Eudocimus ruber, and the roseate spoonbill (15), A. ajaia; the keel-billed toucan (16), Ramphastos sulfuratus; and the ruby-topaz hummingbird (17), Chrysolampis mosquitus. Other animals are: a South American river turtle, the Arrau (18), Podocnemis expansa, shown on a giant lily pad (19), Victoria amazonica; the arrow poison frog (20), genus Dendrobates; the bird-eating spider (21), family Aviculariidae; a rare butterfly (22), Heliconius ethillus; a leaf hopper (23), family Cicadellica; and leaf-cutter ants (24), genus Atta. Three epiphytic plants are two orchid genera, Oncidium (25) and Cattleya (26), and a bromeliad (27). Cephaelis (28) carpets the floor.

meaningful if limited to the dense, scrubby vegetation that develops when primary rain forest has been degraded by destructive forms of logging or by cultivation followed by abandonment.

Types of Rain Forest. Rain forests may be grouped into two major types: tropical and temperate. Tropical rain forest is characterized by broadleaf evergreen trees that form a closed canopy, below which is found a zone of vines and epiphytes (plants growing on the trees), a relatively open forest floor, and a very large number of species of both plant and animal life. The largest trees have buttressed trunks and emerge above the continuous canopy, while smaller trees commonly form a layer of more shade-tolerant species beneath the upper canopy. The maximum height of the upper canopy of tropical rain forests is generally about 30 to 50 m (100 to 165 ft), with some individual trees rising as high as 60 m (200 ft) above the forest floor.

The largest areas of tropical rain forest are in the Amazon basin of South America, in the Congo basin and other lowland equatorial regions of Africa, and on both the mainland and the islands off Southeast Asia, where they are especially abundant on Sumatra and New Guinea. Small areas are found in Central America and along the Queensland coast of Australia.

Temperate rain forests, growing in higher-latitude regions having wet, maritime climates, are less extensive than those of the tropics but include some of the most valuable timber in the world. Notable forests in this category are those on the northwest coast of North America, in southern Chile, in Tasmania, and in parts of southeastern Australia and New Zealand. These forests contain trees that may exceed in height those of tropical rain forests, but there is less diversity of species. Conifers such as REDWOOD and Sitka spruce tend to predominate in North America, while their counterparts in the southern hemisphere include various species of EUCALYPTUS, *Araucaria*, and *Nothofagus* (Antarctic beech).

bibliographies of recommended reading are included at the end of all major articles and many shorter ones.

The *New Encyclopaedia Britannica* is the least accessible of the three both because of its sophisticated style and because of its elaborate three-part structure: the Propaedia, which outlines the world of knowledge; the Micropaedia, which provides short articles on many subjects and serves as both a ready reference and an index; and the Macropaedia, which contains in-depth, signed articles. The *Britannica* emphasizes international subjects and historical data. Leisure and previous knowledge of a subject are sometimes necessary to appreciate the abstract discussion, and it is often difficult to find all the material on a given subject because of a complicated and sometimes inadequate system of cross-references. But at times the effort required to use the *Britannica* is worthwhile. Its depth and complexity make it more informative and authoritative in the long run.

The Columbia Encyclopedia is an excellent single-volume reference work that provides reliable information on a wide range of subjects in condensed form. It is particularly useful for quick reference—getting an overview of a person's life or work, discovering the exact location and size of a state or country (there are maps), learning the average size of a particular breed of dog. The articles are cross-referenced, and many of them include lists of books for additional reading.

These are all good encyclopedias. The best one for you will depend on what you want to find out, how much time you are willing to spend, and how much you already know about a subject.

Encyclopedia Indexes and Bibliographies

The general index of a standard encyclopedia may refer you to a number of articles that treat your subject, but you will find that consulting the encyclopedia index will be more productive for some topics than for others. For example, the *Encyclopedia Americana* lists seven subheadings under "Conscientious Objector," while "Woodstock Festival" is included only under "Rock Music." At the end of some encyclopedia articles, you will also find a list of books used or recommended by the author of the article. One encyclopedia may provide a useful bibliography on a subject for which no references are cited in another standard encyclopedia. A case in point is *The Columbia Encyclopedia,* which lists five books on the subject of conscientious objection, while the *Encyclopedia Americana* lists none. You may therefore want to consult all the standard encyclopedias before going to more specialized reference works. Note the following excerpt from a general encyclopedia index:

Motion Picture Association of America 19–539
  Production Code 7–429
Motion Picture Production Code Administration (U.S.)
  19–539
  Censorship 6–167
  Hays, W. 13–901
MOTION SICKNESS (med.) 19–545, 798
  Seasickness 24–490
Motion study (indus. eng.) 15–112, 114
MOTIVATION (psych.) 19–545
  Advertising 1–202
  Altruism 1–639
  Attention 2–656
  Child Development 6–452
  educational psychology 9–708, 712
  Emotion 10–309

Specialized Reference Works

General encyclopedias are the most widely known of the books in the reference section, but their usefulness will be very limited for serious student researchers looking for material on a particular subject. There are many other reference works that you should know about—indexes and bibliographies; yearbooks and almanacs; and numerous specialized reference works, including directories, dictionaries, histories, and specialized encyclopedias. These specialized works will usually offer a more thorough treatment of a subject than that given by a general encyclopedia. For example, you are more likely to find an in-depth treatment of behavioral psychologist B. F. Skinner in the *International Encyclopedia of the Social Sciences* than in the most recent edition of *Collier's*.

The annotated list of reference works in Appendix B will help you identify specialized reference works appropriate to particular research projects.

The Periodical Section

The most relaxed spot in a library is usually the current periodical section, where students can be found sitting in comfortable chairs, reading magazines, or consulting movie schedules. In this area there are two kinds of periodicals: popular magazines and newspapers—such as those you can buy on newsstands—and scholarly or professional journals, which contain articles for specialists and most of which are available only by subscription. Back issues of periodicals are stored in bound volumes or on microform—sometimes in the periodical room and sometimes in the stacks.

Periodical Indexes

Indexes to periodicals are usually shelved in the reference section of the library. To locate material in magazines, newspapers, and journals, you will have to use a variety of indexes. Most libraries have at least one electronic index for finding material in periodicals and newspapers. You will need to find out what your library has to offer. Commonly used electronic periodical indexes are *Periodical Abstracts Ondisc, InfoTrac,* and *Newspaper Abstracts Ondisc.* NEXIS, an online full-text database of thousands of magazines, newspapers, and other media around the world, also gives you access to periodicals. If your college has NEXIS available for students to use, by all means learn what it can do for you. LEXIS is produced by the same company as NEXIS, and in some cases the two databases can be accessed from the same terminal—you may hear them referred to as LEXIS/NEXIS. Electronic indexes can be searched very quickly, but many cover only recent years. There are a number of electronic indexes that academic libraries use, and your library may have one of those mentioned below, or other similar ones. For searching older periodicals, you may need to use bound indexes.

The *Readers' Guide to Periodical Literature* (New York: Wilson, 1900 to date) is useful for finding articles (by subject or author) in 150 popular magazines. Supplements are published every two weeks, so it can be used for very recent publications. Bound volumes consolidate all the entries with a single alphabetical listing. The following is an excerpt from *Readers' Guide:*

MOVING of machinery
 Huge generator moves on planks. il Pop Mech
  103:109 Mr '55
MOVING of structures, etc.
 Cash-and-carry houses. D. X. Manners. il Read Di-
  gest 68:145-7 Ap '56
 Hotel takes a ride. il Pop Mech 103:139 Je '55
 Houses that move around. D. Isaak. Am Mercury
  82:89-91 Mr '56
MOVING of trees. See Tree planting
MOVING picture acting
 Strange doings of actress at practice. il Life
  42:96-8 + Ja 28 '57
 That wonderful, deep silence; difference be-
  tween stage and screen. S. Winters. il Theatre
  Arts 40:30-1 + Je '56
 When you take a screen test. M. Arnow. Good H
  142:38 + Ja '56
MOVING picture actors and actresses
 American women pick: our favorite stars. P. T.
  Hartung. pors Womans Home C 82:12 Je '55
 Amour and the man. pors Sat R 39:29 O 13 '56;
  Reply. D. Beams. 39:23 N 10 '56
 Bells are ringing. L. Lerman. il Mile 44:81-5 + N
  '56
 Bogart on Hollywood. il Look 20:96-8 + Ag 21 '56

Bright young stars in fashions for off-stage
  hours. W. Cushman. il Ladies Home J 72:68-9
  My '55
By any other name. Mr Harper. Harper 210:80-1
  Mr '55
Discovery: British women are beautiful. il Look
  20:26-30 + Ag 21 '56
Fans choose; Photoplay magazine winners. News-
  week 45:90 F 14 '55
Film pioneers' roll of their living immortals. il
  pors Life 40:116-23 Ja 23 '56
Foreign accent in starlets. M. Nichols. pors Coro-
  net 40:44-55 Ag '56
Glamor gallery; Italian screen stars; photo-
  graphs. Theatre Arts 39:72-3 My '55
Greatest stars; Timeless stars; Glamour in our
  time; Star system in 1956; Newcomers. il Cos-
  mop 141:28-37 O '56
Hollywood actors win $80 day for now. Bsns W p
  170 Mr 24 '56
Hollywood and its people. R. Gehman. il Cosmop   — date of periodical
  141:46-51 O '56
Hollywood fathers. il Look 19:38-41 Jl 12 '55
Hollywood hobbies. il pors McCalls 83:16 + O '55
Hollywood revisited. L. Rosten. il pors Look   — pages
  20:17-28 Ja 10 '56
Hollywood tragedies. E. Honor. il Cosmop
  141:38-9 O '56   — author
Hollywood, unhitching post. I. C. Kuhn. Am Mer-
  cury 80:7-11 Ja '55
Hollywood's search for new faces. S. Peck. il pors   — title of article
  N Y Times Mag p28-9 O 7 '56
Hollywood's search for stars. T. M. Pryor. il pors
  N Y Times Mag p 14-15 + Je 12 '55
I make up Hollywood; ed. by P. Martin. W. West-   — name of periodical
  more. il Sat Eve Post 229:17-19 + Ag 4; 30 +
  Ag 11 '56
Idols of Italy. il Look 19:100 + N 15 '55   — illustrated
Look annual movie awards. il Look 17:26-31 Mr
  10 '53; 18:122-4 + Mr 23 '54; 19:100-4 + Mr 23
  '55   — volume

Remember that *Readers' Guide* is limited. It indexes only popular magazines, the kind that depend primarily on advertising for most of their income. If your research is at least in part concerned with popular reaction
to a movie, a book, or even a major political event, then of course you will
use this work or electronic indexes that cover the same material. If you
are investigating the contributions of Betty Friedan and Gloria Steinem to
the women's movement, you will read the books they have written as well
as any articles in scholarly journals, but you are likely to find most of your
material in magazines. *Readers' Guide* is available in some libraries on CD-
ROM or online. If you want to find out the latest information about the
treatment of AIDS, you would want to search the medical journals, using
the index *Medline*. For most research projects, in fact, you will want to consult specialized indexes that will lead you to periodicals that contain articles written by experts in particular fields. Many of these indexes are described in the annotated bibliography beginning on page 359.

Newspaper Indexes

The *New York Times Index* lists all major articles that have appeared in that paper from 1913 to the present; it also indirectly indexes many other national and even local newspapers by revealing the date on which a news item most likely appeared there. It is kept up-to-date with supplements published every two weeks. There is also an index for selected articles for the years 1851–1912. Articles are listed by subject. Entries in recent volumes give the exact location of each article, an indication of length, and usually a brief summary of content. Note the following excerpt from the *New York Times Index:*

MOTION Picture Arts and Sciences, Academy of. See also
Head, Edith, D 7. Motion Pictures—Awards, F 18,19,24,
Mr 12,23,29,31, Ap 1,2,3,12, O 22, D 26
MOTION Picture Assn of America (MPAA). See also
Motion Pictures, Ja 16. Motion Pictures—US, My 24,
O 8. Television—Cable TV, My 15 ⎯⎯⎯ **main heading**
MOTION Picture Daily. See also Television—Programs,
Catch a Falling Star (TV Program), My 10 ⎯⎯ **explanation of how articles**
MOTION Pictures. Note: US and gen material are under ⎯ **are organized**
subject subheads. Foreign material is under geog subheads.
Specific films are under subhead Revs
  See also Pornography (for inclusion). Theater and ⎯⎯⎯ **other suggested headings**
performer names
  Vincent Canby movie quiz; illustrations, Ja 4,II,15:1
  Edwin Bigley, asst to Jack Valenti, pres of Motion Picture
Assn of Amer, reports that Pres Carter viewed some 500
films during his tenure in office, more than double that of any ⎯ **(S) indicates a short article**
previous Pres (S), Ja 16,III,6:6
  Kirk Honeycutt article on Lillian Michelson Research
Library, which provides meticulous background information
for writers, designers, dirs, and art dirs to recreate authentic ⎯ **(L) indicates a long article**
stories, sets, props and costumes (L), Mr 1,II,18:1; comment
on Acme-Dunn optical printer, used to enhance certain
special effects in films; noted developers of printer, Linwood
G Dunn, Cecil D Love and Edward Furer, were recognized ⎯ **(M) indicates an article of**
with Oscar for technical merit; illustration (M), Ap 3,IV,5:1 **medium length**
  Comment on problem of old movie film that fades; Henry
Kaska, spokesman for Eastman Kodak, Larry Carr of Amer
Film Inst and filmmaker Martin Scorsese note preservation
steps that are being taken to improve situation (M), Ap 5,
III,19:1
  Natl Center for Jewish Film is established by Jewish ⎯⎯⎯ **brief summary of article**
Historical Soc: will be located on campus of Brandeis Univ
(S), My 3,70:6
  Gregory Peck comments on acting opposite Sophia Loren ⎯ **author of article**
(S), Jl 20,II,8:3
  Bob Harelson, head of Berry Auction Co which specializes
in movie memorabilia, comments on trends (S), Ag 7,III,8:5 ⎯ **date**
  Universal, Paramount, M-G-M, and United Artists have
joined together to form Lorgn, United Internatl Pictures, to
distribute films abroad (S), O 6,IV,28:6 ⎯⎯⎯ **section**
  Vincent Canby article on effect that society's repression
has on filmmakers' styles; notes works of Frank Ripploh,
Andrzej Wajda, Dusan Makavejev and George Cukor (M),
N 15,II,23:1 ⎯⎯⎯ **page**
  Russell Baker humorous article on how old movies would
change if they were to be produced today; drawing (M), D ⎯ **column**
20,VI,p17

While your library probably has electronic indexes for the *New York Times* and other newspapers, you will need to use bound volumes for older materials.

General Indexes to Scholarly Articles

The following indexes—actually one work with several title changes over the years—cover scholarly articles in the humanities and social sciences from 1907 to the present:

Readers' Guide Supplement and International Index covers articles from 1907 to 1919.

International Index to Periodicals, 1920 to 1965.

Social Sciences and Humanities Index, 1965 to 1974.

Since 1974, this index has been published in the following two parts:

Humanities Index lists articles published from 1974 to date.

Social Sciences Index lists by subject (anthropology, economics, psychology, etc.) articles published from 1974 to date.

Indexes to Specific Disciplines

There are many indexes to specific disciplines, some highly specialized. Some are limited to periodicals, such as the *Art Index;* others combine an index to periodicals with lists of books on particular subjects, such as the *MLA International Bibliography.* A list of specialized indexes appears in Appendix B, along with an explanation of how each might be useful. You may want to explore the shelves of the reference room of your own academic library to discover what specialized indexes your library carries.

Catalog of a Library's Periodicals

After you have located articles you want to consult in periodicals, you need to find out if they are in your library. Libraries catalog periodicals in different ways. Most include periodicals in a central computerized catalog. Others have a separate card or electronic catalog for periodicals. You can easily find out which system a library uses by consulting a reference librarian or a printed guide to the library's resources. All systems, however, will give you the same basic information: which issues the library has; their location in the library, indicated by a call number; and whether they are bound, unbound, or on microform.

If articles that seem particularly important to your research are not in your library, you may want to try to get them from another library. To identify libraries that have a particular periodical, use the *Union List of Se-*

rials, which catalogs periodicals in the United States and Canada through 1965. For articles after that date, consult *New Serial Titles,* which is kept up-to-date by periodic publication. Most academic libraries have a service for obtaining from other libraries copies of articles from periodicals that they do not have. Usually students pay a small fee to cover the cost of copying and mailing the article.

Computerized or Electronic Information Retrieval

Libraries store information in many different forms, including books, magazines and journals (serials), newspapers, computer disks, audio tapes and videotapes, and films. No library's collection is like another's. Libraries also vary in the tools they use to help you find these materials, but most libraries have computers and some of the new electronic tools that make finding library sources easy. Most have the catalogs of their entire collections online or on CD-ROM. Others have only the books cataloged online, while still others have some forms of information cataloged on cards (the card catalog) and others online. Some may have books cataloged in one way, magazines in another, and nonprint material in still another.

Most academic libraries have the ability to search databases that index materials, and the majority have CD-ROMs, or access to a local area network such as CD-LAN, for the most frequently used indexes. It is important to understand how your library organizes and catalogs its materials and what tools it has for finding those materials. There is literally a revolution going on in the ways we retrieve information, and as a student, you will do well to learn what your library has available and to keep up with changes in the libraries you use.

Nonprint media that you can use to find library materials are:

1. Microform (microfiche or microfilm)
2. CD-ROMs
3. Online databases
4. Magnetic tape in a computer mainframe
5. The Internet

To use an index on microfiche or microfilm, you would use a microform reader, a machine designed for the particular product you are using. CD-ROMs are accessed by a specialized computer program (search software) along with a CD-ROM player attached to a computer. To find information in an online electronic database, you may use a computer terminal in the library or elsewhere on campus. Much of the information stored in microforms, CD-ROMs, or databases is also available in print form. Catalogs of libraries all over the world are also available on the Internet.

Photocopying from Microform Readers

Some microform readers have the ability to photocopy material stored on film or tape. Once you have found an article or passage from an article that seems important, you may want to make a copy to use later. If you only need a small bit of information or a very short passage, then you may choose to record it on a note card; but sometimes you will want the whole article. As soon as you make a copy, take care to identify the source, including the date, page number, and any other information you need for your list of works cited.

CD-ROM Information Data Sources

CD-ROM stands for "Compact Disc – Read Only Memory," which means that information is permanently encoded onto the disc so that it can be "read" by a computer with a CD-ROM drive, but cannot be altered in any way. A floppy disk that allows you to add, erase, or change information is usually spelled with a "k," while a read-only-memory compact disc is usually, but not always, spelled with a "c." Each CD-ROM contains an enormous amount of information—up to seven hundred megabytes (hundreds of thousands of pages).

Printing Information from CD-ROMs

CD-ROMs are usually connected to printers. In most cases you can print out information from the CD-ROM simply by striking a key on the keyboard. Take the time to learn how to use all the features of a CD-ROM reader and printer. You may want to print everything on the screen, a whole list of items in a bibliography, or a few selected items. Librarians will help you if you do not understand the written instructions or if the equipment malfunctions.

Advantages and Disadvantages of Using CD-ROMs

The most obvious advantages of using a CD-ROM index compared to its printed version are speed and the ability to focus a search. It allows you to find information much faster than would be possible using books and to search several headings at once. It is of course much more efficient to print out information from a CD-ROM than to copy it by hand from a book. There is no fee for using the CD-ROM once the library has purchased it. It can be used continually and searched again and again, whereas an online computer search can be quite expensive.

There are, however, disadvantages in using a CD-ROM index over its printed version. Most compact disc versions cover a limited number of years (the MLA currently covers 1963 to the present; *Biological Abstracts* covers only 1989 to the present), whereas a printed index is complete. Since there is no standard CD-ROM format or program, it sometimes takes time to learn to use an electronic index, and you may find the written instructions and the program inadequate to get you started. Before you decide to use a CD-ROM, consider whether or not it is likely to be useful. Lisa Lee, for example, decided to use two CD-ROMs: *Biological Abstracts* and *General Sciences Index,* and she did in fact find a few useful articles that way. But the most important articles she found by combing through the bound volumes of *Biological Abstracts,* which provides abstracts (brief summaries) of each article.

Another disadvantage of CD-ROMs is that they can only be used by one person at a time, so that those that are frequently used may not be available when you want them. Some libraries allow you to schedule a particular time to use a disc. Finally, a CD-ROM disc may not be as up-to-date as its online version, and many databases that students can access with an online search are not available on CD-ROMs.

Periodical Indexes on CD-ROM

Most libraries have extensive databases available on CD-ROM. Many of these are electronic alternatives to printed periodical indexes and are available for searching scholarly journals and periodicals in specific disciplines in the humanities, the natural sciences, and the social sciences. Your library will probably have at least some of these indexes on CD-ROM, and you will find them very helpful, especially for finding recent materials. Most CD-ROM indexes do not cover as many years as their print counterparts. Examples of indexes on CD-ROM that are commonly available in libraries include:

Art Index
Books in Print
Biological Abstracts
Business Index
Econlit
ERIC

General Science Index
MLA International Bibliography
PsycInfo
PsycLit
Sociofile

Other Texts and Databases on CD-ROM

CD-ROMs that provide full texts of entire books, sets of related books, or even entire collections are now available. Titles range from *Jewish Classics,* with full texts of the Talmud and other Hebrew scriptures; to a database of African-American poetry from 1760 to 1900 containing the work of more than fifty poets; to *The Wall Street Journal Ondisc,* including the full text of articles from the *Journal* over a several-year period. What makes these CD-ROMs and others like them so valuable to student researchers is that they can be searched for content. For example, you can search the African-American poetry database by topic and easily call up all the poems that mention the Civil War or the word "slavery." It is possible to focus a search to find specific kinds of content, such as poems about slavery that are not also about the Civil War or poems in which the word "slavery" is mentioned within twenty words of a reference to beatings or torture. An invaluable research tool, CD-ROM databases are increasing in sophistication and in number. Find out what is available in your library.

For a description of indexes available on CD-ROMs, see Appendix B. Whenever you use a CD-ROM, you should note what years are covered since they are frequently updated.

CARLA MEDINA

Carla has chosen to write her first paper on Alice Walker's novel *The Color Purple.* She has never used any of the computerized indexes in the library, and so she also makes an appointment with a reference librarian. The librarian asks her a few questions and finds out that Carla wants both critical articles as well as those published in popular magazines. She explains that Carla will be able to conduct her search in two indexes, the *MLA International Bibliography,* which indexes scholarly journals, and *InfoTrac,* which indexes current periodicals and newspapers. Carla's college library has both of these indexes on CD-ROM that cover the years since the publication of *The Color Purple* in 1982. By carefully reading the instructions near the computer terminal, Carla is able to conduct her search electronically and in less than an hour to print out listings for more than twenty articles and essays that seem relevant to her topic.

Here is the first stage of Carla's search—*the MLA International Bibliography* as it appeared on-screen:

```
MLA International Bibliography              Data Coverage: 1/81 thru 12/26/91
                                                                      READY

  SEARCH  |              WILSEARCH                           | NUMBER of
  SET     |              COMMAND                             | ENTRIES

    1     | FIND WALKER, ALICE:(AU) OR WALKER, ALICE:(PS)    |    145
          |              (AU) WALKER, ALICE:.....   6 Entries
          |              (PS) WALKER, ALICE:..... 139 Entries
    2     | FIND COLOR(TI) AND PURPLE(TI)                    |     38
          |              (TI) COLOR..... 207 Entries
          |              (TI) PURPLE.....  56 Entries
    3     | FIND 1 AND 2                                     |     37
          |              (ss # 1) ..... 145 Entries
          +-------------------------------------------------+
          |     37 ENTRIES FOUND                            |
          | HIT ┘ ENTER                                     |
          +-------------------------------------------------+


                                           Mon Jan 27 15:02:36 1992

    F1 - HELP   F2 - END
```

And the beginning of Carla's *InfoTrac* printout:

```
InfoTrac - General Periodicals Index-A


Heading:    THE COLOR PURPLE.
               -(book reviews)

    1.      The Color Purple. (book reviews) by Alice Walker
         rev by James Lovelace
       B v79 English Journal Oct '90 p83(1)

    2.      The color purple. (book reviews) by Alice Walker
         rev by Darryl Pinckney il
       C v34 The New York Review of Books Jan 29 '87 p17(2)

    3.      The color purple. (book reviews) by Alice Walker,
       Anne Carr and  rev by Anne Carr and
       A v111 Commonweal Feb 24 '84 p119(2)
       25F1574

    4.      The color purple. (book reviews) by Alice Walker
         rev by Dolores Leckey
       A v111 Commonweal Feb 24 '84 p125(1)
       25F1579

    5.      The color purple. (book reviews) by Alice Walker
       A- v133 Forbes Feb 13 '84 p25(1)
       21B1317                                      03R1943
```

Carla shows her printout to the librarian, who suggests that she also check *Book Review Index* and the *New York Times Index;* in these Carla finds a few references that she has missed in the electronic search. Her teacher has suggested that she read the chapter dealing with *The Color Purple* in Henry Louis Gates Jr.'s *The Signifying Monkey,* and so she uses the computerized catalog to locate this book in the library's collection.

Before proceeding further, Carla takes the time to make sure she has all the bibliographic information for each source. She cuts out each individual citation from her printout sheet, tapes it to a large note card, leaving room for call numbers and notes about the source. For sources found in printed volumes, she carefully records all the information necessary for a full bibliographic reference.

To identify which articles are in her library, she goes to the periodical catalog and records the call numbers for the available materials. Some are in bound periodicals, others on microfilm. She decides that she has plenty of material and will not need to order anything through interlibrary loan.

Carla's next task is to begin reading the material she has located, to decide how to focus her study, and either to make copies of the essays or to take notes. She sets aside an afternoon in the library and goes to work. After reading through several articles, she decides to focus her study on the voices of the novel and to show how reviewers and early critics of *The Color Purple* were especially attracted to Celie's voice. At the end of the day, Carla has made photocopies of three articles and taken notes from several others. She plans to come back to the library the next day to finish reading and taking notes.

Note: Students using libraries that do not have CD-ROM indexes can conduct the same search using the bound volumes of the *MLA International Bibliography* and *Readers' Guide to Periodical Literature* along with *Book Review Index, Book Review Digest,* and the *New York Times Index.*

Learning When and How to Use the Internet

Information stored electronically can easily be made available outside the library, and you may be able to tap into the vast resources of the Internet in the library, the computer lab, both, or neither. In most libraries, there are librarians who can advise you about using Internet resources for your research project. Computer terminals in libraries are used for particular tasks—some may be strictly for databases stored on CD-ROMs, others for searching the library's catalogs, and still others for e-mail and other Internet and online services. As you get to know your library, find out which terminals are used for what purposes and whether you can access the Internet from any of them.

Finding Sources on the Internet

The advantage of consulting the Internet for information is that its vastness allows people who are skilled in using it to find something interesting on almost any topic. You are likely to find at least one Web site, newsgroup, database, or more that will help you. One disadvantage of using the Net is that unless you have had practice searching, you may not be able to find what you need. Another disadvantage is that it is often difficult to evaluate what you find. Before you decide whether to explore the Net, think about what you are looking for. You may be tempted to spend a lot of time browsing the Net, but remember that you may learn just as much or more by browsing through appropriate sections of the stacks in your library.

Sources Available in More than One Form

Many reference works are available in more than one form—in print, on CD-ROM, and online. Others currently available in print will soon be out in electronic form, and the print version may no longer be available. A student at one institution might use the bound volumes of the *Encyclopaedia Britannica,* while someone at another college might read the same articles by accessing the Internet. Similarly, you might use bound volumes of *Readers' Guide to Periodical Literature,* while a friend at another school might use a CD-ROM version, and another might find the same information through *InfoTrac* or *Periodical Abstracts Ondisc.* It's important for you to know that there are ways to access almost any information you might want as a student researcher; your job is to learn about those reference works available at your own institution.

The annotated list of reference works in Appendix B (pp. 359–82), provides information about the content and available forms of reference works commonly found in academic libraries. You may want to check your library's main catalog to find out which works are available in bound and/or electronic formats.

LISA LEE

When Lisa goes to the library to find books about rain forests, she searches the online computer catalog by subject. The first subject she tries is "forest." Under that heading she finds various subject sub-headings that include the singular word "forest"—so many in fact that it would take her a long time to find the one that includes rain forests. Trying the plural "forests," she finds both rain forests and also two subheadings, "rain forests, Africa" and "rain forests, Amazon basin." Since she is interested in finding general information about rain forests, she looks at the general heading for "rain forests," which yields another general heading as well as many subheadings leading her to materials about rain forests all over the world.

The general heading includes seventeen books listed chronolog-ically in the order they were received by the library. Lisa copies down call numbers for the books that are not checked out. She locates Collins's *The Last Rain Forests* and *Lessons of the Rainforests,* edited by Head and Heinszman.

Lisa then goes back to the online catalog and tries a more specific subheading: "rain forests, ecology." Under that heading she locates other sources, including *The Tropical Forest and Its Environment,* by Longman and Jenik.

Lisa learns that it is best to begin her search with the most spe-cific heading she can think of and then move to more general ones.

The Main Library Catalog

A library's main or central catalog may be in different forms, but almost all academic libraries and most public libraries have an electronic catalog, either online or on regularly updated CD-ROMs, which users can access through computer terminals. In addition to the electronic catalog, some libraries have a card catalog and/or a Computer Output Microform Cata-log (COMCAT). Very large libraries with extensive collections may have all three forms, with parts of the collection accessible through one form or another. For example, rare or old books may be cataloged only on cards, while newer materials are online. Some libraries maintain a catalog in mi-croform as a backup for those times when computers are down. While most students in most libraries will search for source materials by consulting an electronic catalog through a computer terminal, do not assume that every item in a library is cataloged electronically. Before you have the pressure of a deadline, explore the systems your library uses and make sure you know how to find all kinds of material, including new books, special collections, periodicals, newspapers, and electronic texts.

Each item in a catalog is assigned a unique identifying number referred to as the call number. Whether your library uses the Dewey decimal system or the Library of Congress system for classifying books, you will need to record the complete call number before you try to find a source.

For most items in a collection, there will be a separate entry for author, subject, and title. Individual poems, short stories, and essays will not have a separate card if they are part of a book. Longer works of imaginative literature—fiction, poetry, or drama—usually will not have a subject entry, though any type of work might be cited on additional entries for editors, illustrators, or translators.

The Computerized Catalog

The computer catalog always will be accessible by computer terminals in the library, but you may also have access to your library's catalog from terminals in dormitories, other buildings on campus, or even off-campus. The catalogs of many libraries around the world are available through the Internet, and there may be times when you will want to find material in libraries other than your own. Before you use an electronic catalog, follow the directions placed near the terminals. If you have trouble, get help from a librarian or a fellow student. The entries in computerized catalogs may vary slightly from one to another, but within a single catalog entries will follow a standard format like the one below:

```
E807.1 .R572 1971
          Personal author:  Lash, Joseph P., 1909-
                    Title:  Eleanor and Franklin : the story of their relationship,
                            based on Eleanor Roosevelt's private papers / Jospeh P.
                            Lash ; foreword by Arthur M. Schlesinger, Jr. ; introd.
                            by Franklin D. Roosevelt, Jr.
        Publication info:  New York : Norton, 1971.
    Physical description:  xviii, 765 p. : ill., ports. ; 24 cm.
        Personal subject:  Roosevelt, Eleanor, 1884-1962.
        Personal subject:  Roosevelt, Franklin D. (Franklin Delano), 1882-1945.
        Bibliography note:  Includes bibliographical references and index.
                 Held by:  GENERAL LAW
```

Whether you access an electronic catalog by author, subject, or title, you will find exactly the same information.

The Card Catalog

Many libraries do not maintain card catalogs; others keep the card catalog as a backup system or for records that have not been transferred to a computer database. Still others have certain materials cataloged only on cards. Before you consult a card catalog in a library that also has a computerized catalog, you need to know whether the card catalog is kept up-to-date and whether the information you find there is likely to be accurate. Except for works of imaginative literature listed only by author and title, most items in a card catalog will have three different entries: author, subject, and title. The content of the cards will be identical except that the title will be typed at the top of the title card and the subject at the top of the subject card. Note the elements of the following subject card:

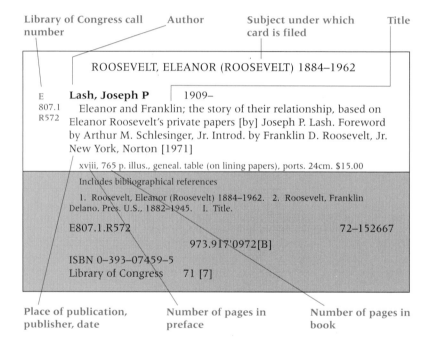

Classification Systems for Library Materials

To locate specific library materials, you need to understand the classification system used by your library. Most libraries use either the Dewey decimal or the Library of Congress system of classification. Although it is not necessary to memorize the classification systems, you will find it easier to use a library if you know which system it uses and what kinds of books are in the general categories.

The **Dewey decimal system** uses a number system to classify books into these ten major categories:

000–099	General Works
100–199	Philosophy
200–299	Religion
300–399	Social Sciences
400–499	Language
500–599	Pure Science
600–699	Technology (Applied Science)
700–799	The Arts
800–899	Literature and Rhetoric
900–999	Geography and History

These major divisions are then subdivided by tens:

000 General Works
010 Bibliography
020 Library and information sciences
030 General encyclopedic works
040
050 General serials & their indexes
060 General organizations & museology
070 News media, journalism, publishing
080 General collections
090 Manuscripts and rare books

100 Philosophy
110 Metaphysics
120 Epistemology, causation, humankind
130 Paranormal phenomena
140 Specific philosophical schools
150 Psychology
160 Logic
170 Ethics (Moral philosophy)
180 Ancient, medieval, Oriental philosophy
190 Modern Western philosophy

200 Religion
210 Natural theology
220 Bible
230 Christian theology
240 Christian moral and devotional theology
250 Christian orders and local church
260 Christian social theology
270 Christian church history
280 Christian denominations & sects
290 Other and comparative religions

300 Social Sciences
310 General statistics
320 Political science
330 Economics
340 Law
350 Public administration
360 Social services; association
370 Education
380 Commerce, communications, transport
390 Customs, etiquette, folklore

400 Language
410 Linguistics
420 English and Old English
430 Germanic languages   German
440 Romance languages   French
450 Italian, Romanian, Rhaeto-Romanic
460 Spanish and Portuguese languages
470 Italic languages   Latin
480 Hellenic languages   Classical Greek
490 Other languages

500 Pure Science
510 Mathematics
520 Astronomy and allied sciences
530 Physics
540 Chemistry and allied sciences
550 Earth sciences

560 Paleontology Paleozoology	780 Music
570 Life sciences	790 Recreational and performing arts
580 Botanical sciences	
590 Zoological sciences	**800 Literature and Rhetoric**
	810 American literature in English
600 Technology (Applied Science)	820 English and Old English literatures
	830 Literatures of Germanic languages
610 Medical sciences Medicine	840 Literatures of Romance languages
620 Engineering and allied operations	850 Italian, Romanian, Rhaeto-Romanic
630 Agriculture	860 Spanish and Portuguese literatures
640 Home economics and family living	870 Italic literatures Latin
650 Management and auxiliary services	880 Hellenic literatures Classical Greek
660 Chemical engineering	890 Literatures of other languages
670 Manufacturing	
680 Manufacture for specific uses	**900 Geography and History**
690 Buildings	910 Geography and travel
	920 Biography, genealogy, insignia
700 The Arts	930 History of ancient world
710 Civic and landscape art	940 General history of Europe
720 Architecture	950 General history of Asia Far East
730 Plastic arts Sculpture	960 General history of Africa
740 Drawing and decorative arts	970 General history of North America
750 Painting and paintings	980 General history of South America
760 Graphic arts Printmaking and prints	990 General history of other areas
770 Photography and photographs	

For example, the numbers 810 to 819 designate American literature, with 813 indicating American fiction. Additional numbers indicate the content of a book. Under the Dewey decimal number is an author number made up of the first initial of the author's last name, a code number assigned to the author's name, and the first letter or letters of the book's title. The combination of the Dewey decimal number and the author number is unique. It applies to one book only. In a library where you have access to the stacks, you can locate a book easily with a complete call number. Note this example for Cleanth Brooks's *William Faulkner: The Yoknapatawpha Country:*

The **Library of Congress system** uses twenty-one major divisions, each indicated by a letter of the alphabet:

A   General Works
B   Philosophy, Psychology, and Religion
C   History and Auxiliary Sciences
D   History: General and Old World
E–F   History: North and South America
G   Geography, Anthropology, and Recreation
H   Social Science
J   Political Science
K   Law
L   Education
M   Music
N   Fine Arts
P   Language and Literature
Q   Science
R   Medicine
S   Agriculture
T   Technology
U   Military Science
V   Naval Science
Z   Bibliography and Library Science

Additional letters and numbers indicate more specific categories, and, as with the Dewey decimal system, an author number designates a particular book within a category. The following call number is for Erik Erikson's *Identity: Youth and Crisis:*

psychology ────────► **BF697** ◄──────── subject (personality)

author's initial ────────► **E7** ◄──────── identifying number

Although it is not necessary to memorize categories and subcategories in the Library of Congress system, you will find it easier to use an open-stack library if you know in a general way where the books in different categories are found.

Deciphering the Code

Volumes are arranged on the shelves:

1. **Alphabetically** by the letter(s) at the start of the call number. The letters come from the Library of Congress classification scheme.

   Example: A (before) AE (before) B (before) BD (before) DA, etc.

2. Then **numerically** by the numbers that follow.

   Example: A6 A23 B299 BF3 BF35

3. Then in **alphabetical and decimal order** by the **second** letter/number combination. On a catalog card or on the book this letter/number combination would be the second line of the call number. The second combination of a Library of Congress call number is arranged as if the number following the letter were a decimal. The call numbers below are arranged in correct order because .28 is smaller than .6 and .68 is smaller than :8.

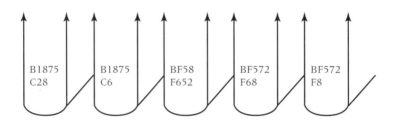

4. Then by **date of publication.** Not all call numbers end in a year. Dates are added to the call number only when a new edition is published or an earlier work is reprinted.

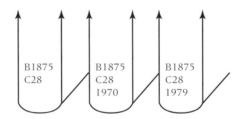

Catalogs of Libraries Around the World

Many libraries around the world have made their catalogs available on the Internet. With a little practice, you can easily access the catalogs of libraries all over the United States, Europe, Australia, and elsewhere. Materials in some libraries may be available to you through interlibrary loan.

Other Book Catalogs

You may want to compile a list of all the books on your topic that you think you would like to consult, even if they are not in your library. Some of them may be available from interlibrary loan, or you may be able to borrow directly from other libraries or friends. There are bibliographies—lists of sources—on many subjects. Many of them are complete books themselves. To find out if there is a published bibliography on your topic or the general subject you are studying, you may consult the *Bibliographic Index,* which is published in cumulative volumes every year; it lists both single-volume bibliographies and those incorporated into books and journals, many of which will not be available in small libraries (see p. 360). Easier to use than the *Bibliographic Index* is Eugene P. Sheehy's *Guide to Reference Books,* which includes an annotated appendix indicating which reference works have bibliographies.

Books in Print is a multivolume work that lists all books in English currently available for purchase by bookstores and libraries. There are volumes that list books alphabetically by author and others that alphabetize by title. Both volumes include complete publication information for each listing. In addition, the *Subject Guide to Books in Print* classifies books by subject and the *Paperbound Books in Print* lists those books published only in paper, as well as those in both paper and hardcover. Any of the volumes of *Books in Print* may be helpful for identifying very recent books that may be ordered but not yet cataloged in your library.

OCLC (Online Computer Library Center) and *RLIN* (Research Libraries Information Network) are enormous online catalogs that provide a listing of the books found in libraries throughout the United States, Canada, and some other parts of the world. Both can be searched by author, title, subject, or identifying number, or in other ways.

The Circulation Desk

The circulation desk is not only the place where you check out books; it is also the place where records are kept on all books that are not on the shelves: those that are checked out, on reserve, or being repaired. Staff people behind the circulation desk can usually tell you where books are and when you can expect to use them. If you have reason to think that a book has been stolen or misplaced, you should report it to the circulation desk.

The Stacks

Libraries shelve books that can be checked out in an area usually referred to as the stacks. In some libraries, the stacks are open, which means that you have free access to the circulating books. You can browse among the shelves, take a book down to skim it, carry it to a library carrel, or check it out. In open stacks, it is easy to find books on a particular topic and to select individual books directly from the shelves. In a library with closed stacks, you must make your selections from the main catalog, fill out a request form, and wait to have a book brought to the circulation desk.

The Microform and Nonprint Collection

Microform is the general term for all information stored as very small images called microimages, which are actually reproductions of printed material—books, newspapers, periodicals, and documents. To use microforms, you must have a machine called a reader, which enlarges the print to a readable size. The most common microforms are microfilm, microfiche, and microprint. Since most libraries have some material on more than one type of microform, you should use the general term when inquiring about these materials. Nonprint material is the term used to refer to audiotapes, videotapes, records, and films. Some libraries store these materials in a separate room near the equipment necessary to use them. You may want to learn to use the machinery before you need to use it under the pressure of an assignment.

The Reserve Book Section

Academic libraries have a section for books that have been set aside for use by students in a particular class. You will, however, usually be allowed to use reserve books in the library, and in some cases, you may be able to check them out overnight. When a book that you want is not on the shelf, you should ask at the circulation desk whether the book is on reserve. In some libraries, reserve books are kept behind the circulation desk; in others, they are in a separate section or even a special reserve reading room.

Special Collections

Library materials that require unusual care are kept in a separate room, often behind locked doors, or in a separate building. Old or particularly valuable books, fragile materials, letters, manuscripts, and all rare publications are usually kept together in the special collections room. There may be times when you will consult material in the special collections or when you will design a research project based on the collections of letters, manuscripts, or other rare or unique materials to which you have access. Once you have discovered what particularly valuable material your library has, you should ask whether it is available to students and what procedures you should follow to use it.

Library Services

Assistance in Finding Information

The circulation department will provide you with information about the whereabouts and availability of circulating books. The reference department will help you answer more specific questions on a wide range of topics. Even after you have studied the annotated list of reference works in Appendix B, you will probably need some guidance about the best reference work to consult for a particular question.

CHERWANDA WILLIAMS

Cherwanda wants to see what she can find in newspapers and magazines about her research topic. She asks the librarian where she can find the *New York Times Index* and the *Readers' Guide to Periodical Literature*, both of which she has used before. The librarian suggests that she try NEXIS, which provides the full text of articles from thousands of newspapers, magazines, and other media. Cherwanda begins by searching for articles about eating disorders and depression and comes up with more than a thousand. All of the articles contain the words "depression" and "eating disorders," but unless she reads them all, there is no way for Cherwanda to know if they link depression and eating disorders. She then refines her search by requesting articles in which the terms "eating disorders" and "depression" appear within twenty words of each other and finds over five hundred, many of which refer to Diana, Princess of Wales. The next time she modifies the request by adding "not Diana" and retrieves about one hundred articles. Scanning these, she comes up with seven articles that she thinks will be useful for her paper. She downloads the articles to a disk and later prints them in the computer lab.

Instruction in Library Use

Many libraries provide pamphlets, maps, and other materials that explain how to use a particular library's services and resources. Some provide tours, workshops, or formal classes in library skills. It is a good idea to look for notices about these services or to inquire at the circulation or reference desk. Your college catalog may explain which of these services are available to you.

Assistance with a Computer Search

Back in the 1980s, before libraries acquired computer terminals and databases that students could access on their own, some schools allowed students to make an appointment with a librarian who would conduct an online search via modem, using a commercial service like DIALOG, which provides access to a number of online databases. While such searches could be very useful, they were often expensive, as students had to pay for online time. It is still possible to conduct this kind of computer search, but because most libraries now provide electronic databases that students can easily access themselves, it is rare that students need to do so and even rare to find libraries that provide the service.

Assistance with Microform, CD-ROM, or Online Sources

While all reference librarians can help you use general reference works, the serial catalog, or the main catalog, most libraries will have particular people trained to help you with electronic sources. It is a good idea to spend some time locating the computer terminals and finding out what you can access through each one. Terminals may be used only to search the library's main catalog online, others to read CD-ROM discs, and still others to access catalogs of other libraries. Terminals are often connected to printers that will provide you with a printout of the information you want. Some may provide full texts of journals, magazines, or articles in reference works. People trained to help you with electronic or machine-read materials are often available at particular times, so it is a good idea to learn their names and schedules.

Study Areas and Storage Space

Certain sections of a library are designated for quiet study, and some libraries have carrels that can be reserved for use by individual students. Most libraries have space set aside for typing. Many also provide lockers where students can leave their books and papers overnight. You will need to take the initiative to find out if any of these services are available.

Copying Services

Using a library's copying service can save time. Most libraries have coin-operated machines that students can use to copy single pages, whole articles, or even chapters in books. Some have staff people who will make copies for you, usually for a small fee. At all times, of course, you will want to respect the copyright laws that make it illegal for you to copy large portions of a book rather than purchasing the book. The law allows you to copy for educational purposes up to a chapter in a book, three articles in an annual volume of a periodical, and a story or a poem from an anthology.

Interlibrary Services

Libraries exchange various services, ranging from reference assistance to copying services. If your library does not receive certain periodicals, you may be able to get copies of articles from them from another library. This service is usually arranged through the reference section, where you will need to fill out request forms and pay a small fee for copying.

You may be able to borrow books from other libraries through a loan system arranged by your college library. To do this you will usually need to consult with the reference librarian, fill out a form, and sometimes pay a small fee. In some cases, you will be able to obtain a book very quickly;

in others, there may be a considerable wait. In any case, ask how long it will take to get the book and respect what restrictions, if any, the lending library places on its use and on the length of time it is lent. Many libraries limit the interlibrary loan service to graduate students and faculty; others provide the service in a limited way to undergraduates. Before you try to find books in other libraries, find out if it is possible for you to borrow them.

Activities

A. On your own take an informal tour of your college library. If a map or other guide is available, use it. Otherwise, you may need to ask a few questions of the library staff before you locate everything. The following activities should lead you to all the sections of the library:
  1. Visit the section where the current periodicals are shelved. Select a popular magazine that attracts your attention and skim it, stopping to read articles that interest you.
  2. Locate the bound periodicals and skim through a single volume, such as a few months of *Life* or *National Geographic.*
  3. Browse through a scholarly journal that interests you.
  4. Find the reference section of the library, identify the reference desk, and find out which staff people are the reference librarians.
  5. Find out how the books in the library are cataloged. Are they on cards, microform, or online?
  6. If the stacks are open, browse among the circulating books and note whether the library uses the Dewey decimal system or the Library of Congress system.
  7. Select a book that interests you, or, if the stacks are closed, select one from the catalog and fill out a request form. Take the book to the circulation desk and follow the procedure for checking it out.
B. Locate the computer terminals and read any material explaining what they do. Find out if there is a computerized online catalog. Locate any computer terminals with indexes to magazines and newspapers. Find out if there are computers for reading CD-ROMs.
C. Go to the section of the library where encyclopedias are shelved.
  1. Select a noncontroversial topic in which most people have some interest, such as "Dogs." Look the topic up in the three major encyclopedias. What differences and what similarities do you note? Are there cross-references within the article? If you wanted to buy a dog,

which article would provide you with the most practical information for choosing the right breed?

2. Choose a subject you feel you know rather well—classic cars, nuclear energy, Nigeria, the Civil War, football, piano composers—and see how much you can learn from reading articles in two encyclopedias. Read carefully to see if you can spot any errors, out-of-date material, or opinions stated as fact.

3. Choose a controversial topic such as abortion and look it up in three encyclopedias, using the index to find all the articles that treat the topic. Note the varied treatments and whether the material in each encyclopedia is current; then make a list of the suggested further reading on the topic in each encyclopedia and compare the sources, noting particularly the dates of each. Do some sources appear in more than one encyclopedia? in all three? Which article gives you the most thorough, up-to-date treatment of the topic?

D. Visit the reference room again.

1. Look up B. F. Skinner in the following reference works: the *American Heritage Dictionary,* the *New Columbia Encyclopedia, Collier's Encyclopedia,* and the *International Encyclopedia of the Social Sciences.* You will find that each is more detailed than the last; as you proceed through each of the last three sources, jot down three facts not found in the previous source or sources. Jot down publication dates of Skinner's major books. Look to see if his work is discussed in more than one entry in the last source, and look up the titles of his works *Walden Two* and *Beyond Freedom and Dignity* to see if they are treated separately. Notice that the *International Encyclopedia of the Social Sciences* also has a *Biographical Supplement* that is indexed separately. You may find so much material in the final source that you will only have time to skim it.

2. Locate the *Readers' Guide to Periodical Literature* and select a volume for a year in which Skinner published a major book (1961 for *Walden Two* and 1971 for *Beyond Freedom and Dignity*). Look up Skinner and note how frequently articles were published about him in periodicals for those years.

3. Find the *Book Review Digest* and skim the reviews of one of these books. Would you be interested in reading the book?

E. Go to the library at a busy time and observe the activities of the people there. Write a paragraph or more describing how people are actually using the library.

F. Evaluate your own library. Make a list of the library materials and services mentioned in this chapter, and then find out which are available in your library. Write a paper in which you describe the resources in your library.

Project Activity

Write a paragraph or more about the library resources that you expect to use for your topic.

USING LIBRARY
SOURCES

4

When you go to the library to research a topic that truly interests you, you may find that your greatest difficulty is limiting the amount of time you spend finding and reading articles and books. It is a good idea to plan the steps of your research and to estimate in advance how much time you can spend looking for library sources. You will probably be more efficient if you allow several hours for each session in the library.

Preparing to Work in the Library

Before you begin collecting library material for a particular project, you will want to do the following:

CHECKLIST 3

Preparing to Work in the Library

1. Find out how to check out books, make an appointment with a reference librarian, order books or articles by interlibrary loan, and get assistance using databases or the Internet.
2. Sign up for classes on using the library, especially electronic sources, including the Internet.
3. Obtain materials such as cards, paper slips, writing pads, scissors, etc.

> **4.** Study suggestions for making source cards (see pp. 73–75).
> **5.** Examine examples of note cards in chapter 6.
> **6.** Decide which style is best for documenting your paper (see pp. 197–99).

USING A COMPUTER IN THE LIBRARY

If you have a portable computer, you may want to take it to the library and record your sources and notes directly on it from the beginning. Before deciding whether you want to do this, read the list of recommendations on pages 114–15 of chapter 6. Some libraries have computers available for students to use.

Selecting Writing Materials

You will save time if you always have enough writing material with you: three-by-five-inch cards for recording sources; five-by-eight-inch cards for note taking; a legal pad for your first draft; pens and pencils; and a large manila envelope, folder, or some other container that you use strictly for your research. To some extent, the kinds of materials you use will be a matter of personal preference. Some students enjoy using different-colored cards so that they can coordinate colors with types of notes or use one color for direct quotations and white cards for all other notes. (This also would help you avoid accidental plagiarism.) You may prefer more flexible slips of quality paper to the stiff index cards. Some students like to use single sides of the pages of a notebook. Regardless of color or size, individual note cards have the advantage of being easy to organize when you are ready to write your first draft, and individual source cards can be quickly put in order to form your list of sources. Whether you use long or short writing pads or small or large note cards should be determined by the scale of your handwriting and the directions of your instructor.

Using the Appropriate Documentation Style

Decide which documentation style you will use for the final bibliography and notes of your paper before you make your source cards. The Modern Language Association (MLA) style of documenting with parenthetical references is illustrated by the short paper in chapter 8, by the papers in chapters 11 and 12, and with complete instructions and sample references in chapter 10. Appendix A provides sample pages from a paper, model references, and detailed instruction for documenting a paper with endnotes or footnotes, a method that is also approved by the Modern Language Association. Chapter 13 provides a sample paper and instruction for using the American Psychological Association (APA) documentation style, used for papers on topics in the social sciences. The sample paper in chapter 14 provides all you need to know to document a research paper using the citation-sequence, or number, system endorsed by the Council of Biology Editors (CBE), a documentation style suitable for papers in the natural sciences. (A list of style manuals sometimes used for other disciplines is included on p. 199.)

Your instructor may recommend a particular style or request that you study these options and choose the one that is most appropriate. In any event, now is the time to review the possibilities and to understand that your subject matter will determine the most appropriate style. To save time later, record bibliographic information as it will appear in your list of sources.

About Style Manuals

This book provides you with the information you need to document papers according to the three major academic styles: the MLA; the APA; and the citation-sequence, or number, system of the CBE. These manuals, established by professional organizations, serve the needs of publishing scholars in the various fields. When you prepare a research paper to conform to the conventions of a particular style, you are practicing to be a publishing researcher by preparing a paper as if it were a manuscript appropriate for publication. Many literary critics, psychologists, medical researchers, marketing specialists, and others who write up their research findings first wrote papers following the standards required for papers presented for publication when they were students. Even if you have no intention of becoming a publishing researcher, the experience of creating a research paper that conforms to professional standards will prepare you for writing papers in advanced courses that require a particular style. Keep in mind that style conventions are designed to help people present research findings in a clear, consistent, and readable way.

Reviewing Available Sources

To narrow your topic as you explore your sources, begin with general sources and move to more specific ones in approximately this order:

1. General reference works such as encyclopedias, bibliographies, dictionaries, and handbooks
2. The main catalog
3. Other book catalogs and specialized bibliographies
4. General periodical indexes
5. Specialized periodical indexes
6. Internet sources

Keep in mind, however, that there are no fixed rules for ordering a search. For his paper on *Rebel Without a Cause,* Michael Gold did follow approximately this order. Lisa Lee, however, began by searching the online catalog for books on tropical forests, and then, after deciding to focus on seed dispersal, she turned to specific periodical indexes: *General Science Index* and *Biological Abstracts.* Lisa also found valuable sources in the bibliographies of scientific articles. Cherwanda Williams, on the other hand, first searched the NEXIS online database for articles about depression and eating disorders, looked for books in the catalog, and then searched for information on the World Wide Web before turning to the CD-ROM indexes where she found most of her material.

Collecting Sources

Finding the sources that you expect to use involves a number of activities that have already been suggested in this book, but it is helpful to review these activities before you begin to take extensive notes. Although you have been advised to move from general to specific sources, you will probably backtrack, and even after you have found most of your material, you may go back to the main catalog or consult an index under a different heading. Always keep a record of your progress, noting specific volumes of indexes as you consult them. Before you conclude this stage of your research, you will want to do the following:

✔ CHECKLIST 4

Collecting Sources

1. Locate and read articles in general encyclopedias, textbooks, and specialized reference works.
2. Consult the list of subjects in *Library of Congress Subject Headings.*
3. Consult the library's main catalog and record titles and call numbers of promising books.

4. Check out appropriate books.
5. Consult other book catalogs and bibliographies.
6. Study general periodical indexes for magazines and newspapers.
7. Explore specialized periodical indexes for scholarly journals, both in bound volumes and computerized databases, and use those appropriate for your topic.
8. Discover which periodicals are in your library and locate the ones you want.
9. Photocopy articles that you feel will be especially pertinent to your topic.
10. Explore the possibility of finding sources on the Internet.
11. Request copies of books or articles in periodicals (using interlibrary loan forms) from other libraries.
12. Locate nonprint material—records, tapes, microform—on your topic.
13. Make a card for each source, using appropriate bibliographic style.

Some of these steps will not be appropriate for all topics. For example, your library may not provide a service for borrowing books from other libraries; there may not be any nonprint material available on your topic; and abstracts (brief summaries) may not be available for journals in the particular discipline you are researching.

Defining and Explaining What You Want to Know

Before you plan your search strategy—the steps you expect to follow in locating material—try to define what you want to know. If you can condense your research questions to a single sentence, you will be able to explain quickly what you want to find out to the reference librarians and others who may guide you to appropriate material. A simple statement of what you want to know can also serve as a guide to keep you on the subject and to help you decide quickly which sources should be profitable and which, though interesting, are in fact irrelevant to *your* project. You might write a summary statement similar to one below.

I want to know:
1. how seeds are dispersed by animals in tropical forests
2. whether people with eating disorders might also be depressed

3. about the people who created the film *Rebel Without a Cause*
4. why *Huckleberry Finn* has been so controversial
5. about Eleanor Roosevelt's work to help women

Librarians and others can be much more helpful if you explain as precisely as possible what you want to know rather than ask general questions. If you want to learn about Eleanor Roosevelt's public activities in the 1920s, say so instead of asking for general information about her life.

Planning a Search Strategy

Try to identify the steps on the checklist above that will be helpful for your topic. For help in devising a search strategy—a plan for locating material—consult the annotated list of reference works in Appendix B and make a list of those that you think will be helpful.

MICHAEL GOLD

Before he makes a plan, Michael makes a list of the steps that led him to his topic:

1. Studied the "Motion Picture" article in the <u>Encyclopedia Americana</u>.
2. Read the chapter on movies in the 1950s in David Cook's <u>History of Narrative Film</u>.
3. Watched a videotape of <u>Rebel Without a Cause</u>.

He then devises the following plan:

1. Consult the <u>World Encyclopedia of Film</u> and the <u>Biographical Dictionary of Film</u>.
2. Check the card catalog under <u>Rebel Without a Cause</u>, James Dean, and Nicholas Ray.
3. Check out books that look promising.
4. Consult the <u>Readers' Guide to Periodical Literature</u> for 1955 and 1956 for reviews of <u>Rebel</u> and articles about James Dean.
5. Ask the reference librarian for guidance.

> After Michael completes these steps, he identifies other areas that he wants to explore and expands his plan to include the following:
>
>   6. Consult the <u>International Index to Film Periodicals</u>.
>   7. Read Robert Lindner's 1944 book, <u>Rebel Without a Cause</u>.
>   8. Consult <u>Book Review Digest</u> for reviews of Lindner's book.
>   9. Check <u>Readers' Guide to Periodical Literature</u> for more recent articles about Dean, Ray, or <u>Rebel</u>.
>   10. Check <u>Essay and General Literature Index</u> for chapters in books.
>   11. Locate and photocopy promising articles.
>   12. Begin reading.

Using a Library Network

There are three major national bibliographic networks: *OCLC* (Online Computer Library Center), *RLIN* (Research Libraries Information Network), and *WLN* (Washington Library Network). These systems link libraries by providing computerized lists of books in the collections of libraries throughout the United States and Canada. A network is useful for a variety of purposes. You may, for example, use it to locate a book that is not available in your library or to verify publication information about a book that you do not have in hand.

Identifying Subject Headings

Certain indexes have their own guides to subject headings (sometimes called a thesaurus). Some include the guide in each cumulative volume; and some—the *ERIC* publications and *Psychological Abstracts*—provide a separate volume for subject headings. Still other indexes use the Library of Congress headings. Before you use an index, study the introductory material to find out how subjects are classified. When you are looking for books on a particular subject or articles listed in indexes that use the Library of Congress system, you should consult the *Library of Congress Subject Headings.* This and other guides may suggest headings that you would otherwise not think to consult.

Finding the Right Date

If you are studying the public response to a movie or a book, you will consult indexes to periodicals published at the same time or shortly after.

Most films are reviewed immediately after they are released, and popular books are reviewed within a few months. If you have trouble finding reviews of a book, you should check at least three years after publication dates since publication of reviews of certain books, especially scholarly ones, may be delayed that long.

To find information on historical subjects, keep in mind that events are sometimes not written about for some time after they occur; some events are of course kept from the public by people who do not want them to be known.

Using Appropriate Search Terms

If you are searching a printed periodical index for articles on a particular topic, then you must know the correct subject heading and the appropriate years to find material. If you are using a computerized database, you will also need to know the correct subject headings. It is possible to refine a search of databases, such as the *MLA International Bibliography, PsycLit,* or *Biological Abstracts,* by broadening or narrowing the terms searched. Some databases allow you to do a Boolean search, using the terms "or," "and," and "not." Some allow you to refine a Boolean search by specifying what terms must be adjacent or near other terms. For example, a student doing research on Dr. Jack Kevorkian's recent campaign to legalize physician-assisted suicide might use the following strategy for finding articles in a database about current news:

1. suicide or euthanasia
2. and doctor or physician
3. and these terms should be within at least fifteen words of the name Kevorkian
4. and the articles should have been published since 1994

To search successfully, you will need to consult the directions provided by a given database.

Printing Source Citations Directly from the Computer

It is usually possible to print directly from the computer terminal the citations for sources that you find in a computer search or on a CD-ROM disc. You may later want to cut these citations and paste them to a card so that you can more easily alphabetize them; organize them according to subject categories; or, if you are using the number system for a scientific paper, arrange them according to the sequence in which you use them in the final paper. Citations taken directly from a database do not always have all the information you will need for your final citation, so when you find the original source, make sure you add any missing details to each reference.

Making Source Cards

Plan to make two kinds of cards from the beginning: *source cards,* for all the information you will need to prepare your bibliography, and *note cards,* for material that you plan to use in writing the paper. Before you begin to make source cards, study the forms for reference citations in chapter 10 for MLA style. If you plan to use the APA style, consult pages 289–97. For the CBE style, see pages 315–19.

As soon as you find the titles of books or articles on your topic, you should make a card for each reference that seems promising. You may be tempted to jot down all the references you find on a single sheet of paper, but it is better from the beginning to use a single card or sheet for each source. Why? Quite simply because it is easier and more efficient in the long run to have a single slip or card for each. There is room on a card to add call numbers and other information, even a note about what someone has told you about a source or a comment to indicate how you have actually used a source. This can be helpful later, since your instructor may ask you to annotate your bibliography, that is, to indicate after each item in your list of sources how you have actually used it. In addition, individual source cards are easy to alphabetize or otherwise organize for the final list of sources.

When you first find a reference to a book that you want to consult, note the author, title, and—if you have found it in the card catalog—the call number. Leave room for publication information of the edition that you actually use. (Note the sample source card below.) Later, when you have the source in hand, you can double-check the spelling of the author and title and then add the place and date of publication and the publisher. Keep in mind that there may be more than one edition of a book in your

A SAMPLE SOURCE CARD

Lash, Joseph. *Eleanor and Franklin.*

New York: Norton, 1971.

✓ **CHECKLIST 5**

Making Source Cards

Source cards can be used in the following ways:

1. To record all the information you need to find a source and to document it for your bibliography or list of works cited
2. To note the value and content of a source
3. To indicate how you have actually used a source
4. To alphabetize for your final list of sources

Source cards that have been used for these purposes can be very helpful to an instructor who wants to monitor your progress.

library, and you may use a different edition from the one you first found cited in a catalog or bibliography. In any case, before you make your first source card, find out from your instructor which documentation style you should use, and record the information as it will appear on your list of sources.

When you make a source card for an article in a periodical—newspaper, magazine, or journal—record all the information needed for the citation in your list of sources. Include date, volume number, and page number, as well as author, title of article, and complete title of the periodical. Consider the following example:

A SOURCE CARD NOTING CONTENT

Woolf, S.J. "A Woman Speaks Her Political Mind."
New York Times 8 April 1928: 3.

Good quotes from a speech by E. Roosevelt.

Roosevelt, Eleanor. "Why Democrats

Favor Smith." _North American_

Review 224 (1927-1928): 472-475.

ELECTRONIC SOURCE CARDS

In addition to your source cards, you may want to start a computer file in which you record your sources alphabetically using the appropriate documentation style exactly as you want it to appear in your final paper. Some word-processing programs have the capability to alphabetize entries and even to arrange the data according to the format required by a specific style such as the MLA or APA. But even the simplest programs allow you to build a list of sources easily, by recording them alphabetically and adding new sources by inserting them in the appropriate place.

If you have a portable computer with you whenever you are collecting material, you may choose to record all the necessary information about sources directly into the computer, eliminating the need for source cards. You may want to set up a template card with prompts to remind you of the information you need to record. For example:

author:
editor:
title of book or article or other source:
part of book used (foreword, chapter, essay, poem):
title of series the book is part of:
page numbers relevant to your topic:
type of source (book, essay in book, article in journal, audio cassette, Web page, etc.):
title of publication or publisher:
place of publication:
volume and/or issue number:
date:

other information (reprint, translator, identifying numbers, Web address, performers, etc.):

There are no rules about how to make a template, but you do want to make it as complete as possible. It is better to have more information than you need than to discover later that you are missing a page number or some other small detail.

Note how Carla Medina has filled in this template for one of her sources:

author or authors: Victor Fisher
editor or editors:
other contributors to the source (translators, writers of forewords, etc.):
title of book or article or other source: "Huck Finn Reviewed: The Reception of *Huckleberry Finn* in the United States: 1885–1897"
part of book used (introduction, chapter, essay, poem):
title of series the book is part of:
page numbers relevant to your topic: 1–57
type of source (book, article in journal, audio cassette, Web page, etc.): journal article
title of publication or publisher: *Mark Twain Journal*
place of publication:
volume and/or issue number: volume number 16, issue number 1
date: 1983
other information (reprint, translator, identifying numbers, Web address, performers, etc.):

You may also want to create note-taking templates. As long as you record all relevant information about a source (as in the forms above), you need add only identifying information to each note. For example, you might make one template for direct quotation and another for paraphrases as in the example below:

subject:
quote:
source:
page number:
or
subject:
paraphrase:
source:
page number:

If you record all your source information on computer, you should print a hard copy of your list of sources and/or make a backup copy on another disk. Most students, however, prefer the convenience of source cards, which they can easily carry about the library. Source cards also serve as insurance against losing your data if disks are lost or damaged.

Taking Preliminary Notes and Classifying Sources

Although most of your note taking will take place later, there will be times even in the earliest stages of your research when you will want to record dates, facts, statistics, or ideas as you read general reference works or skim periodicals or books. You probably will not quote from an encyclopedia or cite it later, since you will seek far more specialized sources dealing with your topic, but writing out a summary of an encyclopedia overview can contribute to your understanding of a topic. When you take notes, iden-

CARLA MEDINA

In the early stages of her research on *The Color Purple,* Carla reads and takes notes on various aspects of the novel, including Celie's unique voice. As she reads through articles about the novel, she chooses to make source cards for those that include a discussion of Celie's voice. Note how on the following card Carla has included all the necessary bibliographic information as well as a brief note about its content:

Harris, Trudier. "On The Color Purple,
  Stereotypes, and Silence." Black
  American Literature Forum 18
  (1984): 155-61.

Critical of the novel's moral vision
and lack of realism, but praises
Celie's voice as "powerful, engaging,
subtly humorous . . ." (156).

tify the source of the note with the first item from the source card—either the author or, when there is no author, the title—followed by the page number (see chapter 6). If you should jot down a complete sentence or even a phrase written by someone other than yourself, make sure that you put quotation marks around it (see pp. 119–20). Make separate cards for notes you expect to use for writing your paper, and put only one note on a card.

It will be easy to measure your progress by classifying your source cards as you go along. Put them in three stacks or mark them with Roman numerals indicating which of three categories they belong in:

I. Sources that you have found and hope to use
II. Those that you hope to find, either by recalling them from users of your own library or by borrowing them from other libraries
III. Those that you do not expect to be able to find

Adding a note now to each reference about its availability and possible usefulness can be helpful later.

It is best to use only one note for each card so that when you are ready to organize your notes you can shuffle and sort them easily into categories. If you take notes directly on a computer file from the beginning, you can easily rearrange them as needed.

Evaluating Sources

In general, specialized journals in which the articles are signed and written by experts are more reliable than those published in popular magazines that depend on advertising to make a profit. This is not always the case, but remember that articles published in weekly newsmagazines are often written under the pressure of a deadline and vary considerably in accuracy, objectivity, and reliability of sources used.

Some magazines are known to publish dependable articles and excerpts from books. Among these are the *Atlantic,* the *New Yorker,* and the *New York Times Magazine.* You may decide to trust an article if it is signed and includes a brief summary of the author's credentials.

Some special-interest magazines are published by private and/or publically funded institutes and societies that are committed to particular goals. *World Watch* is published by the Worldwatch Institute, which has a staff of people committed to disseminating information about recent trends and activities that threaten the environment and the welfare of people everywhere. An article in this publication would probably give you more reliable information on the cholera epidemic in South America than a travel magazine that depends on revenue from airlines that fly there.

Judging the value of a book is not easy. In general a book published by a university press is likely but not necessarily more trustworthy than mass-market books that are written in a hurry to make a quick profit. For example, a book about the bombing of the Murrah Federal Building in Oklahoma City that appeared a few months after the event could not have been very carefully researched. On the other hand, a book written by an expert on terrorism and published two years later would probably be more reliable. But not necessarily. People have many motives for writing books. Some write to reinforce a particular point of view or political position. Others write to persuade readers to think a certain way on issues. Still others report the findings of investigations and research.

Evaluating sources that you find on the Internet, particularly the World Wide Web, is especially challenging since literally anyone can create a Web site, and you will need to use good judgment to decide if the information you find is trustworthy. Information on drug therapy from a pharmaceutical company might not be as objective as information from the National Institutes of Health, but in fact it may be reliable. Information about oil drilling in the Arctic National Wildlife Refuge on an oil company's Web site would most certainly be biased; information on the same subject from an environmental organization or government agency is also likely to be slanted. You would, however, be more likely to get a truthful statement from a nonprofit organization with nothing to gain economically from oil drilling than from the company that intends to profit from it.

The more you learn about a subject, the more you will be able to judge the value of your sources. You will learn to check the book's bibliography, documentary notes, and index; based on what you are learning about a topic, you will be able to discount some books and rely on others. You will certainly want your work to be based on the most authoritative sources available to you.

If you doubt the reliability of a source, you might consider the following questions:

1. *Is it up-to-date?* An article on drug use among teenagers written in 1960 will not tell you much about the drug culture that developed a few years later, though it could be quite illuminating in contrast. An encyclopedia article on computers that lists a bibliography from 1965 and earlier will be worthless to someone studying current computer technology. Keep in mind that current editions of standard encyclopedias often include out-

of-date material. The dates on the sources at the end of an article will usually let you know if the article is current, but not all articles include a list of sources. The difficulty of knowing if some encyclopedia articles are up-to-date is one reason for their limited usefulness.

2. *What are the author's credentials?* You may be able to learn about an author's background and other publications from *Contemporary Authors.* You can often find information about authors with an academic background—usually established scholars who have published with a university press—in the *Directory of American Scholars* or *American Men and Women of Science.* An author's academic or institutional affiliation is often listed on the title page or the jacket of a book. You should be wary, however, of accepting the evaluation of a book found on its jacket or sometimes on pages inserted before the title page. These comments, often called blurbs, may have been solicited from the author's friends, and those quoted from published reviews are of course selected because they are the most favorable.

3. *Is a journal or newspaper known to be generally fair, or is it biased in some definite way?* You might try looking it up in Katz and Katz's *Magazines for Libraries,* which evaluates periodicals and indicates those that have a particular bias.

4. *Does the author have a special interest in the topic that might affect the reliability of the source?* Completely unbiased sources don't exist; individuals filter information through their experience in subtly different ways. Yet you should try to be aware of inherent or obvious biases. The CEO of an oil company would interpret "factual" information about the damage done by oil spills in a very different way than members of a radical environmental organization. You should also learn to recognize *your own* biases and keep them in mind when researching controversial subjects.

5. *Does the source seem adequately documented?* You may be surprised to learn that some books and articles have less documentation than you will be required to have in your paper. Most reliable books, however, will have at the very least a comprehensive list of sources, either after each chapter or at the end of the book. Others will include notes as well. Articles in popular magazines are less likely to indicate their sources than are those in scholarly journals, which will almost always include precise information about sources. You need not necessarily discard a source simply because it lacks a bibliography. A personal memoir, for example, is often based on notes and diaries recorded by the author. Eleanor Roosevelt's account of her career as a social activist would of course be a valuable source, but one that should be treated for what it is: a personal account that is based on memory and private records and that presents the author in the way that she wants to be remembered.

6. *In the case of controversial topics, does a source give a balanced or a one-sided view?* If you know that a topic is controversial, you can usually determine whether a source acknowledges both sides of an issue. For example, an article about the need to move people off welfare and into the workforce that doesn't mention the need for funded childcare programs would probably be biased. You may, however, be unaware of the controversial aspects of a topic. For example, if you were doing research on the conviction of Alger Hiss and you consulted only sources that assumed his guilt, you might never know that there are people who insist on Hiss's innocence. Similarly if you were interested in theories about the origins of homosexuality, you might find considerable material about psychological causes. To understand the extent of the controversy about this subject, however, you would also need to consult studies concerned with the possible biological and neurological factors involved. By beginning with objective sources—encyclopedia articles or other reference works—at the beginning of a project, you can usually discover the controversial aspects of a topic and judge your sources accordingly. Comparing the material in two or more encyclopedia articles can be helpful.

7. *Does the source's language reveal a bias or call the author's reliability into question?* In addition to the other suggestions given here, you should also determine if a source uses confusing language or misleading statistics. Beware of the following:

• *Vague, nonspecific use of language,* such as the word "average." A statement that the average annual income for a group of first-year college graduates is eighteen thousand dollars is meaningless unless we know whether that figure refers to the arithmetic average of all the salaries added together (the mean average); whether it means that half the group makes more than that and half makes less (the median average); or whether more people make eighteen thousand dollars than any other amount (the modal average).

• *Discriminatory language.* Review the accuracy of general or blanket statements about a particular group: "old people," "African Americans," "women." Beware of sources that make definitive statements about the sexes yet use sexist or gender-specific language: "man" for "humanity"; "he" when "he or she" (or a plural pronoun) is more appropriate.

• *Percentages that are misleading.* An advertisement that claims a product contains "30% less fat" does not indicate less than what, while the phrase "95% fat free" leaves you to wonder how much fat that product contains.

8. *Is a book published by a respected publishing house?* This is some-times difficult for the beginning student to discover. If you have never heard of the publishing house, you might ask your instructor about it, find other books by the same publisher and see if you can judge their quality, or look the publishing house up in a book like *Writer's Market* for the current year. This reference work will tell you what a particular house usually publishes, who its target audience is, and what its standards for accepting new work might be.

9. *How was the book reviewed?* (See *Book Review Digest* and other book review sources mentioned in Appendix B.) Checking reviews can also give you some idea of what the book contains and how it might be useful in your research.

10. *Is the source of a Web page or gopher server reliable?* There is much valuable information placed on the Internet by government agencies, non-profit organizations, universities, and foundations. If you do not know the source of a Web page or have reason to think it is propaganda or a disguised advertisement, then you should ignore it in the same way you would a book without an author, a publisher, or a date. Remember that many people use the Web for commercial purposes.

Reading Effectively

Reading an article or a book for research is rarely a matter of reading steadily from beginning to end, word for word. There are times when you will read that way, but even then you will probably first skim through the text, noting its length, chapter or paragraph headings, and sometimes its conclusion. Let us consider various ways of learning from a text, beginning with a short article and ending with a substantial book.

Many articles found in popular periodicals can be skimmed quickly with attention to facts or ideas relevant to your topic. One technique is to read the introduction and the conclusion; a second is to read first sentences of paragraphs; a third is to look for headings, graphs, illustrations, or a summary. Depending on the content of an article, one or more of these approaches may be adequate for you to decide if you want to read more carefully.

Similar techniques apply to skimming a book. A detailed table of contents can tell you a lot, as can a good index. You may also want to look at the introduction and the conclusion of a book. Sometimes books are organized in such a way that you can learn much about their content by reading the beginning and concluding paragraphs of each chapter.

When you find a source that you want to read thoroughly, consider using the PQRST method:*

P: **Preview** a text by quickly surveying it from beginning to end.

Q: Jot down **questions** that you expect to find answered in the source.

R: **Read** it carefully from beginning to end, noting passages you want to use.

S: **Summarize** the thesis and main points of what you have read.

T: **Test** yourself; make sure you understand the source before you use it.

Keeping an open mind is an important part of effective reading. Good researchers may expect or look for certain answers, but they must be open to other possibilities. If you approach a book expecting to find particular answers, you run the risk of misinterpreting it, of finding only what you want to find, of ignoring qualifications and alternative points of view. Just as we can put words in the mouth of another person, so we can misread a text, taking statements out of context and even seeing words that are not there. The best way to avoid misreading is to be aware of the possibility of its happening and to keep an open mind as to what the author is actually saying.

Returning to the Library

Most students will use library resources throughout the stages of reading, note taking, and drafting a paper. By scheduling work time in the library, you can easily look up the new people, places, words, and events that you encounter in your reading. To identify reference works that you may want to consult once your research is underway, study the descriptions of reference materials in Appendix B.

The actual business of conducting research is never quite as systematic as might be inferred from the guidelines of this book. A step-by-step procedure suggests a formula that, if followed carefully, will result in a polished, finished product; but the reality of asking questions and seeking an-

---

*The PQRST method has been used for years to teach study skills (I learned it from my high school English teacher). Recent versions can be found in these texts: Ellen Lamar Thomas and H. Alan Robinson, *Improving Reading in Every Class,* 3rd ed. (Boston: Allyn and Bacon, 1982); George Spache and Paul Berg, *The Art of Efficient Reading,* 4th ed. (New York: Macmillan, 1984).

swers—the essence of meaningful research—is often messy and erratic. You may find yourself wandering down a dead-end road or digressing to a subject that leads away from your topic. The steps suggested here can help you stick to a manageable number of questions and to reach realistic, if qualified or tentative, conclusions.

Activity

Visit your library at a time when it is not crowded (college libraries are usually least crowded during the first hours of the morning early in the term) and do any of the activities below that interest you:

1. If there is a computerized catalog, locate a terminal and use it to locate a book first by author and then by title.
2. Using either a computerized catalog or a card catalog, find out how many books your library has by Rachel Carson, Angela Davis, Norman Mailer, Toni Morrison, Ralph Nader, and D. H. Janzen.
3. Consulting the subject catalog, find out how many books there are about Sigmund Freud, Mikhail Gorbachev, Doris Lessing, Martin Luther King Jr., and Margaret Mead.
4. Look up some of the following medical topics in two general encyclopedias, such as *Academic American Encyclopedia* and *Encyclopaedia Britannica,* and notice which is the more up-to-date and thorough: AIDS, birth control, cholera, cholesterol, cocaine, depression, migraine, radiology, and schizophrenia.
5. Using an index such as *InfoTrac, Periodical Abstracts Ondisc, Newspaper Abstracts Ondisc,* or the *New York Times Index,* look up the following names and note how widely these people have been treated in the media in recent years: Maya Angelou, Hillary Clinton, Princess Diana, Bill Gates, Oliver Stone, and Edward O. Wilson.

Project Activities

A. Make a list of the questions you hope to answer through your research.
B. Try to reduce those questions to a single statement beginning with "I want to know."
C. Study the annotated list of reference works in Appendix B and mark those that you think may be useful to your project. Make a list of those

you have marked, putting them in the order in which you expect to consult them.

D. Design your own search strategy by listing the steps you expect to follow to find library material on your topic and those that will take you beyond the library. (See the next chapter.)

E. After consulting bibliographies, periodical indexes, and the main library catalog, record on index cards the sources that you expect to consult, including all the information that you will need to document your final paper.

F. Choose at least one book on your list and consult *Book Review Digest* to find out how it was reviewed. Write a paragraph summarizing the reviews you find there.

G. Find a Web site with information related to your topic.

USING THE INTERNET AND SEARCHING BEYOND THE LIBRARY

5

Consider the following questions: What is the current interest rate? How did Congress vote on a piece of recent legislation? What are the best-selling books or the most popular movies? Which species have been added to or removed from the endangered species list? Although you can learn a great deal from reading print sources, some of what you want to know—and the answers to these questions—may not yet be available in print. For some questions you might want to consult an electronic news service or a government agency's Web site; for others, you may need to contact an expert by phone, e-mail, or letter. This chapter provides guidance for searching beyond books, newspapers, and periodicals—for consulting current sources on the Internet, requesting information directly from individuals through e-mail or regular mail, or conducting telephone conversations and face-to-face interviews.

The Internet

You might want to think of the Internet as a gigantic pipeline of connected computers. Flowing through it are data, programs, images, sound, video, and text—e-mail, newspaper articles, electronic versions of books, transcripts of speeches, corporate reports, and writings by individuals advocating a cause, telling a story, or sharing information. The one thing that ties all Internet communication together is that it is interpreted and transmitted by computers.

Before Internet access became widespread, student researchers wanting to use electronic resources were limited to what was in the library: online catalogs and a limited number of databases. Interlibrary loan made it possible to gather additional sources, but information was almost exclusively being shared between libraries. The Internet enhances, and potentially expands, the research process by offering access to all kinds of information, much of it new: experts that you can contact by e-mail; online and up-to-the-minute newspapers, magazines, and other news services; government agencies; and research libraries, to name just a few.

The enormous amount of information on the Internet—and it grows daily—challenges our ability to find, evaluate, and use it. How do you, as a student researcher, take advantage of all this potential, while keeping the real limits (such as your due date) in mind? First, you will need to know how to access different kinds of information on the Internet. Then you need to call on your critical skills in order to evaluate what you find—to determine if a source is reliable and the information useful. Above all, don't be intimidated—learning to use the Net can be an exciting part of the research process. You might be amazed at the information you are able to gather and the people you are able to reach. What follows is an introduction to what the Internet has to offer, not a technological how-to guide.

Using the Internet at Your College

The beginning of a research project is an excellent opportunity to start using the Internet, but you will need to take the time to learn about the particular computers and software available on your campus—you might access the World Wide Web from your library, computer lab, or room, while another student might Telnet from home. There are many possibilities. Furthermore, the newest and best software programs available as I am writing probably will be superseded by the time you read this. For advice about using the computers at your own college, contact the experts there.

Just as you walk around the library to find the reference section, the circulation desk, and the stacks, so you will want to locate the computer labs that provide Internet access to students. You will also want to know the people who can help you—librarians, lab assistants, even fellow students. Many colleges offer short classes—in the library, the computer lab, or as part of class work—to introduce you to e-mail, newsgroups and mailing lists, gopher searches, and the World Wide Web. If this valuable resource is available to you, by all means take advantage of it.

Using the Internet for Research

Whether you have your own computer or use one provided by your college, Internet access requires three basic elements: a computer, software, and a link to the Internet. The link can be a telephone line and modem, or a cable link if you have access via the campus network.

To use the Internet effectively, you need to understand the components that are most useful for research: e-mail, newsgroups and mailing lists, gopher databases, and the World Wide Web.

E-mail

E-mail (electronic mail) is the simplest and most widely used feature of the Internet. You may already be sending e-mail to your friends and family; it is also an excellent and efficient tool for contacting experts who might be willing to answer questions about your research topic. People who might be available to help you with your research via e-mail include faculty members at your college, public relations people in businesses, staff people in government and non-governmental organizations, and experts in various fields who provide information as a public service. You can find e-mail addresses in many ways: the media, directories, and on the Internet itself (in some cases, you may have to make a phone call to someone you want to contact, explain what you want to know, and ask for the person's e-mail address). Whenever you use e-mail for research, keep in mind that the person you're contacting is doing you a favor. Explain your project briefly, ask if the person is willing to answer questions, and be specific about what you want to know. Remember that as soon as you receive an e-mail message relevant to your research, print it or copy it and record the date and the sender's name so that you can cite it properly in your paper.

Take care to evaluate what you learn through e-mail. You would not seek information from someone through e-mail unless you believed you would receive reliable information, but you may find that what you learn by asking questions of individuals differs from what you find in journal articles and books.

You may use your e-mail account to telnet to a remote computer that may provide government documents, library catalogs, and other data made available to the public. To telnet you must have the remote computer's address, which you may be able to find through the Web and other Internet sources. For example, to telnet to the Library of Congress, use the following address: locis.loc.gov

Mailing Lists and Newsgroups

Joining a mailing list is somewhat like being part of a large e-mail conference call. When you subscribe to a mailing list, you participate in a conversation that may include people from around the world. There are mailing lists on thousands of subjects, and you may well find one on your topic. To subscribe to a mailing list, you must have your own e-mail account, the name of the list, the address of the list's server, the address of the list itself (the computer where messages are posted), and instructions on how to subscribe. Once you subscribe to a list, every message posted to the list will appear in your e-mail. Note that when you respond to a mailing list message, your posting goes to everyone on the list, not just to the person whose question or comment you are addressing; to send a private message you must e-mail an individual directly. Postings always include the e-mail address of the sender, so mailing lists can be a source of people you might contact individually.

Evaluating mailing list postings presents a challenge, since you might not know anything about the people on the list. Before joining a mailing list, consider whether information you find there is likely to be reliable. Much of what is posted on a list may be valuable only to give you a sense of what people are thinking and asking about a given subject, but you also may find that someone on the list can give you information you can't find elsewhere—leads on reliable books, articles, conferences, and experts on your topic. A mailing list is more likely to be useful for general information than for hard facts.

Newsgroups are very similar to mailing lists, but instead of using e-mail, subscribers consult a special server (computer) that stores newsgroup postings. Postings on a mailing list come to you through your e-mail; those on a newsgroup, like those on a bulletin board, you must actively search out—which cuts down on the number of messages in your e-mail every day. As on a mailing list, postings to a newsgroup include e-mail addresses, in case you choose to contact someone directly. To subscribe and participate in a newsgroup, you must have access to a USENET server. Evaluate newsgroup postings using the same criteria you use for mailing lists. Remember, many groups and lists are like a public bulletin board that no one monitors—anyone can post anything there. Some, however, are monitored, and these will usually provide more reliable information, especially when the monitor is an expert on the subject.

The World Wide Web

The World Wide Web is the graphical and multimedia part of the Internet. A museum's Web site may include pictures of paintings, while a country's home page may link to a sound sample of the national anthem. For individuals, organizations, governments, and businesses, the Web provides an unprecedented opportunity to spread information. Searching the Web on a topic such as eating disorders calls up sources ranging from the personal testimony of someone suffering from anorexia to guidelines for treatment published by a medical school.

You will hear people refer to Web "sites" and "pages." A Web site refers to a collection of linked pages loaded on to a computer that is connected to the Web. For example, a seventh grade classroom, a university, a non-profit organization, or a major corporation might all have Web sites, provided they have access to the right equipment. The Rainforest Action Network's Web site includes their home page and a number of other pages that provide information and educational materials about rain forests around the world.

What distinguishes the Web from other parts of the Internet is its capacity to include graphics, multimedia, and hypertext links. Hypertext formatting allows users to jump from one Web page to another simply by clicking on highlighted words, pictures, or icons. One click may move you to another text document, or to a sound, photograph, graphic, or video.

Every page on the Web has its own URL (Universal Resource Locator). The URL is the address of a page or site and is written according to the following form: http://hostname/path/filename. For example, the address for the Purdue University library is http://thorplus.lib.purdue.edu. If you know the address of a page you want to consult, you can type the address into the Web browser and go directly to the page. If you do not know an address, you can use a search engine like Yahoo or Alta Vista. If your search string is two or more words, make sure that your search engine is treating them as a unit and not finding every mention of each individual word—read the screen directions carefully to save yourself time. Once you find a page that you think might be useful, click on the icon that allows you to access that site and record the URL displayed on the screen so that you can easily find the page from another computer.

Gopher

Designed for searching by topic for information stored in networked computers, Gopher was developed at the University of Minnesota. (It was named "Gopher" for the university's mascot—the name was a good choice since Gopher is used to "go fer" [go for] information.)

Gopher servers (sometimes called gopher sites) are computers all over the world that store information—menus, data, articles, and other kinds of documents—made available on the Internet by universities, organizations, and various agencies. The content of gopher servers is text-based, that is, it is communicated exclusively with words; there are no graphics, sounds, or videos. Gopher menus—tables of contents that help you find documents on the Internet—form a system of menus on general topics, each of which leads you to more specific topics. For example, the "health" menu will lead you to subjects such as the CDC National AIDS Clearing House, the United States Environmental Protection Agency, and the Harvard University Health Gopher. Under the Harvard University Health Gopher, Cherwanda Williams searched for "eating disorders" and found an article that she ultimately used in her paper.

To find information in gopher servers, you can use either Jughead or Veronica. Jughead allows you to search a specific site; Veronica allows you to search multiple servers. In addition to gopher servers, you can also access WAIS (Wide Area Information Server). The major difference between a gopher server and a WAIS server is that a gopher searches file names and a WAIS performs full-text searches of file contents.

In addition to reading files on the Internet, you may want to download files to your own computer or to a disk. The method commonly used for downloading is called FTP (File Transfer Protocol). The process of downloading varies from one platform to another, and you may need help from a specialist on your campus.

As with other sources, you will need to call on your critical skills to determine the reliability of what you find at gopher sites. Documents from college student health centers advising students about safe sex or proper nutrition are probably sound, but there may be better sources for the most up-to-date treatment of eating disorders.

LISA LEE

When Lisa Lee first decides to do her research on rain forests, she goes to the Internet to do some preliminary work. Lisa doesn't know the addresses of any rain forest Web sites, so she uses a search engine. Among the hundred Web pages that her search pulls up is the home page of the Rainforest Action Network, a nonprofit organization concerned about protecting tropical rain forests around the world. She reads about the organization's structure and its various campaigns to protect forests; views photographs of tropical rain forests, of the indigenous people who live there, and of land after the forest has been clear-cut; and learns something about why rain forests are important and how quickly they are being destroyed. Other links lead her to the educational home page of a seventh-grade student in Olympia, Washington; to maps of the rain forests of Queensland, Australia; and to information about medicinal plants in the rain forest. What she learns in this search will prove valuable as background for the more specific research she does later using indexes that lead her to articles in scientific journals.

CHERWANDA WILLIAMS

Cherwanda has Internet access through computers in her college library and in the computer lab. A work-study student in the computer lab shows her the basics, and in a matter of minutes Cherwanda is hooked. Using a search engine, she finds Web sites on eating disorders that give her a general sense of what these disorders are like and how devastating they can be for patients and their families. For example, she finds a page written by a young woman whose thirty-three-year-old sister is dying of anorexia nervosa. The page includes the author's personal suggestions about what family members can do to help someone suffering from an eating disorder as well as addresses and telephone numbers of several organizations that provide information on eating disorders to the public. Cherwanda also finds pages written by individuals suffering from anorexia, bulimia, or both, and in one of these she learns that some people believe that there is a direct correlation between depression and eating disorders.

Of particular use to her is the home page of a doctor who specializes in eating disorders. She clicks on a link to Dr. Myers's discussion of "Eating Behaviors and Mood." There she finds evidence of a connection between depression and eating disorders. She notes Dr. Myers's e-mail address and sends him a message asking about the prevalence and treatment of eating disorders in people with depression. The next morning she has an answer that she later incorporates into her paper.

Cherwanda spends a couple of hours viewing Web pages and printing those that interest her. The lab assistant who helps her explains that she could probably find additional material on the Internet—through gopher servers, for example—but she decides to end her Internet search. She needs to turn to sound scientific research that explores specific aspects of the relationship between depression and eating disorders; she consults the library's catalog for books, and electronic indexes for articles in scientific journals.

Evaluating Internet Sources

Using Internet sources in a research paper requires that you call on all of your critical skills. There are millions of Web pages, on almost every conceivable topic—and much of the material on the Web may be no more reliable than a personal letter, a diary entry, or a joke. Anyone with access to the Web can write literally anything and post it as a Web page. While the same is true, to some extent, of printed matter, most books from reputable trade publishers and almost all books from university presses have gone through a fairly rigorous selection process; they have been read by expert readers, editors, and in some cases even legal advisers to determine the validity of the work. Similarly, most magazines and newspapers make sure that factual information in articles is correct. The selection and editing process does not ensure that a book is reliable, but it does let you know that a book has at least been screened by supposedly responsible people. Since there is no such process for posting material on the Web, you are on your own, and you must be very careful in evaluating and selecting material to consider for your own research.

Before you incorporate Internet material into a research project, be sure to look at it with a critical eye. In some cases the reliability of information is not a concern. For example, a Web page written by a twenty-year-old college student that includes a discussion of her own experience with bulimia may be valuable as a single anecdote, but you should not use it to represent the experiences of others, and certainly not as definitive truth. Web pages written by individuals about their own experiences or opinions are exactly that—and are no more and no less valid than the stories you hear from a fellow student over coffee.

Can you trust that the personal story of the writer of a Web page is true? Usually you can, just as you generally assume that the stories that fellow students tell you about their experiences are true. In both cases you must rely on your ability to judge and determine the validity of what someone tells you. When you are talking to a classmate or other acquaintance you have the advantage of visual cues and tone of voice. You also may know other people who can verify what someone has told you. But you don't have these advantages using the Internet.

Before you conclude that factual information you've learned on a Web page or from a newsgroup is reliable, you need to check out the source. Doing so isn't easy, and sometimes you will need to disregard what you've found because you have no way of validating it. Other times a Web page will include the credentials of the author or the sponsoring organization or institution, which may help you to find out if the information there is valid. Much of the time you will want to seek information from university, government, and respected organizations and publications.

Learning Directly from People

To find the answers to some questions for some research projects, you will have to go directly to people with knowledge about your topic. Whether in an e-mail message, a telephone conversation, a letter, or a face-to-face interview, an expert, unlike a book or a Web page, can talk back to you, helping you to correct your misperceptions, understand what you've read, and find further avenues to explore. Often public service organizations have staff members who are responsible for providing topical and up-to-date information that is not available elsewhere. The League of Women Voters, for example, usually has current information about political candidates, and the Better Business Bureau offers basic information about companies—how long they have been in the community and how well they deal with consumer complaints. If people with special knowledge do not have time to talk to you at length, they may be willing to provide you with reading material or to suggest other people who will talk to you. Even if your research is based largely on printed materials, you will probably want to talk about it with someone else with an interest in your topic.

Deciding When to Ask Questions

Many topics are suited to extensive oral research. The following list will give you an idea of the kind of topics that would be enriched by talking to people and asking them questions:

✓ **CHECKLIST 6**

Evaluating Internet Sources

1. Note the e-mail address of the writer of postings found on mailing lists and newsgroups. The last three letters of an address will at least tell you something about the person—"gov" is a government office, "edu" indicates an educational institution, "org" a nongovernmental organization, and "com" a private company.
2. What evidence do you have that the person posting on a mailing list or newsgroup is knowledgable?
3. Is a Web page posted by an objective source?
4. Is a Web page actually an advertisement in disguise?
5. Is the identifying information about the author of a Web page convincing?
6. While electronic versions of respected publications are as trustworthy as their print versions, what about electronic journals, magazines, and newsletters that have no print counterpart? What evidence can you find to give you confidence in such publications?
7. In the case where you have an e-mail address of an individual or agency, send a message requesting further information.

1. The value of services provided by public facilities—a public health department, a drug rehabilitation center, a public school, the food stamp program, an AIDS information service
2. Job opportunities in particular fields—nursing, computers, the military
3. The function and impact of a business or industrial organization in a community
4. The problems of elderly people confined to nursing homes
5. Public responses to a historical event—the day John Kennedy was killed, the end of World War II, the beginning of the Persian Gulf War, the assassination of Yitzhak Rabin.

Students researching topics like these might spend much of their time asking questions, but others researching topics that depend mainly on written materials can also learn in this way. Michael Gold, for example, has read about the James Dean cult, but it becomes real to him when he talks to people who were teenagers during the time it flourished. Lisa Lee has read about some of the ways that plants and animals in tropical forests interact, but only after interviewing Professor Vitousek, an expert in tropical forests, does she begin to understand that the very survival of some trees depends on the presence of particular animals.

Just as you should not write a research paper using a single book, you should not base your conclusions on what you learn from one person. If you were researching careers in the military, for example, you would want to talk not only to recruitment officers but to people who have been recruited as well.

Contacting People

There are many different ways to ask questions: writing letters of inquiry, sending e-mail messages, making phone calls, or posting notices; arranging an appointment in someone's office, dropping by an office unannounced, or stopping people on the street; arranging a formal interview or asking one or more people to fill out a prepared questionnaire. There are no set rules to tell you which approach is best. Every time you want to learn from other people you will have to consider their personalities, their situations—how busy they are or how free to talk—as well as your relationship with them. Your history teacher, for example, may have encouraged you to stop by during office hours whenever you have a question; the academic dean of the college may be willing to answer your questions if you write a letter explaining what you want to know; and the admissions officer may make an appointment to see you, but may not be specific about what is actually required for admission.

The suggestions and examples in this chapter will serve as a guide to your own research. Some suggestions may be helpful, and others may seem irrelevant to the kind of research you are conducting. In seeking information from people, however, you should observe the rules in Checklist 7.

Posting Notices

In a college community, it is often easy to find people who know about a subject that you are researching. A proven way to make such contacts is to post notices on bulletin boards in the student center, dormitories, or other appropriate places. The notice may include your telephone number and a request that interested people call you, or it may include a space for them to write their names and telephone numbers. The following list suggests the kinds of notices that may yield results:

✓ **CHECKLIST 7**

Contacting People

1. Be respectful of the time and needs of anyone that you question. Never be late for an appointment.
2. Remember that no one is obligated to answer your questions, and that even though many people may be happy to talk to you, they do so as a courtesy.
3. Be courteous in return, even if you are angered by a response.

1. Wanted: people who are willing to talk about their experiences in the Persian Gulf War.
2. I am interested in talking to students who have feminist mothers. Do you, or do you know anyone who does?
3. I am collecting campus folklore. Please telephone me if you know any stories about strange or funny happenings on this campus.
4. I am trying to construct a profile of the typical college student's eating habits. Will you help?

Finding Organizations to Contact

If you live in a city, you have many places to visit where you will find people with special interests, but even small towns have organizations that exist to inform the public. Students researching some aspect of business may want to visit the chamber of commerce. Those studying a foreign country may want to contact a consulate, cultural organization, language school, airline, or even a restaurant connected with or run by people from that country. For almost any topic that you research, someone in your community probably would like to talk about it. If you are exploring the role of unions in a factory town, consider calling the local chapter of the AFL-CIO. If you are studying some aspect of early childhood development, you may be able to visit a Montessori school. For students of medical topics, there are public service organizations—Alcoholics Anonymous, the American Diabetes Association, the American Heart Association, an AIDS information service—that provide information to the public. Other organizations, such as mental health associations or councils that deal with drug abuse or children's issues, exist primarily to educate the public. In many communities public service agencies can help you identify specific organizations that may be helpful. If you are looking for a nursing home to visit, contact the local community council on aging. The yellow pages of the telephone book list a variety of such organizations under "Social Services." In some communities, the United Way has an information and referral service that directs people with specific questions to appropriate organizations. Many national organizations have Web sites that include telephone numbers and addresses of local offices.

Reaching the Right People

Identifying appropriate people to question requires more thought for some topics than for others. If you are researching an event that has occurred in the last fifty years, you may want to talk to people who remember the event; but to choose the right ones, you will want to consider how old they were at the time of the event. For example, a man who was in college when the Depression hit will remember it much differently than will someone who was a child at the time. People who were in their teens in the 1960s will respond differently to questions about hippies or the antiwar movement than will people who were in their late thirties. A woman who was sixteen when the Beatles first came to America will probably remember them more vividly than someone who was ten years older.

Age is only one consideration in determining a person's ability to answer a question. A person of appropriate age with little interest in public events might talk about Martin Luther King Jr., but probably would not remember Angela Davis. A person who actually fought in the Vietnam War probably will not be a good source for information about the antiwar movement; some people who survived Nazi concentration camps might feel reluctant to discuss the Holocaust, while others may want to share their experiences.

It is important to try to find out how people have learned what they know. Are they amateurs or professionals? Do they have a vested interest in a subject? Do they have personal experience or second-hand knowledge? While you might reject a rancher as a reliable source of information about the health risks of eating beef, you might seek out such a person for information about cattle breeding.

Choosing an Interview Method

Once you have identified the people who are willing to talk to you, you still have to decide what approach to take. Should you ask them to fill out a questionnaire, to answer a series of prepared questions, or to answer questions as they come up in conversation? Sometimes a written questionnaire can help you to identify what a person is likely to know or be willing to talk about, but generally questionnaires have a limited use, and it is usually best to follow up a written questionnaire with a face-to-face conversation. Some people—particularly government officials and administrators who speak for an organization or bureau—will only answer prepared questions to which they have agreed in advance.

If you decide to use a questionnaire with a group of people, make sure the group is large enough to provide meaningful results. Also take care that the group you question is representative of the larger population to which you intend to apply your conclusions. For example, if you want to find out if people who live in middle-class neighborhoods are willing to recycle their newspapers, you would question a significant but manageable number of people currently living in a number of different such neighborhoods. Those you question would need to include people of different ages and both sexes. Five people would not be enough, five hundred would be unmanageable for most students, while fifty would probably help you reach significant conclusions.

Questionnaires that rely on short answers often lead to false or meaningless conclusions. In his study of *Rebel Without a Cause,* Michael Gold might ask a number of people who were teenagers when the movie first came out to fill out a questionnaire about their memories of the movie in which they would indicate whether or not they thought the movie influenced them. But people who said yes would not really tell Michael very much unless he knew what kind of influence they were referring to. Did they wear red nylon jackets? rebel against their parents? engage in delinquent behavior? To find out, Michael would have to ask people to explain their answers.

Writing Letters

There will be times when you will want to ask questions by writing a letter. Many important people—government officials, politicians, writers, and even entertainers—employ people to help them handle their mail. While such people are not likely to grant you an interview, they may answer a letter. Remember that the mails are often slow; for that reason, you should write letters as soon as possible, always indicating the time restrictions of your research. If you can find a person's e-mail address, you may want to try that first before sending a letter through the mail.

When you write an administrator of a charitable organization, an editor, a writer, or other individuals, you should always include a self-addressed stamped envelope. There are no fixed rules about when to include postage, but usually government offices have a budget for answering mail. In general, you should think about the convenience of the person from whom you are requesting information.

There may be times when you will write a letter to request an interview. In addition to your address, you may want to include your telephone number along with the times when you can be reached or a time when you will call the person. Often people who have received a letter informing them of the purpose of your research and suggesting a convenient time will be receptive to an interview.

MICHAEL GOLD

Michael decides to write a letter to the president of a company that distributes *Rebel Without a Cause*. His questions are pointed and specific, and his letter is effective.

```
            Box 5012
            Brooklyn, NY 11210

            February 21, 1995

            Mr. Jack Lusk, President
            Swank Motion Pictures, Inc.
            201 S. Jefferson
            St. Louis, MO 63103

            Dear Mr. Lusk:

            I am writing you at the suggestion of Beverly
            Cooper, who works in the media center at Brook-
            lyn College. I am doing a research project about
            Rebel Without a Cause, directed by Nicholas Ray.
            I know your company distributes the film, and I
            would like to know how often the film is shown.
            Is it still popular? Do you send it all over the
            country?

            Since the deadline for my paper is March 13, I
            would be very grateful if you could answer this
            letter in the next ten days. I have enclosed a
            stamped self-addressed envelope for your conve-
            nience.

            Yours sincerely,

            Michael Gold

            Michael Gold
```

Within a week after sending the letter, Michael receives answers to his questions that he is able to incorporate into his paper (see pp. 236 and 238).

LISA LEE

Lisa writes a letter to Professor Peter Vitousek, whose lecture first got her interested in the subject of rain forests.

```
333 Ocean Avenue
Santa Cruz, CA 95064
January 7, 1995

Professor Peter Vitousek
Department of Biological Sciences
Stanford University
Stanford, CA 94305

Dear Professor Vitousek:

I will be in the audience when you speak at my
college on January 21, and I would very much
appreciate an opportunity to ask you a few
questions after the lecture. I am doing a
research project about seed dispersal in
tropical forests, and there is still much I do
not understand about this very complex topic. I
know that you are very busy, and I will not take
very much of your time.

I will be wearing a black sweater and will sit
near the front of the lecture hall.

Yours sincerely,

Lisa Lee
Lisa Lee
```

> Lisa's request is also successful; Professor Vitousek answers her letter, suggesting that she introduce herself after the question-and-answer session.

Making Telephone Calls

Whenever you telephone someone to obtain information, remember to be considerate of that person's time and privacy. If you go through a secretary, identify yourself, explain briefly why you have called, and ask when it would be convenient for the person to talk with you.

There may be times when you will make phone calls to ask questions requiring short answers: Do you employ part-time help? How large is the book collection in your library? Do you offer training in computer programming? When is the next meeting of the National Organization for Women? How many organizations does the United Fund support in this community? In cases when you need a quick answer, it is best to ask the question, express your appreciation, and hang up.

CARLA MEDINA

When Carla is doing research about *The Color Purple,* her roommate, who is taking a course in African-American women's literature, suggests that she talk with the instructor for the course. Carla calls Professor Miller during her office hours and opens the conversation as follows: "My name is Carla Medina, and I'm writing a paper on *The Color Purple* for my English 110 class. I'd like to ask you a few questions about the novel. Is this a convenient time?" In just a few minutes on the telephone, Professor Miller answers Carla's questions, and though the answers do not appear in the final paper, this conversation helps Carla understand some of the ways that critics have approached and analyzed the novel.

Making Appointments

Whenever you ask people for favors, it is best to do so at their convenience—which means making appointments. On a college campus, most faculty members who post office hours expect students to drop by or call during those hours. If you have more than a few brief questions, however, ask for an appointment. If you have trouble getting in touch with someone, leave a message with his or her secretary or a note on the office door. Simple courtesy and consideration of other people will lead you to the best way to arrange an interview. Most people in a college community will cooperate with an interview request if they have time and feel that they can be of help to you—and if your request is courteous and appropriate.

Conducting a Successful Interview

Before you begin an interview, whether on the telephone or in person, be prepared to record what you want to remember, either by writing it down or by tape recording it. At the very least, you should have a pencil and note pad with you to jot down brief notes. You do not want to borrow a pencil, of course, or keep someone waiting on the telephone while you look for a piece of paper. There are instructions at the end of this chapter for recording information you receive by talking to people. In addition, the different kinds of note cards described in chapter 6 can be adapted to oral research. There may be times when you want to quote a person directly, paraphrase a response, or summarize a whole interview.

Asking the First Question

A very specific question at the beginning of an interview can limit the whole process by locking the interviewer into a narrow focus. Usually when you are interviewing people, you want to ask initial questions that are general enough to allow them to reveal their attitudes and special interests. You also want to ask questions or make simple observations that invite a response.

Usually, however, if someone has agreed to talk to you about a topic, you should state in a straightforward way what you want to know. Explain your project, and then ask a general question to begin.

Leading People to Talk

In most cases, you will learn more from people by leading them to talk than by rigidly sticking to a prepared list of questions. Keep in mind that people are individuals and that they have unique experiences as well as specific information they can give you. The following questions and responses are often productive:

What can you tell me about . . . ?
What do you remember about . . . ?
Can you explain that to me?
Tell me what you mean.
Can you help me understand?

This last response may be helpful if you encounter hostility or when people tell you that you cannot possibly understand what they mean. In the long run, one way to ask questions will work for you, and others may seem strange. You want to find a way to say "talk to me" to the person you want to learn from, and you want to say it in a way that is natural to you and appropriate to the situation. Usually, if you can lead people to talk about a subject that interests them, you will be able to get them to tell you what you want to know.

Developing Patience

Hearing what people have to say, rather than what we want to hear them say, is not always easy. Discovering the special interests of others and uncovering the significant experiences that have informed their lives call for care and sensitivity. Learning to recognize what people are willing or able to talk about takes practice, and you may have a few failures before you succeed. One of the most difficult tasks is to know when and how to respect people's privacy. If you are too cautious about asking personal questions, you may never learn anything from others; on the other hand, if you probe too deeply or too quickly into private matters, you may alienate some people. To find out if an issue is too personal for an individual, you may ask, "Do you object to talking about . . . ?" And indeed some people do. Here are some final suggestions that may help you in speaking with people:

✔ CHECKLIST 8

Developing Interviewing Skills

1. Listen carefully for details and ask the person to elaborate on those that seem important.
2. Avoid interrupting with your own suggestions.
3. Use requests like "tell me more about that" when you want the person to focus on a detail.
4. Try to ask questions in a neutral way that does not indicate what you think.

5. Assume the attitude of a willing student. Do not be afraid to show your ignorance.

6. Do not push when someone seems reluctant to answer a question. You can always come back to subjects later if the person becomes more open with you.

7. Keep an open mind.

Recording Oral Responses

There are three common ways of recording and storing information from oral sources. One, appropriate to brief interviews, is to listen carefully and then to write down what you want to remember immediately afterward. The second is to take notes during the interview; the most accurate is, of course, to make a tape recording. You will have to decide which method is most appropriate for each situation.

Taking Notes

For very short interviews and for times when people object to the use of a tape recorder, you may choose to jot down notes as you listen. Notes are particularly useful for proper names that you want to remember and for questions that you want to come back to. For more extensive note taking, you may plan in advance how to organize what you hear. One way is to divide a sheet of paper in half—one side for generalities, the other for details. If you think you will quote what someone says, make sure you have an accurate record. If possible, have the person read and verify what you want to quote.

Making a Tape Recording

An audio tape recording is easy to make. You simply ask permission to make the tape, set up the recorder in a convenient place, and turn it on at the beginning of an interview. The only disadvantage of using a recorder is that some people may not speak as frankly in the presence of a recorder as they would otherwise. Most people, however, are not troubled by a recorder and soon forget that it is there. When you want to make a recording, you should consider the following:

> ### ✔ CHECKLIST 9
>
> ## Recording an Interview
>
> **1.** It is best to ask permission for the taping in a positive way. You might simply say, "I would like to record our conversation. Is that all right with you?" When asked this way, most people will agree.
> **2.** Plan ahead: Make sure that you have enough tape and either an extension cord to assure easy access to an electrical outlet or a battery-powered recorder.
> **3.** Label your tapes carefully.

A video recorder is much more difficult to use, and many people are considerably inhibited when they are being videotaped. If you have access to a video recorder, however, there may be times when you will want to use it. For example, your media department may provide videotaping services of lectures by visiting speakers, including the question-and-answer session afterward. It is a good idea to get written permission from a lecturer before making a recording.

Transcribing a Recording

If you decide to write out a recorded interview, you may be surprised at how long it will take. If your side of an interview has consisted of short questions and responses, an hour of tape may turn out to be as many as twenty typewritten pages. Often when we talk, we repeat ourselves, sometimes three or four times, so you may want to listen to the tape once, and then go back to select what you want to copy down.

A Sample Interview

LISA LEE

Lisa is well prepared for her interview with Professor Vitousek. During her preliminary reading about tropical rain forests, she keeps a list of questions about topics she does not understand. From these questions—a long list—she carefully chooses fewer than twenty that are relevant to the subject of seed dispersal and animals. Before the interview, she makes a list using a word processor, beginning with general questions and progressing to more specific ones. When she prints the list, Lisa leaves space between the questions to jot down notes, and with the questions secured to a clipboard, she goes up to Professor Vitousek after his lecture, introduces herself, and begins the interview. Immediately afterward, she goes back to her word processor and reconstructs Professor Vitousek's answers. The following is Lisa's reconstructed version of the interview:

LISA LEE: I have done some general reading about tropical nature, but for the last two weeks, I have focused on the interrelation of animals and plants in Central and South American forests near the equator. I'd like to ask you some questions, but first, please tell me how much time you have.

PROFESSOR PETER VITOUSEK: Let's see how much we can accomplish in twenty minutes.

LEE: I understand that many tropical plants could not survive without the help of animals. I'd like to know which animals are most essential to the propagation of seeds.

VITOUSEK: You need to understand that animals serve plants in three important ways: They pollinate plants so that they can produce seeds, they transport seeds away from the parent tree, and they change seeds in ways that allow them to germinate. As for dispersing seeds, some animals are more important than others. In general, birds are the most effective, mammals next, and then bats.

LEE: I have just read *Tropical Nature* by Adrian Forsyth and Ken Miyata. I learned about strategies that plants use to attract pollinators. For example, some attract nocturnal animals by producing large white flowers. Do trees employ similar strategies for the dispersal of seeds?

VITOUSEK: Yes. Bird-dispersed plants might produce small red fruit with seeds encased in fruit pulp. Birds swallow the fruit whole, their stomachs remove the fruit, and the seeds are eventually defecated. Trees that attract large mammals produce large fruit that falls to the ground, where large animals can find it.

LEE: Do particular trees have strategies to attract particular animals?

VITOUSEK: As much as you can say that a plant can have a strategy, yes. In attracting pollinators, the size and depth of flowers are factors. Darwin argued, based on the depth of a flower in Madagascar, that there must exist a moth with a tongue more than a foot long that pollinates it, which few believed until that moth was found.

LEE: Clearly trees do not have brains, but sometimes they act as if they do. I've learned that some will ripen when certain dispersers are abundant. How do they "know" that the animals are present?

VITOUSEK: They probably "know" only if the animals are consistently present at a particular time of year. It's really a matter of evolution by natural selection. Those trees in the population that fruit when particular animals are abundant have more offspring and ultimately win out over trees that fruit at other times.

LEE: I have been reading about treefall gaps. Could you explain exactly what scientists mean when they refer to gaps and tell me why gaps are important?

VITOUSEK: Gaps form when a tree that is up in the canopy of the forest falls, often knocking down other trees in the process. That allows sunlight to penetrate to the normally shady soil surface, which in turn allows rapid plant growth.

LEE: I think that it is important for some seeds of large trees to end up in treefall gaps. Do trees have a way of attracting animals that are likely to visit the site of a treefall?

VITOUSEK: That question is harder to answer. Many animals frequent treefalls, but I don't know any specific examples of large trees that grow away from gaps and produce fruit that is selected by gap-dwelling animals in particular.

LEE: Other than carrying seeds from one place to another, how do animals facilitate the germination of seeds?

VITOUSEK: Mainly by removing the fruit pulp from the seed and by scarifying the seed, either mechanically as they chew, or chemically through the action of stomach acid on the seed coating.

LEE: Tell me a little more about scarification. Is it always necessary?

VITOUSEK: To scarify simply means to break down the seed coat partially. This is required for germination by seeds of a few species and it hastens germination in many more. However, there are many species for which it doesn't matter at all.

LEE: Help me understand something about the digestive process. I've learned that some vegetarian animals (the red howler monkeys, for example) require more time for seeds to pass through the digestive system than for omnivores. Do we know how this lengthy digestive process affects seeds?

VITOUSEK: I don't really know anything about that.

LEE: How much is actually known about how the digestive process of particular animals affects the viability of seeds?

VITOUSEK: There is still much we do not know about this. Relatively few specific pairs have been studied. We know about a few pairs, such as the jicaro tree and the horse; seeds of this tree were originally eaten by now-extinct animals that lived in Central America more than ten thousand years ago, but they are now eaten by horses. We know that these seeds are still viable after passing through the digestive system of the horse. We also know that some of these seeds are further dispersed by the spiny pocket mouse that takes them from the horse dung. Many are destroyed when the mouse eats them, but a few survive. You may want to read the articles published by D. H. Janzen about this.

LEE: I wonder about birds that regurgitate seeds. Is the seed made more or less viable by that process?

VITOUSEK: I don't really know about this either. We could extrapolate from other studies and guess that it is likely that a seed would be affected by stomach acid in ways that in some cases make the seed more viable.

LEE: I am also interested in what happens to seeds that are neither defecated nor regurgitated, but hoarded. I know that agoutis hoard seeds. What chance do these seeds have of germinating and growing to sizable trees?

VITOUSEK: Animals hoard seeds because they plan to eat them later, but hoarded seeds are not always eaten. Agoutis might forget where seeds are hoarded, or they might have the misfortune of being eaten themselves, by an ocelot, for example.

LEE: Are animals that are strictly carnivorous ever involved indirectly in dispersing seeds? Do they, for example, kill and eat other animals that have seeds in their guts, and then later defecate viable seeds?

VITOUSEK: I don't know. That's an interesting question. Perhaps someone will find out by examining the feces of jaguars, for example.

LEE: What are the greatest threats to the future of effective seed dispersal?

VITOUSEK: Extinction of animals and loss of forest that seeds could disperse to. There have been some very good studies done in Mexico that found how the forest changes when particular mammals and birds are largely destroyed by hunting. In many areas the guan, a large bird, has been hunted to the point that it no longer disperses large-seeded trees effectively. We don't yet know how this will affect populations of these trees, but the effect is not likely to be good.

LEE: What effect would widespread loss of animal life have on a forest that is otherwise unchanged?

VITOUSEK: Specific plant species would be unable to disperse and would ultimately be lost, and others would become more abundant due to decreased grazing by animals.

LEE: The impression I have from my reading is that scientists know very little about this complex subject. Is that true?

VITOUSEK: That's a little strong, but only a little. We would like to learn a lot more about particular trees and animals. We need more examples and detail. With more specific examples of how animals interact with plants, we hope to generalize more effectively.

LEE: What are the most urgent questions?

VITOUSEK: What will be the effect of losing animals on the way the whole forest functions? Can we find ways to keep animals in the forest in the face of rapidly growing human populations?

LEE: Our time is up. Professor Vitousek, this has been very helpful. Thank you very much.

VITOUSEK: It was my pleasure to help you. This is a very important subject you are studying. Don't stop here.

Activities

A. Explore the resources of your community by looking through the yellow pages of the telephone book. Consult the following headings and make a list of places you would like to visit:

Art galleries
Athletic organizations
Bookstores
Libraries
Political organizations
Restaurants
Special schools for children
Social service organizations
Theaters
Colleges and universities

B. Talking to the appropriate people in your community would help you learn about each of the following topics. Choose one or more of these to investigate by making contacts and asking questions.

1. Shelters and soup kitchens for the homeless
2. Drug rehabilitation programs
3. Birth control clinics
4. AIDS testing and prevention services
5. Waste disposal
6. Recycling facilities
7. Animal shelters
8. Dog trainers
9. Abortion clinics
10. Anti-abortion organizations
11. Handicap access in buildings open to the public
12. Public transportation for the handicapped
13. Scholarships for students with special needs
14. Scholarships for minority students
15. Language-training programs for recent immigrants
16. Services for immigrants from the former Soviet Union
17. Support for starting a small business
18. Procedures for getting a business license
19. Medical care for the uninsured
20. Medical insurance for students

C. Choose one subject you would like to know more about, and make a list of questions to use for an interview. Conduct an interview, writing up the results from your notes or tape recording.

D. Choose keywords from the list above and search for Web sites. Using an appropriate search engine, you will probably have success looking for information on homeless shelters, drug rehabilitation, birth control, AIDS, recycling centers, animal rights, abortion, and scholarships.

Project Activities

A. Think of someone who would be able to give you information about your topic that you cannot find in other sources. Write a letter or send an e-mail message to that person in which you explain the purpose of your research project and request information.

B. Think of some aspect of your topic that you might learn about through an interview and make a list of the questions that you would like to have answered. Then think of a person who could help you; try to arrange an interview.

C. Make a list of relevant words or names and use them to search for information on the Internet about your topic.

RECORDING
INFORMATION

6

The early stages of research include three kinds of activities: **choosing and narrowing a topic, collecting and studying sources,** and **taking notes.** To explain how to go about accomplishing these tasks, it is helpful to present them as steps that follow one after another. But in reality these steps overlap. You may find when you are making notes that you need more sources; and as you evaluate your notes, you may discover that though you have narrowed your topic, you must focus it even more. You will be a more successful researcher if you allot sufficient time, after you have collected sources, to alternately skim and read material, take and classify notes, go back to your sources, and, when necessary, gather new material.

Taking Notes

Taking notes is an essential part of learning, studying, and researching; but it is not always easy to know when to take notes or how much to record. The way you take notes is to some extent a personal choice and depends on your study habits and how you learn. For example, some students are able to listen more attentively to a lecture if they take notes throughout, writing down most of what the speaker says; others prefer to jot down a few key words and phrases that they later use to reconstruct or summarize a lecture. In some cases, you may want to take down only what you do not know; in others, you may want a record of whatever a particular person says. The same is true for reading. Some students prefer to record main ideas as they read, others to make a few jottings and to summarize the whole at the end. At times, you may simply want to jot down only the facts that you do not already know about a specific topic. Taking notes for a research project can help you learn about a topic as well as provide a record of the facts and ideas to be used in a final report of that research.

USING A COMPUTER FOR TAKING NOTES

If you have access to a good word-processing system, taking notes directly on computer can make the task of writing a paper easier. You can organize notes according to headings and subheadings, sort them using keywords, and move paraphrased material or quoted material directly from note files into the body of the paper. Many students and professional writers prefer to do their note taking manually and don't type anything into a word processor until they are ready to write a first draft. Others like to turn to the computer as soon as possible. If you have a computer that you can use for note taking, take the time to set up a system for ordering your material in advance.

There are several computer programs that are dedicated to note taking, and if you have such a program you will want to consider using it. It is possible, however, to create a system of taking notes within almost any word-processing program that has a good search feature. Just as some people like to take notes in a notebook and others prefer index cards, people have different styles for taking notes on a computer. The following suggestions might help you decide how to organize your notes:

1. Use keywords at the beginning of each note so that you can easily find all the notes on a given topic by using the search feature.
2. Indicate the kind of note you have taken, i.e., a direct quote, statistics, a paraphrase, an idea of your own. Doing this will remind you what each note is and help you search and find, for example, a quote or a statistic.
3. Identify the source (first item in the bibliographic citation, such as author or authors, or title when there is no author) and the page number so that you can easily find all the notes from one source just by searching for the first item in the citation.
4. Leave sufficient space or page breaks between notes so that you can tell where each one begins and ends.

The following is a note on a computer file that Cherwanda Williams made:

> heading: self-esteem
> type of note: quotation
> source: Sellers, Waligroski, p. 1004
> "Self-esteem is central in many psychological theories of depression. A deficiency in self-esteem has been postulated to be crucial to the development and course of depression."

Cherwanda could locate this and other cards dealing with self-esteem simply by searching for "self-esteem." She could also find all other notes she made from this article by searching for "Sellers, Waligroski," and she could find all her direct quotations by searching for "quotation." She could also use the copy and paste (or cut and paste) features of her word-processing program to move the quotation directly into her draft.

At some point you may want to print out all your notes and organize them from hard copy. You can highlight the different headings of your topic with coded colors (e.g., blue for depression, red for eating disorder, green for treatment). Printing the notes may make it easier for you to see how much material you have on each aspect of your topic, and if necessary, to add to or revise your notes.

Taking Notes on Paper or Cards

Before taking notes in your handwriting, you will do well to plan ahead and decide what materials to use and how to organize and store your notes. Some writers take notes directly into a three-ring binder. If you have only one note for each sheet, then you will later be able to sort the individual sheets as you organize your findings.

Many students prefer to take notes directly on index cards, which are easy to store, stack, and classify. Some students like to file such cards into categories, making it easy to see what is missing in their research findings.

CARLA MEDINA

When she was doing preliminary research for her paper on *The Color Purple,* Carla found that early critics focused on three main aspects of the novel: the voices of Celie and Nettie, its moral issues, and its upbeat vision. Carla took notes on these three categories, but when she sorted her cards she found she had considerably more material on the novel's voices than on the other two categories. Based on this evaluation of her sources, Carla decided to focus on the novel's voices.

Remember that you will have two kinds of cards for recording information. You will have a set of **source cards,** one for each source with all the information needed for documentation exactly as it will appear in your list of sources at the end of your paper. You will also have a set of **note cards.** Keep your source cards with you for easy reference, so that when you begin to take notes, you can identify the source of each with the first item of the source card—the author's name or the title when there is no author.

You may not take all of the kinds of notes described in this chapter, but you probably will find most of the suggestions helpful. There are, however, a few rules that should be followed by all student researchers:

CHECKLIST 10

Taking Notes

1. Document each note, clearly indicating the source on each card at the top. You will be taking too many notes to be able to remember where each came from.
2. Stop before making each note and ask yourself if it is really relevant to your topic.
3. Before you make a note from a passage, decide whether you need to quote it entirely, whether you can paraphrase it effectively, or whether it should be included in a summary.
4. Clarify with proper punctuation or abbreviations whether a note is a direct quotation, a paraphrase, an original observation, or a fact of general knowledge.
5. To save time and insure accuracy, you may want to photocopy passages of more than a few lines.
6. Pause from time to time and evaluate your progress: Sort your notes into categories, consult your bibliography cards to identify which sources you have not read, and make a list of what you still have to do.

Photocopying

At times you will find it very convenient to have an exact copy of material that you expect to use. You can, however, waste time and money by copying material before you are sure that you will use it. After you have sufficiently narrowed your topic and identified most of your sources, you may want to consider what you would like to photocopy. Most libraries have machines that will copy directly from microform materials such as newspapers on microfilm. Since it can be particularly tedious to copy by hand from microform materials, you probably will want to have copies made for articles and passages that are crucial to your research. You may also find it helpful to photocopy magazine or journal articles that you would like to be able to study carefully or come back to when you are working outside the library. But before you do, take the time to evaluate each source. Read through an article carefully and decide if it's relevant to your topic; then ask yourself the following questions:

✔ CHECKLIST 11

Photocopying Printed Sources

1. Is this source important?
2. Will I be able to find it later?
3. Do I need all of it or just a small part?
4. Would it be better simply to take a few notes?
5. Would I learn more from taking notes?

Once you have made a copy, be especially careful to record *on the copy itself* all the details necessary to identify the source. For journal articles, note the author, title, date, page number, volume number, and issue number (if each issue is paginated separately).

Documenting Notes

To document your sources in a final paper is to cite—with a list of sources at the end of a paper, with parenthetical or numerical references within a paper, or with endnotes or footnotes—the books, articles, interviews, or other sources you have used to obtain information. It is important that you document each note as you make it by indicating both the **source** and the **page number.** Since your bibliography cards include complete documentary information—author, title, place of publication, date, etc.—you do not need to repeat it on your note cards. All you need is an identifying word or two and a page number. For many sources, you can simply use the last name of the author. When there are two works by the same author, you may choose to use both the author's last name and a key word from the title; if there is no author, a shortened version of the title is adequate.

Identify your own ideas as well as facts of general knowledge with an appropriate code. For example, if you use your initials for your own observations and GK for general knowledge, you will later know exactly what conclusions you have reached independently, what seems to be generally known, and what is the unique property of another author.

Other precautions will help you avoid confusion when you begin to write your paper. You will find it helpful to have only one reference per card. Each card should have a general subject heading as well as a reference to the source:

subject
heading   source
                                                  page no.

Use conventional quotation marks along with large marks in the margin of a card to avoid mistaking a direct quotation for a paraphrased passage.

In the beginning, you may be tempted to copy everything that interests you, but it is important that you select very carefully which material you want to record and what is the best form for each note. You will probably make cards for the following: **quotations** (p. 119), **paraphrases**

(p. 120), **interpretations** (p. 126), **summaries** (p. 128), **lists** (p. 129), **statistics** (p. 129), **original ideas and conclusions** (p. 131), and **facts of general knowledge** (p. 132). In the early stages of research, you are more likely to quote directly; as you learn more about your subject, you will know how to assimilate and paraphrase material; and toward the end, you will probably interpret your sources and reach some conclusions on your own.

Quoting

To quote is to reproduce exactly someone else's words. Always put quotation marks around quoted matter, including short phrases and key words. In addition, large quotation marks in the margin of a quotation card serve as a double precaution against accidental plagiarism—mistaking someone else's ideas, information, or manner of expression for your own thoughts or conclusions.

Personal   Roosevelt, E.

                                            My Story

                                            p. 308

"In all our contacts it is probably the sense of being really needed and wanted which gives us the greatest satisfaction and creates the most lasting bond."

It is very easy to misquote—to leave out a word or phrase or to write the wrong word—when you are copying a passage. Double-check each quotation after you have finished transcribing it. For particularly long passages, you may want to have photocopies on hand to verify the quotations as you prepare the final draft.

In a research paper, it is best to use only a few quotations, selecting those that are expressed in a highly imaginative way, that are particularly characteristic of the person you are quoting, or that for any other reason you want to preserve in the original. No one, for example, would want to paraphrase John Kennedy's famous words in his inaugural address: "And so, my fellow Americans, ask not what your country can do for you; ask what you can do for your country." No paraphrase could be so concise and memorable. Another example of words that should not be changed is this moving appeal in *You Learn by Living,* by Eleanor Roosevelt: "You gain strength, courage and confidence by every experience in which you really stop to look fear in the face. . . . You must do the thing you think you cannot do."

A few direct quotations, carefully placed, can contribute authority to your paper and can make it more lively and interesting. You should certainly quote striking and memorable statements such as the two examples mentioned above. In other cases, however, when you are considering using a direct quotation, ask yourself what purpose the quotation will serve and whether it would be better to express the idea in your own words.

Some writers make the mistake of stringing together a series of quotations that they have not fully understood. If you find that most of your notes are direct quotations, you need to stop and decide how you are likely to use them. Try putting some of the quotations that you think you will use into your own words, explaining what they mean and what conclusions they have helped you reach. Before you write your first draft, sort your note cards and decide which direct quotations should be kept in their original form and which should be incorporated into your own prose. Make sure that you know exactly what each quotation means and how and why you are using it.

Paraphrasing

To paraphrase is to reproduce the exact sense of a written passage or oral statement in your own words—to convey accurately the ideas, facts, or attitudes of someone else in words that are natural to you. A paraphrase may be clearer or more concise than an original passage or statement. Paraphrasing is a necessary skill for reporting research findings, but it is more than that. You paraphrase in your own mind as soon as you finish reading a passage and try to review what you have read; and you paraphrase when you tell someone about an article you have read or a lecture you have heard or when you answer a question on a history test based on information your instructor has given you in class. In each case, you are restating someone else's ideas. The skill with which you paraphrase is a measure of what you know. If you read a paragraph and are easily able to put the ideas in your own words, then you have a good understanding of what you have read.

In the course of a research project, you will often want to restate in your own words the exact meaning of a passage. Paraphrasing helps to clarify ideas as well as identify the material you expect to use in your final research report. And by recording facts and ideas in your own words, you develop your own style: a form of expression that is natural to you.

In the beginning, you may find it difficult to paraphrase, but the more you know about a subject, the easier it is to assimilate and restate what you read. At first, you may have trouble putting unfamiliar words, names, and concepts in your own words. Rather than quoting long undigested passages, it is better simply to make a note indicating a passage you think you will want to paraphrase when you know more. Note the following example:

Lash, E + F 280-82

Discussion of Eleanor's involvement with the Women's Trade Union League.

Come back to this later.

You also may want to make a photocopy of material that seems important, but which you are not ready to paraphrase.

Once you are familiar with a subject, you will probably be able to write effective paraphrases of significant passages, but even then it is not always easy to know when to take the time to record a passage in your own words and when to make yourself a note about where certain information can be found. To avoid wasting time and effort trying to assimilate and paraphrase material that you will never use, when you come to a passage in your reading that seems important, ask yourself if it is really relevant to your topic. If so, you may want to take the time to record it clearly and fully in your own words while remaining absolutely faithful to the meaning of the original.

You may want to introduce a paraphrase with an identifying transition:

```
Eleanor Roosevelt believed that . . .
In his study of children, Robert Coles found that . . .
According to Lash, . . .
John Mack argues that . . .
```

Below are excerpts from books followed by accurate paraphrases. Note how each paraphrase avoids using even a phrase from the original source.

ORIGINAL PASSAGE FROM ROBERT COLES'S
The Moral Life of Children

Children know and favor the concrete. An abstract moral issue is hard for them to comprehend as thoroughly real and pressing. Thus it was that Sue did her best to make some concreteness for herself, for me—that unforgettable painting.

PARAPHRASED NOTE

moral issues   Coles 275

According to Coles, children prefer to think in concrete images since moral abstractions seem unreal and irrelevant to them. Sue's memorable painting was the result of her effort to make her feelings concrete for him and for herself.

ORIGINAL PASSAGE FROM JOSEPH LASH'S
Eleanor and Franklin

Among the organizations she turned to in the hope of being able to help improve the world was the League of Women Voters, the successor to the National Woman Suffrage Association. Its leaders had emerged from the long suffrage struggle as militant advocates of better working conditions for women, children's rights, reform of the political process, and peace.

PARAPHRASED NOTE

> organizations   Josh 353
>
> The League of Women Voters, one of the organizations Eleanor Roosevelt joined, evolved from the National Woman Suffrage Association. Its leaders, who had all been engaged in the fight for woman's suffrage, took on new causes: improved conditions for women in the workplace, political reform, rights of children, and peace.

ORIGINAL PASSAGE FROM ALICE WALKER'S
In Search of Our Mothers' Gardens

During the sixties, political assassinations, the Civil Rights Movement, and the Vietnam War turned many people away from concern about atomic weapons and toward problems they felt they could do something about.

PARAPHRASED NOTE

> nuclear threat   Walker 343
>
> Alice Walker argues that in the sixties, political upheavals, social injustice, and the war in Vietnam — problems they felt they could do something about — absorbed the attention of many people, distracting them from the problems posed by nuclear weapons.

Consider how this note card combmines paraphrase with a quotation:

ORIGINAL PASSAGE FROM DOUGLAS T. MILLER
AND MARION NOWAK'S *The Fifties:*

> Three classic youth-problem films of the fifties were released in 1954–55: *The Wild One*, with Brando's moving portrayal of the tough but sensitive motorcycle gang leader; *Rebel Without a Cause*, the James Dean vehicle that took delinquency films out of the slums and into the suburbs, and *Blackboard Jungle*, which unequivocally associated delinquency with rock music. Although these films vaguely hint at larger social ills, they fail to explore them, and imply . . . that serious rebelliousness has no real cause but can be attributed to individuals.

PARAPHRASED NOTE

Rebel   Douglas and Nowak 333

Douglas and Nowak contend that like *The Wild One* and *Blackboard Jungle*, two other classic films of the mid-fifties, *Rebel without a Cause* only hints at real social problems, but unlike the others, it moved delinquency from the "slums and into the suburbs."

Effective paraphrasing requires concentration and practice. You may have to write more than one draft to capture the substance of a passage entirely in your own words. At some point, however, you may be surprised to discover that you can write a paraphrase that is actually clearer than the original.

MICHAEL GOLD

In his research on *Rebel Without a Cause*, Michael finds he has to understand a passage fully in order to put it in his own words. His own paraphrases sometimes make more sense to him than the original. In the following example, he decides that he has also improved on the source:

ORIGINAL PASSAGE

Dean's appeal   Astrachan 17

"But in each of the Dean roles, the distinguishing elements are the absence of his knowing who he is, and what is right and wrong. Dean is always mixed-up and it is this that has made him so susceptible to teenage adulation."

MICHAEL'S VERSION

Dean's appeal   Astrachan 17

James Dean always played a character who is unsure about his own identity and about moral issues. Teenagers are particularly attracted to this young man's portrayal of doubt and confusion.

Sometimes you may want to quote a word, phrase, or clause within a paraphrase as in the following note:

Public life   Roosevelt, E.
                                                      My Story
                                                      297

Although she was slow to become a public person, and
even slower to take up the cause of women's rights, she
eventually referred to herself as an "ardent citizen and
feminist."

Paraphrasing often overlaps other forms of note taking, such as interpreting—making sense out of a statement or passage—and summarizing—reducing a longer work to its main points. The more you know about a topic, the more you will be able to interpret what you read.

Interpreting

Interpretation begins as soon as you start to say what something means, to draw conclusions from facts, to explain why certain information is significant. For example, in Tamara Hareven's *Eleanor Roosevelt: An American Conscience*, Roosevelt is quoted as follows: "I don't have any more energy than anyone else. But I never waste any of it on regrets." This statement could be interpreted to mean that Roosevelt was driven to work and to do what she conceived of as her duty. It also might be used as evidence of her determination always to look forward to possible accomplishments rather than backward to failures.

Our appreciation of a book, a film, a political statement, or a psychological theory usually is increased if we are aware of its context. Michael Gold's understanding of *Rebel* grows as he learns something about the

MICHAEL GOLD

The way we interpret a person's words often depends on what else we know about that person and about the time in which the statement was made. The following example is from the first chapter of Robert Lindner's *Rebel Without a Cause . . . The Hypnoanalysis of a Criminal Psychopath.* Michael first copies it word for word:

> History has assigned to this country and her allies the task of cleansing civilization of the predatory creature whose typical history is presented in this volume. Psychological science has provided us with an instrument to study him closely and at first hand; to examine him thoroughly as we would a virulent bacillus; to dissect him and obtain his measure; perhaps even--assisted by those great social forces which are beginning to clear the slime and muck of underprivilege and economic expediency--to make of him a good citizen in a new world.

Later, Michael interprets this quotation in the following note:

> Robert Lindner's <u>Rebel Without a Cause</u> was published in 1944, a year when the whole world was all too aware of the evil--in the form of Adolf Hitler--that the psychopathic mind could create. Lindner was an idealist; he thought of his work as a contribution to the fight against fascism, and he hoped that his study would help change the social conditions that create the psychopathic personality in the first place. He wanted to change society by changing its individual victim: "to make of him a good citizen in a new world. . . ."

To reach this interpretation of the original passage, Michael notes the copyright date, 1944, and infers that the book was written during World War II. He then associates "the predatory creature" with Hitler and fascism and concludes from the last sentence that Lindner was a social reformer. It is always a good idea to know the date of your sources, and sometimes that knowledge will be essential to interpretation.

time in which it was made; and by considering the historical context of the controversies about *Huckleberry Finn,* both at the time it was published and in the last few decades, Carla Medina can begin to understand what the fuss is all about.

Summarizing

Summarizing, like paraphrasing, is a process of putting someone else's material in your own words. Rather than the careful rewriting of an original passage, a summary may be jottings, sentence fragments, or a loose outline of the main ideas of anything from a short passage to an entire book. After reading a dense paragraph, the introduction or conclusion to a book, an essay, or a magazine or newspaper article, you may want to condense what you have read by writing down the main points.

The following note is a summary of a newspaper article that reported the main points of a speech that Eleanor Roosevelt gave in 1929:

> Women   "Mrs. Roosevelt
>   Prepares,"
>   2
>
> Eleanor Roosevelt advised women who want to enter politics that they must work up through the ranks, rigorously educate themselves, and be willing to work a little harder than men. Women should seek office only because they are competent to do the job, not because they are women.

The ability to summarize—to restate concisely the main facts, ideas, or episodes of a longer work—is a useful skill for all kinds of learning, and it is *essential* for writing research papers. Whenever you summarize, you must choose what is essential and what can be omitted. In most cases, you will delete illustrations, examples, and analogies; and you will discard passages intended to attract the reader's attention, to entertain, or to persuade. As with all note taking, you should stop and ask yourself if a passage is relevant to your topic before you take the time to summarize. To summarize, you may choose one of the following forms:

A list of words or numbers
A series of phrases or clauses
Several loosely connected sentences
An informal paragraph
A polished paragraph
A series of paragraphs

Summaries may require several note cards. To avoid confusion, number each card directly above the source in the upper right corner.

Collecting Data: Lists and Statistics

Making a list is a way of recording information in an abbreviated form. There will be times when you will want to make a list from a single source—the main points of a book or, from an encyclopedia article, the titles and dates of publication of a novelist's major works. But not all lists will come from a single source. The information in the note below was gathered from two sources:

Although you have been advised to put only one note on a card, there may be times when you want to consolidate facts from different sources on a single card (as in the previous note), indicating the sources in order in the upper right corner or in parentheses after each item. Students doing many kinds of research jot down lists: of organizations Eleanor Roosevelt belonged to and positions she held; of important films of the 1950s; of countries with nuclear weapons; of animals that disperse seeds; of controversial novels.

You may want to use a separate card for noting numerical data:

Bachman study   Beardsley and Mack
                                                    83

Male high school seniors who
say they often worry about the nuclear
threat :

1976: 7.2%
1982: 31.2%

You have been advised to beware of the misuse of statistics; used properly, however, statistics can help you make sense of what you learn. One of the most common kinds of statistical studies is the sampling of a group of people to determine their behavior, opinions, or income. The results of such studies are usually expressed in percentages. Assuming that they are based on reliable sampling, statistics are significant to certain studies and essential to others. The list below gives examples of research topics and statistical information that might be significant to them:

1. Women Living in Poverty: statistics from the Fourth World Conference on Women held in Beijing, China.
2. The Economics of the Popular Recording Industry: the percentage of recordings that are pirated
3. Interpreting the Gross Domestic Product: the percentage that is related to true productivity and that which is generated by illness and catastrophe
4. The Popularity of Movies about Teenagers: the percentage of moviegoers who are under twenty-one

5. The Consequences of Deforestation: the percentage of the world's tropical forests that are destroyed each year

---

Recording Original Observations and Conclusions

Throughout the process of research, you will want to make cards on which you record your own thoughts and observations. The note below, for example, is an effort to explain contradictory statements in different sources. The student, Linda Orton, has used her own initials to indicate that the ideas are hers:

> E. Roosevelt's motives   L.O. 10/9/91
>
> The articles in Ency. Americana and Brittanica state that ER entered public life to help FDR. Both she and Lash say that she was urged to work to keep the Roosevelt name before the public while FDR recuperated. However, as a public person ER pursued her own interests and not necessarily those of her husband. Perhaps she used her husband's illness as an excuse or defense for doing what she really <u>wanted</u> to do anyway.

If you date each card right under or beside your own initials, you will have a record of the evolution of your own thoughts about your topic. Some students find that their research leads them to conclusions different from what they had originally expected; others discover evidence that supports their original ideas about a topic. For example, Michael Gold expected to find that the success of *Rebel Without a Cause* was due to the personal charisma of James Dean and the attraction that he held for teenagers who grew up in the conservative 1950s. But in fact he discovers that the success of the film was much more complicated and depended on the contributions of a number of people. On the other hand, Lisa Lee expected to find that animals are important to the welfare of plants, and she finds that some animals are not only important, but essential to the survival of certain plant species.

Stating General Knowledge

You do not need to cite a source for notes recording information that most people already know or information that is found in a number of books and articles on a subject. That Eleanor Roosevelt was the wife of Franklin Roosevelt, the niece of Theodore Roosevelt, and the mother of five children are all facts of general knowledge. The following note gives another piece of general knowledge:

GK

Eleanor Roosevelt was First Lady for twelve years, from 1933 until 1945.

From time to time, you will make cards to remind you of facts that you have absorbed from a number of sources, which you assume that anyone with a basic understanding of your topic would know and which can readily be found in general reference books. Many students have difficulty deciding what is general knowledge and what must be documented with the appropriate source. Before making a note of general knowledge, ask yourself the following questions: *Is this information available in a variety of sources? Would most people familiar with the topic know this information?*

Knowing When to Document

The list below should help you distinguish between statements of general knowledge and paraphrased information that must be documented. The first item under each number is a statement of general knowledge; the second, a paraphrase with the source indicated in parentheses; and the third, a full citation for the source.

1. *General knowledge:* Rachel Carson wrote *Silent Spring.*
   Paraphrase: Forty states passed legislation restricting the use of pesticides within two years of the publication of Rachel Carson's *Silent Spring* in 1962 (Hodgson 402).
   Citation: Hodgson, Godfrey. *America in Our Time.* 1976; New York: Vintage, 1978.
2. *General knowledge:* The Amazonian rain forests are being destroyed at an alarming rate.
   Paraphrase: The part of the Brazilian Amazonia known as Acre, the remote region where Chico Mendes lived and was assassinated, has undergone severe destruction in the last decade (Maxwell 39).
   Citation: Maxwell, Kenneth. "The Mystery of Chico Mendes." *The New York Review of Books* 28 Mar. 1991: 39–48.
3. *General knowledge:* Betty Friedan, author of *The Feminine Mystique* and *The Second Stage,* is associated with the beginning of the women's movement.
   Paraphrase: Betty Friedan and other moderate feminists recommended working for change through the established political and legal channels (Hodgson 411).
   Citation: See 1 (*citation*).
4. *General knowledge:* Many people in the late sixties questioned the wisdom of American involvement in Vietnam.
   Paraphrase: Among the many young men who attempted to avoid the draft during the Vietnam War were some 172,000 conscientious objectors, most of whom worked for two years in an alternative public service (Baskir 41).
   Citation: Baskir, Lawrence M., and William A. Strauss. *Chance and Circumstance.* New York: Vintage, 1978.
5. *General knowledge:* Japan bombed Pearl Harbor on December 7, 1941.
   Paraphrase: One of the consequences of the bombing of Pearl Harbor and the subsequent declaration of war by the United States was the detention of tens of thousands of Japanese Americans in relocation camps (Kelly 786).
   Citation: Kelly, Alfred H., and Winfred H. Harbison. *The American Constitution.* 5th ed. New York: Norton, 1976.
6. *General knowledge:* High levels of serum cholesterol can contribute to heart disease.

Paraphrase: Cholesterol is carried through the blood by high-density lipoproteins (HDL), which appear to help remove excessive cholesterol from the body; low-density lipoproteins (LDL) and very-low-density lipoproteins (VLDL) keep cholesterol circulating in the blood (Brody 64).

Citation: Brody, Jane. *Jane Brody's Nutrition Book.* New York: Norton, 1981.

Avoiding Plagiarism

To plagiarize is to take the language, ideas, or conclusions of another person and to represent them as one's own. Plagiarizing, paraphrasing, and documenting need to be understood in relation to each other; most people never have to be concerned with plagiarism as long as they learn to paraphrase correctly, to distinguish general knowledge from information that must be documented, and to document with care.

Some students come to college confused about what plagiarism is. Perhaps in grammar school they dutifully copied an article from an encyclopedia, turned it in to the teacher as a report, and received an A. Even in high school, they may have written papers that included phrases, sentences, or even paragraphs that were copied from books or articles without using quotations marks and citing the sources. At the college level, this is absolutely unacceptable. You must always make perfectly clear which of the words and ideas that you are using were taken from someone else.

You should also avoid plagiarizing accidentally. Some students think that they are paraphrasing correctly when in fact they have retained the sentence structure of the original source or even a phrase or an unusual use of a word. At times, people plagiarize accidentally when they sincerely forget what was their own idea and what they learned from other people. You will need to take special care to avoid plagiarizing sources you find on the Internet. Because it is possible to download electronic files directly onto a disk and then to transfer part or all of that material into your paper, it is very easy to plagiarize both intentionally and accidentally. Deliberate plagiarism is of course very serious and usually detectable by most instructors. Accidental plagiarism is another matter. To avoid accidentally introducing the exact words of an electronic source into your paper, print out any part of a source you think you want to use, then treat this information as you would any printed source, paraphrasing on note cards any parts

LISA LEE

Consider the following passage from Norman Myers's book about tropical rain forests, *The Primary Source,* a work that Lisa consults when she is doing background reading for her project:

> Even more to the point, I feel, as an individual—not as a scientist or a conservationist, but as a human being—that this is a splendid time to be alive, when, at long, glorious last, we can penetrate to the furthest reaches of tropical forests, not only their remote heartlands but also the zone that, paradoxically, has remained more concealed from us than have the depths of Amazonia or Borneo and that forms the forest canopy scores of meters above the ground: the last, great unexplored frontier of life on Earth.

This passage does not contain facts so much as the author's expression of his strong feelings of excitement about the upper level (canopy) of tropical forests. Lisa wants to use the phrase "the last, great unexplored frontier of life on Earth" for her final paragraph and so she correctly quotes it exactly and gives the author full credit (see p. 333).

The following use of the same passage, however, would be plagiarism. Imagine that a student, who is concluding a paper on rain forests, has read this passage and adapts it as follows:

```
Rain forests are truly amazing territory for those who want
to explore what may be the only unexplored frontier left on
the Earth.
```

Even though the passage is used in a new context with different sentence structure, the student has still plagiarized. The phrase "unexplored frontier," and the idea that rain forests or their canopies may be the last, belongs to Norman Myers and he must be given credit.

that you want to integrate into your own writing, and selecting the portions that you want to quote directly. Make sure to set off or enclose direct quotations in quotations marks.

You will never plagiarize accidentally if you observe the rules in Checklist 12:

✔ **CHECKLIST 12**

Avoiding Plagiarism

1. Document all material from other sources, including direct quotations, paraphrases, summaries of facts, statistics, lists, charts, and illustrations.
2. Exempt from documentation only material of general knowledge and your own thoughts and conclusions.
3. Review your note cards and sources after you have finished your paper to make sure that you have not unconsciously confused someone else's ideas with your own.
4. Put a pair of large quotation marks on either side of a quotation note so that there will be no confusion in your mind about which notes are quotations.
5. In your final paper, carefully observe the conventions for quoting (enclose short quotations in quotation marks and set off longer ones) so that there will be no question about where a quotation begins and ends.
6. Paraphrase and summarize by completely casting information and ideas in your own words and style, inserting quotation marks within your paraphrase or summary whenever a unique word or phrase is retained from the original source.
7. Observe all the rules of the particular documentary style that you use.
8. Document the source of information retrieved electronically as thoroughly as you do print material.

Activities

A. Turn back to the *Academic American Encyclopedia* article on "jungle and rain forests" (pp. 34–35).
1. Choose a paragraph from the article and paraphrase it.
2. Reword part of the same paragraph, but retain the author's wording in a phrase or clause. Be sure to indicate this wording with quotation marks. Remember that whenever you use an author's words without giving credit, you are plagiarizing.
3. Make a list of the main points of the article.
4. Summarize the article in a single paragraph.

5. Note any statements in the article that are general knowledge. Remember that statements of general knowledge do not have to be documented in a research paper.

6. Note a phrase, clause, or sentence that you would quote in a research paper.

B. Read the short paper on Eleanor Roosevelt that begins on page 175. Using a light pencil, put a "q" beside each quotation, "gk" beside statements of general knowledge, and "c" by any original conclusions of the author. Indicate in the margin how many sources are used in each paragraph.

C. Study the five sample papers in chapters 11, 12, 13, and 14.

1. Note how each uses quotations. Which uses the most? Which the least?

2. Select a quotation from one of the papers and paraphrase it, trying to retain the sense of the original.

3. Write a brief summary—approximately one hundred fifty words—of Carla Medina's paper on *Huck Finn* (see p. 268).

Project Activities

A. Choose one of your notes that is a direct quotation.

1. Paraphrase it by objectively restating it in your own words and retaining the tone of the original, carefully avoiding any expression of your own opinion.

2. Using the same quotation, or selecting another, write a paragraph in which you combine paraphrase with interpretation.

B. After you have finished taking notes from all the sources that you have collected, stop, take stock, and evaluate your progress. The process of reading, taking notes, questioning people, and perhaps reading again may have led you to rethink your original intentions. Follow the steps on the next page to determine whether you need to redefine your topic:

1. Check each note card and make sure you have recorded all the information you need to identify the source in your paper.

2. Look over your note cards and make a list of the possible approaches to your topic.

3. Sort your cards to determine which aspect of your topic you have learned the most about.

4. Make a list of questions that you still need to answer.

5. List your next steps.

7

ORGANIZING
MATERIAL

There are so many different ways to organize knowledge, and studying a topic always involves a struggle to make connections and to discover relationships. When you first try to order facts and ideas, you will probably discover for yourself what you actually know about a topic. You then have the task of trying to organize what you have found to make it clear to others. Working carefully in the preliminary stages of organization will help you to write a final paper that is clear and logical.

Sorting Note Cards

Ideally you have been assessing your progress all along, but when you have finished collecting materials, talking to people, reading, and taking notes, you will want to stop and systematically evaluate what you have done.

Sometimes students sort their notes only to discover that they have a miscellaneous collection of facts; if this happens to you, you should select the category that most interests you and return to your sources for more information or, if necessary, collect more sources. One student spent several days reading and taking notes on the subject of running. When he stopped to sort his note cards, he found that they fell into these categories:

Sprinting
Recreational jogging
Competitive running
The benefits of jogging

The Boston Marathon
Famous runners

After examining the categories, he discovered that he really had a little information on several different aspects of a large subject and that none of the categories related to each other in a meaningful way.

This student could have strung his notes together haphazardly, beginning with recreational jogging and ending for no particular reason with the Boston Marathon or famous runners. But the result would have been little more than a mishmash of facts. So, instead, he looked at his sorted

---

✔ CHECKLIST 13

Organizing Your Material

To begin organizing your thoughts, consider doing the following:

1. Clear out enough space—a table, desk, your bed, or even the floor—to spread out notes, computer printouts, books and photocopies of articles. Arrange them in categories.
2. Eliminate materials that are not relevant.
3. Consider making two categories: "yes" and "maybe."
4. Set aside the "maybe" stack and evaluate and further categorize the material you know you want to use.
5. Using your computer or a note pad, make a list of the main points you want to make about your topic.
6. Write an introductory paragraph in which you open the discussion of the main points and present a thesis you intend to explore.
7. Consider whether the sample papers are appropriate models for your topic. Will you write an argumentative paper like Cherwanda Williams's paper on depression and eating disorders or Carla Medina's paper on *Huck Finn?* present your findings in a scientific format like that followed by Lisa Lee? analyze a literary text as Carla does in her paper on *The Color Purple?* or narrate a process using both topic categories and a rough chronological order as Michael Gold does in his paper about *Rebel Without a Cause?*
8. Go back through your own notes and sources, record the points you want to make, and experiment with different ways of organizing them.

MICHAEL GOLD

Michael began his study of *Rebel Without a Cause* intending to learn about the success of the film and the contribution that James Dean made to it. When he categorizes his note cards, he discovers that in addition to material about Dean and the film's success, he has learned about the people who made the film—the director, the writers, the actors. He has learned about the James Dean cult; and he has also discovered that although many people associate the film with Dean, he was actually only one of many people who brought *Rebel* to fruition.

cards and chose the category that interested him the most: the benefits of jogging. He then went back to his sources and found additional information on that more limited topic. After discarding the irrelevant notes and taking new ones, he found that he could sort the notes he now had into four main categories: weight control, muscular development, psychological health, and cardiovascular fitness. Note the balanced outline (p. 148–49) that he eventually made.

Testing Your Hypothesis

Most people begin a research project with some idea of what they will find. Michael Gold, for example, expected to find that the success of *Rebel Without a Cause* was due to the charisma of its leading actor, James Dean, but he discovers that many other factors contributed to the film's success. This discovery leads him to discard a single hypothesis, to raise a number of questions, and to keep an open mind.

LISA LEE

Lisa began her research on animals in the rain forest with the notion that the plant/animal relationship is one-sided. She thought that while trees are useful to animals, providing them with shelter, food, and a place of safety from predators, only a few animals assist plants, mainly by pollinating them. Lisa soon discovers that this assumption, or implied hypothesis, is inaccurate, and that many animals are essential to the survival of plants. She then develops a working hypothesis that the plants and animals are mutually interdependent.

Although Lisa takes notes from articles in the library, she also photocopies some articles. As soon as she has identified information relevant to her topic, she types her notes into her computer.

CHERWANDA WILLIAMS

Cherwanda actually began work with a tentative hypothesis that her research supported. After observing the behavior of a friend who seemed to be depressed and whom she suspected might be bulimic, she wondered if there was a relationship between eating disorders and depression. She discovered that many researchers investigating the two disorders found that there is indeed a connection between them.

Before you begin to outline your findings, you should pause and ask yourself whether you still have one or more working hypotheses or a preliminary thesis that you think your findings will demonstrate. If so, write it out, and then go back to your sorted notes and test it. If Michael Gold had written out his original hypothesis—that *Rebel's* success is due to its leading actor—then he would easily have seen that his research could not support that statement. It is a good idea to make a list of any preconceived ideas you have and to test them against your notes to make sure that you do not distort your findings in order to prove yourself right. Ask yourself the following questions:

CHECKLIST 14

Testing Your Hypothesis

1. What did I expect to find when I began research?
2. What did I actually find?
3. If these two are different, what led me to change my mind?
4. If they are the same, have I ignored any evidence that might suggest a different conclusion?

It is possible that your original expectations and your conclusions will be the same, but most researchers find that their original ideas are altered more than once. This of course does not always happen in the systematic way suggested by the list of questions above, since a single article or even a sentence in a text may change your way of thinking.

Developing a Controlling Idea or Thesis Statement

You will be able to control and shape your material more effectively if you can explain in a sentence or two exactly what your paper will be about. This statement of what you intend to demonstrate in your paper is the thesis, and everything in your paper should contribute to that goal.

The Thesis Statement

After you have sorted your note cards and decided that you have enough material to write a report, you may want to write out what you think will be your thesis statement, the controlling idea of your paper.

MICHAEL GOLD

After he sorts notes and before making an outline, Michael writes:

> Rebel Without a Cause was created over a period of years, developing from the dedicated collaboration of many people who brought different points of view and experiences to the project, and it influenced the behavior and feelings of a large number of young people who were united by their infatuation with James Dean.

By keeping this statement in mind both when he outlines his material and when he starts writing his first draft, Michael is able to decide which notes are relevant and which, though they are interesting, should be set aside. Trying to stick to a controlling idea makes it easy for Michael to discard notes concerning Dean's irrational behavior and his similarity to Marlon Brando.

After he writes a first draft based on this controlling idea, Michael examines what he has written, revises it—bringing the information about the Dean cult to the beginning—and writes a new thesis sentence:

> Rebel Without a Cause was really the product of the
> imagination, the creative energy, and the plain hard work
> of a group of people--the director, writers, actors, and
> technical experts--who compose the community of a film.

This thesis allows Michael to use the information about the Dean cult in his introduction, to qualify it in the fifth paragraph, and to focus in the remainder of the paper on the various people who contributed to creation of the film. He is able to use the information about the film's interpreters in a final section leading up to the conclusion.

Not everyone is able to identify a controlling idea after sorting note cards. Some students need to write out an introductory paragraph before they can identify a single thesis or main idea that directs the progress of the finished product. Others discover a controlling idea only after they have begun writing.

Some students, like Cherwanda Williams, need more than one sentence to express their thesis. The process of trying to get down your first ideas may help you to discover an approach to your topic and a way of relating the different aspects of your study to each other. The first draft of an introductory paragraph may simply be a way to get started. After you have written it, you may be able to sketch out a preliminary outline. Later you may want to revise it and incorporate it into a more polished introduction.

Expository or Persuasive Thesis

The controlling idea or thesis statement of a research paper may be expository or persuasive, or a combination of the two. An **expository** thesis simply states what the paper is about in a sentence that suggests that what follows will be interesting and informative. A **persuasive** thesis also states what the paper is about, but in a manner that shows that the author is taking a stand, making an argument, hoping to change the reader's beliefs or move the reader to action.

Linda Orton's thesis statement in her paper about Eleanor Roosevelt is expository:

> Her many activities included work to improve the lot of
> disadvantaged women and to help all women develop their
> potential.

This precise statement alerts the reader that the rest of the paper will provide information about Eleanor Roosevelt's work for women.

Not every paper includes a single-sentence thesis statement. Because Lisa Lee's paper follows a scientific format, her main points are summarized in the abstract at the beginning (see p. 321). She could combine these, however, into the following thesis statement:

> Whether a seed will grow to a mature tree depends on features of
> its parent, the treatment it receives from animals, and the
> availability of the space and light necessary for growth.

Cherwanda Williams uses three sentences to present a thesis in a clear and precise way, and she incorporates into the last sentence her view that people with eating disorders should be tested for depression and treated for it if it is found:

> Recent research findings reveal a correlation between eating
> disorders and depression. This correlation is strong enough to
> suggest that people suffering from eating disorders may also be
> depressed. Therefore they should be tested for depression; those
> who are found to be depressed should be treated for both
> disorders.

This more complex statement of intent allows Cherwanda to present her evidence in a way that will persuade readers that the correlation between the two disorders needs to be considered by medical professionals who treat patients suffering from both disorders.

Michael Gold's thesis is a combination of persuasion and exposition:

> Rebel was really the product of the imagination, the creative
> energy, and the plain hard work of a group of people--the
> producer, director, writers, actors, and technical experts--who
> compose the community of a film.

In his paper Michael Gold puts together the story of all the people who helped to create the film, and at the same time he argues against the idea that James Dean himself was responsible for the film's success.

Many good research papers have both expository and persuasive elements, but there can be dangers in overemphasizing either mode. By writing a purely expository paper, you may leave your reader thinking "So what?" Some students work very hard researching a topic, but they fail to present the material in a way that convinces readers of its importance. Their papers are nothing more than a collection of facts.

One effective form of persuasion is the presentation of interesting facts in such a way that readers are able to reach their own conclusions. Lisa Lee presents her findings objectively without using excessive emotional appeals. Her readers can easily conclude that the protection of tropical animal species is essential to the preservation of plant life. The first step in many persuasive projects is to educate, to give people the facts they need to understand the importance of a subject.

A straightforward scientific paper like Lisa's usually does not pull on the heartstrings. A paper whose intent is to move people to action immediately might include more imaginative elements to motivate readers—a description, for example, of an animal watching its habitat destroyed by fire. When you use such persuasive strategies, you will want to be as careful with facts as you are in an objective scientific paper. Lisa Lee, however, also does more than simply lay out the facts; she makes it clear that what she has to say is important and that her readers should be interested. If you are genuinely interested in a subject—as were all the students whose papers are in this text—then you will be able to make that subject interesting to your readers. Almost all successful persuasive writing requires careful research and thoughtful presentation of research findings.

There are some dangers to conducting research with the intention of using it to write a persuasive paper. You may be tempted to oversimplify a complex subject, to select only the evidence that proves a thesis and ignore the rest. You probably should not begin a persuasive paper until you yourself have been persuaded by what you have found.

Writing an Introduction

There are no hard and fast rules about when you should write the introduction to a paper, but some students who have difficulty organizing material find that the effort to write an introduction results in a kind of unconscious organizing. The draft of an introduction may serve as a skeleton outline that, as you review your notes, you can elaborate and develop. It is usually a good idea to draft an introduction very early on, to analyze the main points in an introduction, and then to determine what should be eliminated and what needs to be expanded. Give yourself time for this process to take place. After you have reviewed and organized your notes, and perhaps even after you have constructed what you think is your thesis sentence, open a new computer file or choose a clean notebook and begin writing. What comes out may surprise you and may help you shape your paper. A preliminary draft of an introduction can be useful even if you discard it later and write another.

Although you may use more than one paragraph for the introduction to your paper, your first paragraph must do double duty. It must help announce what the paper is about, and it must get the reader's attention. Readers will probably continue to read if they are convinced that what they will learn from the paper is both interesting and important.

Following the Standard Outline Format

The standard outline format that is used in most disciplines is simple and logical. It alternates between numbers and letters, using Roman numerals for major categories of a paper, capital letters for the subheadings under the major categories, Arabic numbers for details under the subheadings, and lower-case letters for any breakdown of the details. Each subordinate heading is indented, beginning immediately under the first letter of the first word of the larger category. You should be able to adapt this pattern to any topic:

    I. [First major category]
        A. [Subheading]
        B. [Subheading]
    II. [Second major category]
        A. [Subheading]
            1. [Detail]
            2. [Detail]
                a. [Breakdown]
                b. [Breakdown]
        B. [Subheading]
    III. [Third major category]

Another form—often used in technical writing or for papers in business and the sciences—is the decimal outline:

    1. [First major category]
        1.1. [Subheading]
        1.2. [Subheading]

2. [Second major category]
   2.1. [Subheading]
      2.1.1. [Detail]
      2.1.2. [Detail]
         2.1.2.1. [Breakdown]
         2.1.2.2. [Breakdown]
   2.2. [Subheading]
3. [Third major category]

Many topics can be organized using only one level of subdivisions under the major categories. An outline that includes even minor details is more than a plan; it is really a distilled version of a complete paper that will later be cast in readable prose. A very detailed outline sometimes requires as much work as a rough draft.

Outlining Your Material

There are different ways of thinking about outlining. For some writers the outline is a strict plan carefully structured before drafting of the paper begins. For others, outlining is a process of discovery that changes as they draft and revise. Michael Gold combines the process of drafting and outlining, Cherwanda Williams writes a complete sentence outline before she begins her first draft, and Lisa Lee organizes her paper according to a scientific format. For her work on *The Color Purple,* Carla Medina decides that her paper will have three parts and an introduction (see p. 166). Her outline for the *Huck Finn* paper is ordered chronologically as she traces first one side and then the other of the controversy about the novel (see p. 266). Instructors vary in their requirements about outlines. Some teachers may not even ask to see your outline, some may want only the final outline, and still others may want to check the drafts of outlines in order to advise you as you organize the paper. Keep in mind that an outline is a tool to help you shape your material, not a hurdle that you must get over to meet a requirement. If you are having trouble making an outline, you may need to reconsider your thesis statement and to reexamine your sources to find out what you have really learned.

Constructing an Outline

An outline is both an organized description of your research findings and a plan for the report you will write about your research. An outline of what you have found may reveal irrelevant material or point to aspects of your topic that need more research. A final outline of what you intend to write about may go through several stages as your ideas develop. Most people are able to construct an adequate plan using words or, at most, phrases to indicate the main points or topics they plan to cover. A sketchy topical outline allows you to develop ideas as you compose, whereas a detailed sentence outline requires that you develop your ideas primarily in the outlining process. Some people, however, do prefer to organize their material in complete sentences before they begin to compose.

The kind of outline you use should be determined by the subject you have researched, the amount of factual evidence you have to support your points, and the nature of your own thought processes. For most people, there is an interaction among writing, thinking, and organizing. As you proceed with the writing of a paper, you will probably revise your outline more than once, rearranging the order of topics, adding evidence, deleting irrelevant material.

Balancing an Outline

Your paper will probably be more effective if you try to present your findings so that the different parts are about the same length. If you are researching two books, for example, you should give approximately the same space to each. The student who once had such a hodgepodge of miscellaneous material on the subject of running eventually focused his study and constructed this perfectly balanced outline:

```
                    THE BENEFITS OF RUNNING

    I. Weight Control
        A. Aids self-control
        B. Expends calories
        C. Suppresses appetite
        D. Encourages a healthy diet
   II. Muscular Development
        A. Improves tone
        B. Enhances contours
        C. Increases strength
        D. Improves endurance
  III. Psychological Well-Being
        A. Aids sleep
        B. Inhibits depression
        C. Increases strength
        D. Intensifies vitality
   IV. Cardiovascular Fitness
        A. Strengthens heart
```

        B. Lowers blood pressure
        C. Changes blood lipids
        D. Improves circulation

   The parts of an outline are often not as symmetrical as they are here, where each category has an equal number of subcategories. Research findings may not fall into categories with equal and parallel subheadings, and it is a serious mistake to try to force your material into a neat outline. To do so is to distort your findings and to suggest a false logic and even false conclusions. It is much better to have a sketchy, unbalanced outline that is an accurate reflection of your findings than a neat but misleading one. But an outline that is very unbalanced may indicate serious problems in organization.

   Some topics can be planned from the beginning in such a way that the findings will necessarily suggest a balanced outline. For example, a student who wanted to learn something about jazz and who decided to study two representative musicians from four cities where jazz has flourished constructed the following outline:

                    THE MANY FACES OF JAZZ

        I. New Orleans
           A. King Oliver
           B. Sidney Bechet
       II. Chicago
           A. Tommy Dorsey
           B. Glenn Miller
      III. New York
           A. Dizzy Gillespie
           B. John Coltrane
       IV. San Francisco
           A. Gerry Mulligan
           B. Chet Baker

This outline is geographical in that each main category is a city where jazz was important, but there is also a chronological principle at work: jazz began in New Orleans, moved up the river and on to Chicago, then became popular in New York, and finally emerged on the West Coast. Often, as with the jazz outline, the best organizing principles for research findings are inherent in the topic and in the way the research is conducted. An anthropologist studying the economic significance of various animals in a peasant community might naturally order her findings by reporting on one animal at a time, moving from the least important to the most important. Many students, however, begin to explore a subject without a fixed idea of what they want to find out; and in such cases, it is best to keep an open mind about how to organize research findings, allowing, as Michael Gold does, the material itself to suggest its own order.

Using an Organizing Principle

There is usually more than one way to organize the same material. You might, for example, shape your findings by ordering events as they happened, by showing how two or more elements are alike and different, by making general statements and then supporting them with concrete evidence, or by setting up a problem and demonstrating solutions. With the exception of the opening paragraphs that deal with the cult that developed after Dean's death, Michael Gold largely organizes his material chronologically, telling the story of the making of *Rebel Without a Cause* as it happened. Carla Medina organizes her discussion of *Huck Finn*, around the two arguments, discussing the novel's critics first, then its defenders. Within these two categories she organizes her discussion chronologically.

Cherwanda Williams organizes her paper logically, beginning with a discussion of two common disorders followed by definitions of the diagnostic criteria for each, an overview of the research that links the disorders, and finally a discussion of treatment options. Lisa Lee, on the other hand, organizes her material using the guidelines of a scientific format. Your organizing principle may emerge unconsciously as you struggle with your material, and a carefully constructed thesis will usually call for one or another treatment. Michael Gold's research focuses on a process and therefore invites a temporal ordering.

Revising an Outline

MICHAEL GOLD

Michael organizes his study of *Rebel Without a Cause* rather easily. He first watched a videotape of the film and read the book that gave it a title. After a period of reading, taking notes, photocopying articles, and marking relevant passages, Michael categorizes his notes and writes his first preliminary thesis sentence:

> Rebel Without a Cause was created over a period of years,
> developing from the dedicated collaboration of many people
> who brought different points of view and experiences to the
> project, and it influenced the behavior and feelings of a
> large number of young people who were united by their
> infatuation with James Dean.

He decides that he can organize his paper chronologically, telling the
story of the creation of the film from beginning to end. He then sorts
his cards into stacks representing those people who contributed to
the film's production, those who were influenced by it, and those
who have interpreted it. He arranges them chronologically and produces the following outline:

THE COMMUNITY OF A FILM: REBEL WITHOUT A CAUSE

   I. The Beginning
       A. Robert Lindner's Rebel Without a Cause
       B. Warner Brothers' purchase
       C. Lindner's contribution
  II. The core community
       A. The director
       B. The producer
       C. The musical director
 III. The screenwriters
       A. Problems
       B. Leon Uris
       C. Irving Shulman
       D. Stewart Stern
  IV. The actors
       A. James Dean
           1. Relationship with Ray
           2. Improviser
       B. Natalie Wood
       C. Supporting actors
   V. Influence
       A. The original fans
       B. The Dean cult
       C. The interpreters
       D. Conflicting views
       E. Problems of evaluation

When revising the first draft based on this outline, Michael decides to rearrange his material. By moving the information about the Dean cult to the introduction, Michael can stress that what many people know about the film—James Dean and his impact—is only part of the story. Studying his outline, he retitles the other categories and rearranges the material, emphasizing the different stages of the film's development in a more effective way. His new outline looks like this:

```
    I. Rebel's followers and creators
       A. Rebel's impact
       B. The Dean cult
       C. The creators
   II. A collaborative effort: the beginning
       A. Robert Lindner and Warner Brothers
       B. Nicholas Ray
  III. The writers
       A. Odets and Uris
       B. Shulman
       C. Stern
   IV. The actors
       A. James Dean
       B. Natalie Wood
       C. Others
    V. The interpreters
       A. Conflicting views
       B. Problems of evaluation
   VI. Rebel's place in film history
       A. Appropriate categories
       B. Need for reevaluation
```

LISA LEE

After Lisa has checked out several books, read and photocopied more than a dozen articles on seed dispersal, highlighted relevant passages, taken notes both on cards and in a computer file, and carefully recorded information from books that she would soon have to return to the library, she prepares to organize her material. She prints the notes she has on a computer disk and then clears her desk. She then assembles all of her sources and classifies them into four general categories: introductory material, plants, animals, and environmental factors. She enters all her references into a computer file, using the correct bibliographic style.

With all this material organized in front of her, Lisa opens an "outline" file and begins typing. Following a format recommended for scientific papers, she decides that her paper will have seven parts: an abstract, an introduction, a discussion of the methods she used to find her materials, three main parts in which she explains her findings, and a conclusion. Since an abstract and conclusion cannot be written until the main body of the paper is complete, Lisa does not subdivide them. A version of this outline is incorporated into her highly structured paper.

```
  I. Abstract
 II. Introduction
       A. State of research
       B. Various methods of seed dispersal
III. Research methods
       A. Search of indexes
       B. Examination of lists of references
       C. Focus of studies used
 IV. How plants facilitate dispersal
       A. Schedule of ripening
       B. Influence of disperser's feeding behavior on
          ripening
       C. Size of fruit crop
       D. Availability of fruit during times of scarcity
  V. Factors determining a disperser's effectiveness
       A. Degree to which digested seeds survive
       B. Rate of passage through the gut
       C. How the animal handles seeds while eating fruit
       D. Failure to retrieve hoarded seeds
 VI. Other factors that impact the fate of a seed
       A. Presence of seed predators
       B. Number of seeds in dung pile
       C. Adequate light and space: treefalls
VII. Conclusion
```

Lisa is now ready to begin drafting her paper. As soon as she finishes this outline, she opens a computer file and begins.

Writing a Sentence Outline

CHERWANDA WILLIAMS

At her instructor's suggestion, Cherwanda writes a sentence outline. By thinking through her entire paper in advance and putting down her main points in complete sentences, Cherwanda is able to organize complex material.

I. The incidence of both eating disorders and depression is on the rise.
   A. The disorders are widely treated in the media.
   B. There is an increasing amount of research available on the disorders.
   C. Major universities organize Eating Disorder Units in their Medical Schools.
II. The diagnostic criteria are established in the DSM-IV.
   A. There are four criteria necessary for diagnosis of anorexia nervosa.
   B. There are five criteria necessary for diagnosis of bulimia nervosa.
   C. There are seven criteria necessary for diagnosis of a major depressive episode.
III. A significant amount of research indicates that there is an association between the two disorders.
   A. The relationship may be influenced by cultural factors.
   B. The relationship may be explained by biochemical factors.
   C. The relationship may be explained by low self-esteem.

IV. There are certain treatment methods supported by
    research.
    A. Drug therapy for eating disorders includes
       antidepressants.
    B. Rates of success differ for treatment of anorexia
       and bulimia.
    C. A combination of cognitive behavioral and drug
       therapies are effective for bulimics.

Activities

A. Read the short paper about Eleanor Roosevelt at the end of chapter 8 and sketch out an outline of the main points.
B. Turn to page 253 and read Carla Medina's paper "The Voices of *The Color Purple*." Outline her main points. Is there another way she might have organized the same material?
C. Consider the branching diagram on page 15 that Lisa Lee uses to recall what she already knows about environmental issues. Translate the topics on the diagram to a standard outline format. Which categories are incomplete? What might you add? Can you add subheadings?
D. Look back again at the encyclopedia article on pages 34–35. Outline the main points using either a standard outline or a branching diagram.

Project Activities

A. Sort your notes into categories and eliminate those not obviously related to your topic.
B. Is there more than one way to organize your notes? Choose the one that seems best and sketch out an outline of your findings.
C. Write out a statement of what you intend to demonstrate in your paper. Do you expect to write an expository or a persuasive paper?
D. If you plan to write a persuasive paper, sort your notes, choosing those that will most effectively advance your argument.

COMPOSING AND REVISING

8

You begin writing your paper the first time you paraphrase a written source or jot down a summary after an interview. By the time you sit down with a clean sheet of paper, several stacks of notes, and an outline, you will already have written drafts of small parts of your paper. Nevertheless, the task of taking this raw material and crafting it into smooth, readable prose lies ahead. Even though you may have an outline that seems orderly enough, you still must arrange the bits and pieces that you have collected into logical sentences and paragraphs, creating a coherent pattern. Shaping your material requires constant attention to the way one sentence relates to another, as well as to how each relates to the whole. From the beginning, it is good to make your points as clearly as possible, using all the transitions, definitions, and explanations that are necessary for meaning.

Getting Started

Before you start to write, try to have the materials, the space, and the time you need to write at least three hundred words—a good beginning.

Many writers like to compose first drafts in longhand, using a pencil for easy erasure. If, however, you write best with a favorite pen, by all means use it. A long legal pad is good for drafts because you can use every other line, leaving space for revision, and still have several sentences on a page.

Find a surface—a large desk, a dining room table, or a card table—where you can line up your note cards, stack books, and lay out your writing materials. You will save time if you find a place where you can leave these materials until your paper is complete; but if roommates, family members, or others are likely to distract you, it may be best for you to pack up and head for the library.

You will probably get more done if you can allot at least three hours for a writing session. If possible, allow yourself a little more time than you think you will need and plan to take a break after about an hour and a half or when you get tired.

USING A WORD PROCESSOR

There are many advantages to beginning the composition process directly on a computer. Whether you are going to use a computer from the beginning or after your project is well underway, you may want to consider the following recommendations:

1. Make sure the computer and printer you plan to use are in good working order.

2. Make sure that you know how to indent, delete, and insert words and passages; move blocks of texts within a file and from one file to another; and save, copy, and delete files. Practice the format commands—underlining, spacing, setting margins, and numbering pages. Finally, print a file to see the results.

3. If you already know how to use these features of a word processor, you may use it for brainstorming, recording sources, taking notes, organizing findings, and outlining or planning a paper. If you do so from the beginning, you can open multiple windows and move ("copy and paste") material from a note file directly into the paper.

4. If you find your ideas running dry on a particular section of your paper, you can quickly scan your notes for new ideas.

5. As soon as you have completed a draft of your paper, you may want to print out a hard copy. Many writers find they can make revisions more effectively on a printed copy than on the computer monitor.

Imagining the Reader

All writers need to consider for whom they are writing. Scholars who write for professional journals assume that their readers are people like themselves, specialists who share a vocabulary and a common body of knowledge. Microeconomists, behavioral psychologists, or medieval historians might report their research in a way that only others in their fields can read with ease. In the course of your research, you may have found articles or books that you could not make much sense out of simply because their authors used many words you did not understand.

Most students, however, do not write up their research findings for specialists. Unless your instructor specifies a reader for you, it is usually advisable to think of your audience as someone who wants to learn about your topic, but who knows little about it. You may find it helpful actually to imagine a particular person who fits that description, a classmate or family member who is interested in what you are learning but who has no context or special vocabulary for understanding it. Michael Gold, for example, does not write for movie buffs only, but for anyone who has even a slight interest in movies. He imagines a reader who may not even have seen *Rebel Without a Cause.*

Being Consistent

From the beginning, you want to strive for consistency—selecting a verb tense, a level of word choice, and a tone that you carry throughout your paper. You should also be consistent about the mechanics of writing. When there are variant spellings of a word, for example, choose one and use it consistently; or when you are documenting your sources, choose one style of documentation and use it throughout the paper.

Developing a Readable Style

Your main consideration when you choose your words and construct your sentences should be readability. You want to write so that others can understand what you have to say as easily as possible. Some students are tempted to use a specialized vocabulary or long and obscure words because they want to sound intelligent; but it is best to concentrate on communicating what you know clearly rather than on showing off what you have learned.

What you write will be more readable if you create a voice that is natural to you, so that when you read what you have written, it sounds like you when you are trying to explain something that is important. Of course you will not use slang, which is often natural to informal speech, but which is also often vague and imprecise. One way to test the voice of what you have written is to read out loud or, even better, into a tape recorder. If your voice sounds pretentious or insincere, you will probably want to work on your style. Once you have completed a portion of your paper, read it carefully and ask yourself the following questions:

CHECKLIST 15

Developing a Readable Style

1. Have I used long words where shorter ones would have been just as effective?
2. Have I been general where I could have been specific?
3. Have I tried to show off what I know rather than to say clearly and precisely what I mean?

If the answer to even one of these questions is yes, you probably need to try more consciously to compose sentences and paragraphs that others can read with ease.

As you are composing your paper, take care to use gender-inclusive language. Writing prose that does not use sexist language is easy if you follow these guidelines:

CHECKLIST 16

Using Gender-Inclusive Language

1. Use masculine pronouns only to refer to individual men or to groups of people that are *exclusively* male.
2. In order to avoid the awkward "he or she" and "his or her," consider changing singular nouns to plural as in the example below:
   A student who finishes his or her project early . . .
   Students who finish their projects early . . .
3. Use nouns that are not gender-specific: *server* instead of *waiter*, *firefighter* instead of *fireman*, *spokesperson* instead of *spokesman*.

The National Council of Teachers of English has drawn up guidelines for avoiding sexism in writing. To order a copy of them, ask for *Guidelines for Nonsexist Use of Language in NCTE Publications* (NCTE, 1111 Kenyon Road, Urbana, IL 61801. Stock No. 19719).

Planning Ahead

Budgeting time is important at every stage of research, and it becomes crucial as you begin to write. Not only do you need time for composition and revision, but you need adequate time in between these steps. When your first draft is finished, it is a good idea to set it aside before you revise it. When you come back to a draft after some time, you will usually be able to see where it needs improvement. The time required for writing papers varies enormously, but the schedule below is adequate for most people writing a paper of approximately ten pages.

CHECKLIST 17

Budgeting Time

1. Writing the first draft: two to three days or five three-hour sessions
2. Laying the first draft aside: one day
3. Revising and typing the second draft: one day
4. Laying it aside: one day
5. Revising and typing the finished paper: one day

Writing the First Draft

Whether you write in longhand, use a typewriter, or compose on a word processor, writing your first draft should be a process of trying out alternatives, marking some out, and starting over again and again. Even if you are working from a detailed outline, you will probably experiment with different ways of presenting your research as you write. A handwritten or typed first draft should in fact be messy, reflecting numerous efforts to improve your writing—to say it better—as you compose. The way in which you introduce your sources and give credit for information can, however, help you present your findings and argue your thesis.

Writing in Your Own Voice

Think of your paper as being mainly written in your own voice. You are explaining in your own words what you have learned and what you have concluded. Whenever you paraphrase or summarize the words of the writers whose articles and books you have studied, you must try to do so in a way that is natural to you, in words that you might use, while being careful to indicate your sources in the text of your paper so that it is perfectly clear which are your thoughts and ideas and which are those of others.

Citing Sources as You Compose

From the beginning, cite each source as you use it and make sure that you have all the information needed for a complete citation in the bibliography. Every quotation, every paraphrase, every fact that you have learned in your research should be identified in the text of your first draft. Sometimes you may want to begin a paragraph or a sentence with the name of the author or authors of a source you are using:

```
Joseph Lash concludes that . . .
Tamara K. Hareven offers another view.
Bernard Bailyn et al. explore . . .
Davidson and Lytle demonstrate that . . .
```

Always cite the page number when you refer to a part of a source rather than the whole and place the page number of the source at the end of a clause or sentence as you compose:

```
In Eleanor and Franklin, his best-selling Pulitzer Prize-winning
biography, Joseph Lash explains Eleanor Roosevelt's role in the
League of Women Voters (355).
```

```
As Eleanor Roosevelt has written, "It is probably the sense of
being really needed and wanted which gives us the greatest sat-
isfaction and creates the most lasting bond" (308).
```

When you do not mention the author's name in the text, include it in the parenthetical reference along with a page number:

```
During Franklin's convalescence, Eleanor assumed the responsibil-
ity of keeping the Roosevelt name before the public (Hareven 20).
```

Always make it clear where a paraphrase ends by putting the page number at the end of several sentences or a paragraph taken from the same part of a source. See the first full paragraph on page 176.

Note how sources are cited in the sample paper at the end of this chapter, and see page 161 for further examples of ways to introduce sources.

If you are writing a paper using the APA style or the citation-sequence system of documentation recommended by the CBE style manual, you will include other information in the text of your paper as you compose—date of publication for APA and a number for each source in the number system. See chapter 13 for APA and chapter 14 for CBE style.

The following rules assume that you are using the documentation style recommended by the Modern Language Association, but the principles apply to other styles of documentation as well. These rules should help you with the technical aspects of integrating sources into a coherent text. For examples, see the marginal notes in the short paper at the end of this chapter.

✔ CHECKLIST 18

Citing Sources

1. Make perfectly clear the exact source of all material except facts of general knowledge and your own ideas and conclusions.
2. Indicate sources within the text when you can do so smoothly and always when you need to clarify which are your own ideas and which you owe to someone else. When you refer to material from a particular page number of a written text, you will have to give the page number—in parentheses or in a note.
3. After direct quotations indicate the source either in parentheses or with a note number that will correspond to a note at the bottom of the page or on the endnote page or to an item in your list of sources.
4. Place references after paraphrased material in such a way that there is no doubt about the source. In paragraphs that depend entirely on a few pages of a single source, cite the source at the end of the paragraph.
5. When you use two or more sources in a paragraph, use as many citations as are necessary for clarity.

Providing for Notes as You Compose

If your paper requires either explanatory or documentary footnotes or endnotes, indicate in your draft where you expect to place the note, using an asterisk, a circle, or some other code. In the margin, place the page number and any other information necessary to write a complete note later. Unless you are using a word-processing program that keeps up with the numbers of notes and automatically renumbers them, make sure that numbers in the text correspond to the appropriate notes.

Integrating Quotations with Your Own Words

Learning how to combine your own words with someone else's is as necessary as learning the technicalities of documentation. The best guide for doing this effectively is again your own voice. Quote only when it is important to capture another person's voice or exact words, and know enough about your subject so that you can smoothly move from your own ideas and words to those of another person. Remember, this is *your* research paper. The sources you use and the quotations you include are intended to back up and explain your thesis. You are not just compiling data—you are interpreting and reporting your findings.

You may choose to quote a word, a phrase, a sentence, or several sentences, but in any case, you should retain the exact spelling and punctuation of the original. When you use quotations, it is important that you do so smoothly, making sure that your sentence is grammatically correct and that any quoted material appears exactly as it does in the original. Short quotations—not more than four lines—should be incorporated into the text of your paper. They may be integrated in a variety of ways:

At the beginning of a sentence:

> "The very best of human possibilities," according to George
> Eliot in <u>Daniel Deronda</u>, is "the blending of a complete personal
> love in one current with a larger duty" (685).

Following an introductory clause:

> A character in George Eliot's <u>Daniel Deronda</u> refers to marriages
> as "all the wondrous combinations of the universe whose issue
> makes our good and evil" (812).

With an introductory clause followed by a colon:

> Joseph Lash stresses the complexity of Eleanor Roosevelt's char-
> acter: "She was the teacher, the moralist, the dreamer, but she
> was also highly practical" (386-87).

Combined with paraphrase in the same sentence:

```
Lash argues that because of Franklin's career, Eleanor's "prod-
dings and probings had to be carried on in a way that would not
embarrass him politically" (387).
```

Note how short quotations are integrated into the sample paper at the end of this chapter (pp. 175–80).

Long quotations of more than four typed lines are usually set off with a colon with no quotations marks and indented ten spaces from the left margin. The right margin does not change. Do not add extra space before or after the quotation, but simply double-space throughout. If the long quotation is all from one paragraph, do not indent further (see the long quotation on page 177), but if you are quoting two paragraphs, indent the first line of each three more spaces:

```
Dickens's descriptive power is evident in the opening lines of
Little Dorrit:
          Thirty years ago, Marseilles lay burning in the
     sun, one day. A blazing sun upon a fierce August day
     was no greater rarity in southern France then, than at
     any other time. . . .
          There was no wind to make a ripple on the foul
     water within the harbour, or on the beautiful sea
     without. The line of demarcation between the two
     colours, black and blue, showed the point which the
     pure sea would not pass; but it lay as quiet as the
     abominable pool, with which it never mixed.
```

Avoiding Padding

You may be tempted to pad a research paper, to put in all the interesting bits of information you have found, even when they do not directly relate to the main idea of the paper. If your instructor has asked for a paper of a particular length—perhaps ten pages—you may at first feel that you cannot possibly write so much on your topic and that you therefore will have to use all your notes.

LISA LEE

Before she focused her paper on factors determining the effectiveness of seed dispersal of tropical trees in Central America, Mexico, and Peru, Lisa read and finally eliminated a number of interesting articles that were not directly relevant to the points she wanted to make: about crabs and even fish that disperse seeds, about the ways monkeys seem to organize themselves into groups according to the amount of food available in a given area, and about the germination rates of seeds that have passed through the digestive track of pygmy chimpanzees in Africa. After carefully sorting out this material, she places it in a separate file labeled "Sources not used." She is then able to write a clear, uncluttered paper.

Revising

By writing on every other line on long sheets of paper—such as legal pads—or by triple- or at least double-spacing a hard copy, you will have adequate space for revising sentences and words, but revising paragraphs and the overall structure will sometimes require rewriting on separate paper and cutting up the sheets you have written and rearranging them. Every time you read through your paper, you will probably make minor changes in words and sentences, but the larger structural changes need to be made systematically.

Revising on a word processor is especially efficient because it is easy to move text around. Be sure to save a copy of your file with a new name before you start revising. The cutting and pasting happens simply by giving the computer a command and striking a key. If you think you want to save parts of your draft, you can open a file (labeled "extra") and store them for later.

If you compose your paper on a word processor from the beginning, you will probably revise all along. When you are ready for a systematic revision of a completed draft, you will probably print out a copy that you read carefully with pencil in hand.

Evaluating Organization

Once you have written a first draft, you should examine it to see if it really reflects what you intended to say. The first step is to compare your preliminary outline—the one you made before you began to write—with an outline of what you have written. The surest way is to go through your draft and to write down in abbreviated form—words and phrases—what you have actually written, making a new outline of the draft itself. Then consult your original plan. Are they the same? Which is better?

CARLA MEDINA

Carla has decided to organize her paper on *The Color Purple* by first treating the critical reception of the novel, then analyzing the ways Celie speaks and gives voice to others, and finally considering how Celie's ability to speak for herself and others is related to her development as a person.

Once Carla has decided how to organize the major points she wants to make, she is able to write the first draft and prepare her list of references in two days. Since Carla composes the whole paper directly on a word processor, she prints out the paper and sets it aside.

After reading her first draft of the paper, Carla decides to add a paragraph describing the novel's form and content so that what she says about the novel's voices will make sense to someone who has not read the novel. (See the second paragraph of her paper on p. 253.)

Rearranging the Parts

Rearranging the parts of a rough draft may require drastic methods: taking a paragraph from the middle and putting it in the introduction, for example. Sometimes you can indicate changes in the margins, but often you will want to make the change by cutting up your manuscript and pasting or taping sections on new sheets, leaving space for writing transitions to connect one part to another. Once you are working with a word processor, you will find it easy to revise, but you still may want to make changes on a printed copy before entering them into your computer. Numbering the pages of your draft, even though you know these will not be the final page numbers, makes it easier to change or add material during revision. If, for example, you write a paragraph that you want to insert in the middle of page 12, number it 12a and place it after the original page 12, indicating clearly in the text where you want to insert it.

Eliminating Unnecessary Material

You may be reluctant to strike through sentences and paragraphs that you have worked so hard to write, but most rough drafts include extra words, sentences, and even larger units that you later admit are really not necessary. You may have to force yourself to mark through repetitive or irrelevant passages (if you're working on computer, you can save sentences you like in your "extra" file). Tell yourself that your writing will be more effective if it is not repetitive and if each part contributes to the whole. Then read through your draft looking for what you can strike through without weakening your meaning. Notice how Michael Gold cuts the passage below from forty to twenty-two words:

Original

According to Kreidl, it was Leonard Rosenman, the musical director of <u>Rebel</u>, who suggested the thirty-one-year-old Stewart Stern
as a replacement for Shulman. At last, Ray had found a collaborator with whom he could work until the film was finished.

Revision

Leonard Rosenman, the musical director of <u>Rebel</u>, suggested the
thirty-one-year-old Stewart Stern, who worked with Ray until the
film was finished.

Since Michael's preceding paragraph ends with a statement about the break between Shulman and Ray, there is no need to repeat it, and nothing is lost with the other cuts (see p. 242).

Lisa Lee cuts her paper by eliminating largely speculative material about coevolution of plants and animals since the studies she read on this subject did not really contribute to the points she wants to make. In the following passage, she paraphrases a quotation that seemed confusing, and she retains the one that seems most understandable.

Original

John Terborgh, for example, suggests the possibility that the
keystone plant species may "act over evolutionary time as deci-
sive factors in the evolution of whole faunal assemblages," but
he urges that this possibility "be regarded as wide-eyed speculation."

Revision

John Terborgh suggests that keystone plant species may determine
how groups of animals act over time, but he urges that this possibility "be regarded as wide-eyed speculation."

Clarifying Meaning

Ask yourself if you have expressed what you want to say as clearly as possible, and then reread your paper from the point of view of an interested reader who does not know very much about your topic. Sometimes what is clear to you may not be clear to someone else. Because you have become familiar with a topic, you may find it difficult to decide whether what you have written will make sense to someone who has not studied the same material.

Improving Paragraphs

The goal of all revision is clarity. When you examine a paragraph to see what improvements you can make, first identify the main idea and then decide if you have developed it as clearly as possible. Do you need more explanation? Is there irrelevant material that belongs elsewhere or not in your paper at all? Is the order effective? Sometimes when you have doubts, you may want to write another version and choose between the two.

Improving Smaller Units

Although you will probably change some sentences and words as you revise the larger units of your paper, it is advisable to go through it at least once just to improve diction (word choice) and sentence structure. The following list suggests a procedure for revising that you may find helpful:

1. *Vary the length of your sentences.* If most are approximately the same length, try to achieve more variety either by combining short sentences or by breaking down long ones.
2. *Use the active voice.* Whenever possible, structure sentences so that the subject is followed by an active verb. Note the following example from Michael Gold's paper:

ORIGINAL

```
Rebel was directed by Nicholas Ray.
```

REVISION

```
Nicholas Ray directed Rebel.
```

You can easily locate passive verbs by looking for "is," "was," and other forms of the verb "to be." (But the passive voice is not taboo. It can be used effectively both to vary sentence structure and to emphasize the object rather than the subject—as I have done in this sentence. Instead of beginning another sentence with "You can use," I decided to emphasize the passive voice.)

3. *Tighten sentences you have stretched with unnecessary clauses or phrases.* These examples may help you revise:

ORIGINAL

```
The difficulty of dealing with screenwriters who are uncoopera-
tive often delays the production of a film.
```

REVISION

```
Uncooperative screenwriters often delay film production.
```

ORIGINAL

```
James Dean's fans were characterized by an excessive degree of
sentimentality regarding his memory.
```

REVISION

```
Dean's fans sentimentalized his memory.
```

4. *Simplify unnecessarily complex verb forms,* as in the following sentence:

ORIGINAL

```
Rebel Without a Cause was to have been based on a book by Robert
Lindner.
```

REVISION

```
Robert Lindner's book was the original inspiration for Rebel
Without a Cause.
```

5. *Avoid unnecessarily long or vague words.* Whenever you can, substitute a short, easily understood word for an unnecessarily long or obscure one, as in the following:

ORIGINAL

Eleanor Roosevelt endeavored to improve living conditions for indigent people who were deprived of the benefits of society.

REVISION

Eleanor Roosevelt worked to improve the lives of the poor.

6. **Check for repetition.** Do you use certain words repeatedly? If so, search for good synonyms to provide some variety. You may find a thesaurus, a dictionary of synonyms, or a regular dictionary helpful to remind you of other appropriate words. But, of course, you should never use a word unless you are confident that its meaning will be clear to your reader.

Revising for the Last Time

Ideally, you should consolidate your revisions in a second draft on a word processor. If you set this second draft aside for a day and then come back to it, you will certainly find that there are more changes you want to make. Once again you will want to examine the organization, the transitions, the paragraphing, the sentences, and the choice of words, making changes directly on the draft. Some students run into difficulty at this stage. They are unable to complete their revisions because they feel there is always more to be done, always something more they can do to improve their paper. While it is true that no writer ever produces the perfect paper, there must come a time when you realistically judge that you have done all you can to improve the paper in the time allowed. Three important steps in revision remain:

✔ CHECKLIST 19

Revising for the Last Time

1. Check and correct spelling, looking up any words of which you are unsure.
2. Check and correct punctuation, reading through once concentrating on punctuation and capitalization. Use the rules in chapter 9 for guidance.

3. Make final alterations in the documentation. If you are using documentary notes—a number after each reference corresponding to an endnote placed after the main body of your paper or to a footnote placed at the bottom of the page—you are ready to put in the numbers as soon as you are sure that there will be no more rearranging, deleting, or adding of material. This is usually one of the last steps before you type the final copy. It is also a good idea to check your sources against your note cards to see if you have made any errors in page numbers, quotations, or other details.

Examples of Revision

The following passages show the process of revision. The typed passages were taken directly from rough drafts, and the revisions are indicated in longhand.

1. From Michael Gold's paper:

~~It was~~ Leonard Rosenman, the musical director of <u>Rebel</u>, ~~who~~
<ins>who worked</ins>
suggested the thirty-one-year-old Stewart Stern, ~~as a replacement~~
<ins>with</ins>
~~for Shulman. At last~~ Ray ~~had found a collaborator whom he~~
<ins>film was finished, bringing together the ideas of previous</ins>
~~could work with~~ until the ~~end. Apparently it was Stern who~~
<ins>writers with his own.</ins>
~~synthesized the various ideas that fed into the finished script~~.

Note how Michael has reduced the number of words, simplified the language, and generally made the original passage more readable.

2. From Cherwanda Williams's paper:

<ins>has</ins>   <ins>substantial</ins>
Although there ~~have~~ been ~~signficant amounts of~~ research

on the correlation between eating disorders and depression,
<ins>remain,</ins>
~~there remain~~ a number of questions ~~left to be answered. One~~
<ins>such as</ins>
~~of these questions is~~ whether depression causes eating

disorders,~~eating disorders cause depression~~ <ins>or Whether for</ins> ~~Another question~~

some people both are true(.)

is whether ~~there are some~~ depressed people who develop eating

~~disorders~~ and then get even more depressed ~~and vice versa~~.

3. From Lisa Lee's paper:

species of

Countless | trees in ~~regions of the world known as~~ tropical

rain forests depend on the activities of animals for ~~their own~~

survival. Animals ~~serve trees by their pollination activities,~~ _Carry pollen,_

~~by~~ eating insects that prey on leaves and bark, and ~~by~~

transport~~ing~~ seeds to locations in the forest where they may

have a chance to germinate; some will grow to saplings; and a

few, maybe only one from a solitary tree, will find the space

and light necessary ~~for it to be able~~ to soar to the top of the

forest.

Note how Lisa has removed unnecessary words, divided the second sentence, and expressed the activities of animals as three parallel verbs: carry, eat, and transport.

A Sample Short Paper

LINDA ORTON

Composition

The decision to focus on Eleanor Roosevelt's efforts to help women allows Linda to direct her reading, but when she finishes her research, she finds that she has taken notes in several areas that do not directly relate to her chosen topic. Yet she still thinks she might be able to use some of that very interesting information. Her first rough draft includes information about Roosevelt's parents and her education, as well as speculation about what motivated her to live as she did. This first draft is too long and unorganized.

Linda decides to cut the parts about Roosevelt's childhood and her psychological development. She is then able to concentrate on Roosevelt's public accomplishments. Her second draft, however, is still not focused enough.

Revision

Revision often involves excluding information that may be very interesting, but that is really irrelevant to the research topic. The passages below show Linda revising by eliminating material that is not directly related to her topic.

ORIGINAL

Among the young men who were attracted to Eleanor was Franklin Roosevelt. Soon they were secretly engaged. Their engagement coincided with Eleanor's increasing interest in social reform, which resulted in her going to work in a settlement house in one of New York's slum districts.

REVISION

In 1902, at about the time she became involved with Franklin, Eleanor began to work as a volunteer at the Rivington Street Settlement House in one of New York's slum districts.

ORIGINAL

For some years after she was married, Eleanor's life was filled with raising her five children, meeting the demands of her domineering mother-in-law, and running a complicated household.

REVISION

For some years after she was married, Eleanor was occupied with family obligations.

Linda finally decides to outline the main points that have to do with Eleanor Roosevelt's public activities on behalf of women. When she does this a clear thesis sentence emerges:

```
Her many activities included work to improve the lot of
disadvantaged women and to help all women develop their po-
tential.
```

Steps Leading to Linda's Paper

1. Is asked to write a short research paper exploring the work of a public figure; reads the article on Eleanor Roosevelt in the *Encyclopedia Americana* (p. 19).
   - Consults the card catalog under "Roosevelt, Eleanor" and finds three books about Roosevelt's concern for women's issues.
   - Uses the *New York Times Index* to find several articles about Roosevelt's work for women.
2. Decides to focus on Roosevelt's efforts to help women and directs her note taking accordingly; writes a first draft, focuses her topic, and revises her paper (p. 172).

Thesis sentence

Orton 1

Linda Orton
Professor Shostak
English 102
25 October 1994

Eleanor Roosevelt: Blazing a Trail for Women

Eleanor Roosevelt was the First Lady of the
United States for some twelve years, but she was
much more than that. Long before she became First
Lady, she was working for a better society: Her many
activities included work to improve the lot of
disadvantaged women and to help all women develop
their potential. In 1902, at about the time she
became involved with Franklin Roosevelt, she began
to work as a volunteer at the Rivington Street
Settlement House in one of New York's slum
districts. There she taught young women who could
not regularly attend school because of their long
working hours. This experience, Eleanor's first
extended contact with poverty and its demands,
helped shape her social conscience, according to
Joseph Lash (E&F 98); it also exposed Franklin to
real poverty for the first time (E&F 135).

For some years after she was married, Eleanor
was occupied with family obligations. As Franklin's
career developed, she assumed more of the
responsibilities of the wife of a government
official. During this time, she did not join the
widespread movement to help women get the vote. Even

MLA citation style

Note short quotation integrated into
paraphrase.

when Franklin voiced his support for women's
suffrage in 1911, Eleanor "considered men superior
beings" (E&F 173), and she remained--in Joseph
Lash's words--"anti-suffragette, and vigorously so"
(E&F 168).

World War I offered Eleanor the opportunity to
reenter public life. As head of the Naval Department
knitting project, she supervised more than forty
groups of women who knitted woolen clothing for
soldiers (E&F 213). In the first volume of her
autobiography, This Is My Story, Eleanor writes that
it was her war work and her activities immediately
following the war that caused her to change her
ideas about women's suffrage: "Soon after
[ratification of the Nineteenth Amendment] I
undertook work which proved to me the value of the
vote. I became a much more ardent citizen and
feminist than anyone . . . . would have dreamed
possible" (297).

After the war, Eleanor took projects
specifically concerned with bettering the lot of
women and helping them develop their full potential.
Her interest in education led her to purchase
Todhunter, a school for girls. There she taught a
variety of subjects and struggled to help her
students see beyond their own narrow world (E&F
306-8). During this time, she continued to work for
social reform, specifically for shorter working

Note use of ellipsis points to indicate
omission from quotation.

Quotation of more than four typed lines is
indented ten spaces.

hours and better working conditions for women. Her
concern for women's welfare and an increasing
recognition of her abilities helped her to rise
rapidly to responsible positions in several
organizations, including the Women's Trade Union
League and the League of Women Voters (E&F 281).

    Eleanor found that the various parts of her
rich life enhanced each other. Through her work in
women's organizations, she made friends and learned
skills that proved invaluable in her later work:

> Eleanor not only made friends but she
> learned by doing, a title she used in one
> of her last books. These friendships and
> activities did not replace but
> supplemented her life at home, running a
> large household and bringing up five
> children to whom she had to be father as
> well as mother. (Love, E 85)

This incredibly competent woman, however, was more
than teacher, social reformer, and homemaker.

    After Franklin contracted polio in August 1921,
Eleanor's activities took a pronounced political
turn. During his convalescence, she assumed the
responsibility of keeping the Roosevelt name before
the public (Hareven 20). But she did not give up her
work to help women play a significant role in
society.

    Eleanor began to see suffrage as a means for

Only a single parenthetical reference is
needed since all facts in paragraph are
from the same source.

Orton 4

achieving specific goals: Having gained the vote,
women now had the duty to work for political power
and to work for social reform through the system. In
1921 Eleanor joined the women's division of the New
York Democratic State Committee. Other members
quickly recognized her organizational abilities, and
she soon headed the division's finance committee
(Hareven 26-29).

Joseph Lash concludes that by 1924 Eleanor
Roosevelt was one of the leading politicians of the
state of New York (Love, E 86). On 16 April of that
year, the New York Times reported that she had
helped win the fight for the right of women to
choose their own representatives at the state
convention ("Democratic Women Win"). She also worked
to incorporate issues of concern to women in the New
York State Democratic platform (Love, E 88). The
following year, Eleanor took part in the fight
before the New York State legislature for a forty-
eight-hour work week for women ("Women at Odds"),
and she continued to battle industrial lobbyists on
this issue in 1926 and 1927 (E&F 310).

During these years, Eleanor Roosevelt worked to
increase women's involvement in national politics.
In 1924 she led the struggle to include women's
issues in the Democratic platform at the National
Convention ("Democratic Women to Help"). In 1928 she
headed the bureau of women's activities of the

Page reference is unnecessary with a
newspaper article.

Final paragraph is Linda's own conclusion.

Democratic National Committee and directed the
national women's campaign for Al Smith, the party's
nominee for president ("Mrs. F. D. Roosevelt").

In 1928 Franklin was elected governor of the
state of New York, and Eleanor found herself with
new responsibilities as the wife of the governor.
While she felt that she should no longer hold
official positions in certain organizations,
especially within the Democratic party, Eleanor
continued to work for women's rights and social
reform (Rice 5). On a national radio broadcast in
1929 called "Women in Politics," she advised women
to get involved in politics and to "work a little
harder than men" since they "have a new trail to
blaze" ("Mrs. Roosevelt Prepares").

Eleanor Roosevelt is widely recognized for her
aggressive and creative approach to her
responsibilities as the wife of the president of the
United States. A little investigation reveals,
however, that she was an independent thinker and a
leader in her own right. She blazed many trails
through the wilderness of social injustice; her work
with women and for women formed one of those trails.

**Even though some lines may appear short,
try not to hyphenate words at the ends of
lines.**

MLA-style Works Cited

```
                                            Orton 6
                        Works Cited
"Democratic Women to Help on Platform." New York
     Times 31 Mar. 1924: 2.
"Democratic Women Win." New York Times 16 Apr. 1924:
     2.
Hareven, Tamara K. Eleanor Roosevelt: An American
     Conscience. Chicago: Quadrangle, 1968.
Lash, Joseph P. Eleanor and Franklin. New York:
     Norton, 1971. Referred to in the text as E&F.
——. Love, Eleanor. Garden City: Doubleday, 1982.
     Referred to in the text as Love, E.
"Mrs. F. D. Roosevelt Urges Peace Work." New York
     Times 4 Aug. 1928: 4.
"Mrs. Roosevelt Prepares to Unite Democratic Women."
     New York Times 9 Nov. 1929: 25.
Roosevelt, Eleanor. This Is My Story. New York:
     Harper, 1937.
Rice, Diana. "Mrs. Roosevelt Takes on Another Task."
     New York Times 2 Dec. 1928, sec. 5: 5.
"Women at Odds on 48-Hour Bill." New York Times 26
     Feb. 1925: 23.
```

Activity

Note the thesis sentence of Michael Gold's paper on *Rebel Without a Cause* beginning on page 236. How much can you cut out of the paper that does not directly relate to the thesis? Hone your revision skills by trying to shorten this paper.

Project Activities

For Students Who Have Organized Their Notes

A. Write a paragraph—perhaps one that would be appropriate as an introductory paragraph to your research paper—that explains the main findings of your research. Set it aside and come back later to revise it.

B. Write a sentence that reduces your findings to a single controlling idea.

C. Imagine your readers. Write a paragraph in which you indicate the kind of readers you are writing for—how much they know about your topic, how interested they are, and what you will need to explain for your research to make sense.

D. Compose a rough draft, skipping lines to leave room for revision.

E. If you have composed your first draft on a word processor, print out a hard copy and set it aside for later.

For Students Who Have Finished a Draft

F. After setting your draft aside for at least a few hours, go over it and mark passages that need to be reorganized, sentences that can be improved, and words that should be replaced.

G. Go through your draft and cut unnecessary words and shorten lengthy sentences.

H. Reread the section on revising in this chapter, make a checklist for revising your own draft, and go through your paper again, doing all you can to improve it.

PRODUCING THE
FINAL PAPER

9

Your final paper should be as neat and accurate as you can make it. A paper that is correct and readable is more effective than one with noticeable errors and will help persuade your reader that you have been correct and diligent in your research. After you have worked so hard, you will want your final paper to display the time and care that have gone into your entire project.

Working on a word processor, you can easily design an attractive, readable document. You can change a number of settings—margins, spacing, pagination, headers and footers, type sizes, and typefaces (or fonts)—and import or create illustrations, tables, graphics, and even photographs. Use these features only in ways that are consistent with the style you are following and when they actually enhance the quality of your paper; avoid the urge to use them simply because they look good. Before you print your final paper, make sure you have made the appropriate decisions about each of these features.

Margins

Word-processing programs automatically set margins (automatic settings are called "default" settings). In most cases, however, you can alter the settings to create more or less white space around the text of your paper. Standard preset margins in all styles are one inch from the top, the bottom, and the sides of the paper—even with a ragged right margin, that is, when the lines will be of uneven length. (The only way to make the right margins even is by justifying the text. This is not recommended, however, because it can result in unsightly space between words). If your instructor asks you to widen the margins (perhaps for comments), you can change the margins at any time before you print the paper.

Spacing

Research papers using any of the three documentation styles should be double-spaced throughout. This includes quotations, footnotes, endnotes, and the list of works cited. Double-space between titles (of the paper, works cited, or notes) and first lines. If you like to single-space your drafts, remember to reformat for double-spacing before you print.

Title and Other Identifying Information

MLA style does not require a title page, although your instructor may ask for one. If you use MLA style, type your name, your professor's name, the name of the course, and the date one inch from the top of the first page, on four separate double-spaced lines, flush with the left margin. See pp. 236, 253, 268. If your instructor requests a title page, use the same information and center it, beginning about a third of the way down the page. APA style does use a title page, which in addition to centering the complete title, author, and any other required information, includes a running head—a shortened version of the title—that appears in the top right corner of each page on the same line and just before the page number. See page 298. CBE also requires a title page, which includes the complete title, author, and date.

Numbering Pages and Creating Headers

The three styles illustrated in this book have slightly different rules for numbering the pages of a paper. Papers following MLA style are numbered in the upper right corner, from the first page to the last page of the works cited. Page one of a paper following APA style is the title page; following pages are numbered consecutively through any appended tables or illustrations to the end. Papers using the CBE citation-sequence, or number system, begin page numbering with the first page of text (the title page is not numbered). If your instructor asks you to include an outline, place it at the beginning of the paper. Outlines of more than one page should be numbered with lowercase roman numerals.

Most word-processing programs allow you to set headers that automatically insert page numbers and words—your name, for instance—on each page of your paper. MLA style calls for the writer's last name in the header; APA style requires a shortened version of the title.

Choosing Fonts and Point Sizes

Most word-processing programs offer a variety of typefaces, or fonts (designs of characters) in different sizes, measured in points (1/72 of an inch). Choose a standard typeface, such as Times Roman 12, that is easy to read and doesn't call attention to itself.

Tables and Illustrations

In papers documented using MLA style, tables and illustrations are inserted in the text of the paper as close as possible to the part to which they refer. Such material is labeled and numbered consecutively according to type, and the source of each is indicated immediately below. All tables are simply labeled "table" as in this example:

Table of Demonic Imagery

Category	Manifest Demonic	Parody Demonic	
		Group	*Individual*
Divine	[Satan]	Stoicheia Tou Kosmou	Antichrist
Spiritual or Angelic	1) Fire-spirits 2) Demons of Tempest	False gods	Moloch, Baal, Dagon, etc.
Paradisal	Waste Land and Sea of Death	Tree and Water of Heathen Power	
Human	Those Cast Out	"Great Whore" (Heathen Kingdoms)	Nero, Nebuchadnessar, Antiochus
Animal	Dragons of Chaos (Leviathan, Rahab; etc.)	Beasts of Prey or Fertility	Deified Animal (Bull, Serpent)
Vegetable	Harvest and Vintage of Wrath	Vegetation Gods and Earth-Mothers	
Mineral	Ruins	Heathen City (Babylon, Rome)	Tower of Babel

Source: Frye, Northrop. *The Great Code: The Bible and Literature* (New York: Harcourt, 1982).

All charts, drawings, graphs, maps, photographs, and other visual materials are labeled "Figure"; a selection from a musical score is labeled "example." Type all such material flush with the left margin, number the individual items with arabic numerals, give the source and any notes immediately afterwards, and indicate notes with lowercase letters (a, b, . . .) to prevent confusion with notes to the text of your paper.

Tables and figures are commonly used in research papers in the social sciences documented using APA style. If your research paper requires extensive illustrative material, or if you are constructing your own illustrations, you will want to consult the chapters in the APA manual that deal with tables and figures. Most student papers will use at most a few tables or figures, usually taken from scholarly journals. APA requires that these be labeled, numbered, and placed at the end of the paper after the reference list. You may group them in separate appendices, called Appendix A, B, and so on. Tables and figures that are grouped in an appendix will have the letter of the appendix as well, as in "Table A1" below:

TABLE A1
Fertility Declines in Selected Countries, 1960–89

Total Fertility Rates

Country	*Population 1989*	*1960*	*1989*	*Change*
	(millions)	(average number of children per woman)		(percent)
China	1,104	6.0	2.4	−60
Mexico	87	7.2	3.8	−47
Brazil	147	6.2	3.4	−45
Indonesia	185	5.6	3.5	−38
India	835	6.2	4.3	−31

Note. From "China's Baby Budget," by Jodi L. Jacobson, *The World-Watch Reader*, 1991.

Other illustrations—charts, drawings, graphs, and photographs—are labeled "figure," numbered consecutively with arabic numbers, and followed by a brief description of the figure. When the source of an illustration is not clear from the text of the paper, type and underline the word "Note," at the bottom of any figure or table and follow it with a period and a full citation of the source using APA citation style.

Style

Since you will follow the documentation requirements of one style (MLA, APA, or CBE), you need to study a sample paper and follow the model citations that illustrate the style. For MLA, see chapters 10–12; for APA, chapter 13; and for CBE, chapter 14. Even if you have recorded your citations in the appropriate form from the very beginning, you will want to check each item before you print the final copy of your paper. Remember to use a title page for APA and CBE styles.

Making Final Corrections

Errors and awkward passages are often easier to spot on hard copy, so when you feel your paper is finished, you may want to print out a working draft to proofread for the last time. Go through the paper carefully, looking once again at spelling, punctuation, consistency of tenses, agreement of subjects and verbs, and finally the accuracy of documentation. Consult a standard handbook to resolve questions and, if your word processor has a grammar checker, by all means use it. Never rely entirely on spell checkers—they can't determine meaning and they are limited by their dictionaries. You may still need to use a dictionary to double-check proper nouns and words like "their" and "there."

This is your last chance to make stylistic changes—to substitute a familiar word for an obscure one, to change a sentence from passive to active voice, to delete unnecessary words. If you read your paper out loud, you may discover awkward sentences that you can improve. Time taken to read your paper carefully at this point can make a difference.

Paper and Other Materials

Don't wait until the last minute to assemble what you need to produce the final copy of your paper. Assuming that you have access to a good printer, all you need is a supply of the appropriate 8 1/2- by 11-inch paper. For last minute small corrections, you may want a pen with black ink and some liquid paper.

Proofreading Symbols

Many instructors use the symbols below for correcting papers, but they're also useful for clearly marking changes in a draft before printing out—or retyping—the final version of your paper. Below the symbols is a portion of a draft with corrections marked.

ˇ Apostrophe or single quotation mark
⌣ Close up (basket ball)
↗ Comma
ℰ Delete
∧ Insert
¶ Begin a new paragraph
No ¶ Do not begin a new paragraph
⊙ Period
"⟨ ⟩" Double quotation marks
Space
∽ Transpose elements, usually with *tr* in margin (thier)

Huck Finn's reputation may have be gun with pictures rather than words. One of the illustrations was altered at the printer's presumably as a joke, to show Uncle Silas "in a flagrant act of indecent exposure"(David 269). The offending obscene picture was corrected, but a New York newspaper published the story, creating undesirable publicity and perhaps starting the idea that the book was improper and inappropriate for children (Egan 9). Publication was delayed and the Christmas season was missed (Blair 336–70). When the editor of Century magazine published extracts from the novel in December, January and February of 1884–85.

Checking Punctuation

Before you check for punctuation errors, keep the following rules in mind;
they cover the questions that most students have about punctuating research papers.

The Period

- Use a period to mark the end of straightforward sentences and to mark
  the end of some abbreviations: 2:00 A.M., Ms. Check the dictionary
  when you are in doubt about punctuating abbreviations.

- In quotations, place the period inside quotation marks: I think I know what Lewis Thomas meant when he said, "There is really no such creature as a single individual." When a quotation is followed by parentheses, however, place the period after the parentheses: "A director shows the way. He does not manipulate his actors" (Dalton 232).
- Use a period after indirect questions: Eleanor Roosevelt's friends often asked how she was able to accomplish so much.
- Single-space after a period at the end of a sentence.
- Single-space after personal initials: J. I. M. Stewart.
- Do not space after the period within an abbreviation: Ph.D.
- Do not space before commas or other punctuation that follows an abbreviation: Sherwyn M. Woods, M.D., Ph.D.
- Place periods after numbers and letters used to itemize:

1. Exercise vigorously at least three times a week.
2. Eat a diet high in carbohydrates and low in fat.
3. Sleep between six and eight hours a night.
4. Avoid nicotine and excessive amounts of caffeine and alcohol.

The Question Mark

- Place a question mark at the end of direct questions: What does it mean to be an adult?
- Place the question mark outside quotation marks if the quoted part of the sentence is not a question. Have you read a short story by William Faulkner called "The Old People"?
- Place the question mark inside the quotation marks if the quoted part of a sentence is a question, even when the sentence itself is not: Robert Lindner was in town to give a lecture entitled "Must We Conform?"
- Put a question mark inside the quotation marks if both the quotation and the sentence are questions: He turned and asked, "Have you read a novel by Horace McCoy called *They Shoot Horses, Don't They?*"
- Double space between a question mark—or the quotation mark after a question mark—and the first letter of the next word.

The Exclamation Point

- Exclamation points are usually not effective in research reporting. If you have used one, try to find another way to stress the importance of your statement. For example, instead of "Eleanor Roosevelt was a great lady!" it would be more effective simply to write "Eleanor Roosevelt was one of the most important women of this century."

- The rules for placing exclamation points inside or outside quotation marks are the same as those for question marks (see above).

The Comma

- Use a comma after lengthy introductory phrases or clauses: Since he won the Nobel Prize, Gabriel García Márquez has become increasingly popular in the United States.
- Use commas to set off modifying clauses that give extra (nonessential) information: Doris Lessing, who has written a number of powerful realistic novels, has recently written a series of novels that she calls space fiction.
- Do not use commas when such a clause is essential to the meaning of the sentence: The work of Lessing's that I find most intriguing is *The Golden Notebook.*
- Use a comma before a conjunction (and, but, so, etc.) that joins two independent clauses (complete sentences): I wanted him to write about the contemporary novel, but he chose to write about poetry instead.
- Use a comma to separate items in a series: Her computer components include two disk drives, a monitor, a keyboard, a high-speed printer, and the main computer chassis itself.
- Use a comma to set off other words or phrases that rename, contrast with, or qualify other words or phrases that are not essential to the meaning of the main clause:

1. An appositive or parenthetical phrase: Norman Cousins, the long-time editor of the *Saturday Review,* believes that if people can understand a problem, they can solve it.
2. A phrase of contrast: Swimming, not jogging, is the best sport for overall fitness.
3. Qualifying words placed in the middle of a sentence: Many people became disillusioned, seriously disillusioned, in the sixties. Ralph Nader, however, proved that an individual can influence public policy.

- Single-space after a comma, except before closing quotation marks: "Dave," he said, "what is the matter with you?"
- Place a comma inside quotation marks except when the quotation is followed by parentheses: He wanted to make a film shot through with "conflict" (Thomson 15), and he achieved that through the conflicts of real people.

The Semicolon

- Use a semicolon to join closely related independent clauses: Most young people in the fifties conformed to society's expectations; most of their counterparts in the sixties rebelled.
- Use a semicolon between two independent clauses that are joined together by conjunctive adverbs like *however, nevertheless,* and *therefore:* Successful students keep up with their assignments; however, they also make time for recreation.
- Use a semicolon between items in a series when at least one includes commas: Among the many musicians and actors who help people in need are Willie Nelson, who raises money for Farm Aid; Wynton Marsalis, who encourages inner-city youth to get involved in music; and Whoopi Goldberg, Robin Williams, and Billy Crystal—all advocates for the homeless.
- Single-space after a semicolon and place it outside closing quotation marks.

The Colon

- Use a colon to introduce a list or an example, when it is not preceded by a preposition or a form of the verb *to be:* Each student should write a report on one of these artists: Mary Cassatt, Auguste Renoir, Henri Matisse, or Pablo Picasso. *Or:* Imagine a typical early painting by Picasso: large sculptural nudes, primitive African motifs, distorted faces, flattened forms. *Or:* Three kinds of music were popular among college students in the fifties: rhythm and blues, jazz, and rock and roll.
- Colons or commas may be used to introduce quotations, but colons are usually best when the introductory material is longer than a few words and when the quotation itself is fairly long, as here: The president of the senior class concluded the graduation address with the following words: "Students today face many challenges. The question is not what will the world do for us, but how we can prepare ourselves to meet the needs of a complex and demanding society."
- Use a colon to introduce a second clause that amplifies the first: Many students have unusual jobs: One of my classmates is an animal trainer and another a lace maker.
- Single-space after a colon and put it outside quotation marks.

Quotation Marks

- Put quotation marks around quotations of three lines or less of verse or four lines or less of prose when they are incorporated into the text of your paper (see p. 163).
- Set off longer quotations by indenting ten spaces from the left margin. Do not use quotation marks (see p. 164).
- Enclose quotations within quotations with single quotation marks: According to one critic, "George Eliot's favorite poem was Wordsworth's 'Ode to Duty.' "
- Use quotation marks around the titles of short works: essays, poems, short stories, or songs. Quotation marks are also placed around the titles of parts of books: chapters, introductions, and afterwords.

The Apostrophe

- Use an apostrophe to form the possessive as follows: Morrison's novels; an actor's life; Keats's poetry (a single-syllable word ending in "s"); Dos Passos' early work (a word of more than one syllable that ends in an "s" sound); Dumas's plays (a word of more than one syllable that ends in a silent "s"); Terence's comedies (a word ending in an "s" sound and a final "e").

The Hyphen

- Use a hyphen to divide a word at the end of the line. Always break the word between syllables as designated in a standard dictionary, and avoid divisions that leave only one or two letters on a line: adjustment, *not* ad-justment. Divide compound words between the two words: type-writer. Divide hyphenated words only at the hyphen: computer-generated, *not* computer-gen-erated.

The Dash

- Use a dash to add information that interrupts the flow of a sentence: The growing concern about the environment—a concern which seemed to go beyond mere politics—resulted in many legislators changing their positions early in 1996.
- Use a dash to add extra information that is itself divided by commas: Some environmental problems—global warming, ozone depletion, deforestation—threaten the entire planet.

- Use a dash to set off a word or group of words that summarizes what comes before: Among Michael's friends were drummers, pianists, vocalists, guitarists—all kinds of musicians.
- To type a dash, use two hyphens. Do not space before or after.

Parentheses

- Use parentheses for the same purposes that you use a dash, reserving parentheses for more radical interruptions of a sentence: Looking for a new popular icon (the heyday of Madonna is over), young people are following new stars such as Alanis Morissette.
- Do not space between a beginning parenthesis and the first letter or between the last character and the closing parenthesis: Many young people in this culture (most of them in fact) earn some of their spending money.
- When you include a complete sentence within parentheses as part of another sentence, it is not necessary to capitalize the first letter or to put a period at the end: Young people in the nineties face many serious problems (one of the most frightening is AIDS) that were unheard of by their counterparts in the sixties.
- Other punctuation follows parentheses: In the nineteenth century, mothers tranquilized their hungry babies with opium (a widely used legal drug at the time). After a long, set-off quotation, however, parenthetical documentation is placed after final punctuation (see p. 177).
- A period is included within the parentheses only when the parenthetical statement is completely independent: Historians are only now beginning to try to make sense of the turbulent events of the 1960s. (An early work that tried to interpret some of the ideas and values of the youth culture in the 1960s was Theodore Roszak's *The Making of a Counter Culture.*)

Brackets

- Use brackets to insert an editorial comment or explanatory name or word within a quotation: One biographer has concluded that "even though he suffered from a prolonged illness, he [D. H. Lawrence] never lost his love of life."
- If you change the capitalization of a letter in a quotation, place brackets around the letter to indicate the change: Steffi Sidney has said of Nicholas Ray that "[h]e wanted the movie to come from *us*, rather than from his direction."

Ellipsis Dots

- Use ellipsis dots within a quoted passage to indicate that part of the quotation has been omitted: On April 8, 1928, the *New York Times* quoted Eleanor Roosevelt as saying that if women "expect equal political preferment . . . they must study history, economics and political methods, and they must mix with their fellow human beings."
- If the omission comes at the end of the sentence, add a period before the ellipsis dots: Eleanor Roosevelt argued that women interested in becoming involved in politics "must study history, economics and political methods. . . ."
- Use ellipsis dots at the beginning of a sentence only if it is not clear that something has been left out.
- Space before, between, and after the individual ellipsis dots.

Underlining

- Use underlining where italics would be used in a printed text. Underline titles of complete works—books, films, radio and television programs, plays, operas, and long poems published as books. Underline titles of periodicals (newspapers, magazines, and journals) and works of art (paintings and sculptures) as well as the names of ships, aircraft, and spacecraft. If you use a computer and printer that allow you to italicize, you may want to check with your professors to see which they prefer.

Spacing of Punctuation

- The following lists summarize standard rules on the spacing of punctuation.

No Space

1. After a period within most abbreviations
2. After a quotation mark at the beginning of a quotation or before a quotation mark at the end of a quotation
3. Before punctuation used to divide or end a sentence
4. Before or after hyphens
5. Before, between, and after hyphens used to make a dash
6. After a beginning parenthesis (or bracket) or before a closing one

SINGLE SPACE

1. After the period following personal initials
2. After commas, semicolons, and colons
3. Before, between, and after ellipsis dots
4. Before a beginning parenthesis within a sentence
5. After a closing parenthesis within a sentence unless the parenthesis is followed by another punctuation mark
6. After a period, question mark, or exclamation point at the end of a sentence except when it is followed by quotation marks
7. After quotation marks that follow a period, question mark, or exclamation point

Printing the Final Paper

Once you have completed Checklist 20, you are ready to print the final copy of the paper. If after printing it you find a few small corrections you want to make, do so using liquid paper and black ink. If there are more than a few corrections, make them on your computer file and print the paper again. In any case, you will want to make a copy for your own files.

Binding

Most instructors prefer students to bind their papers with a large paper clip in the upper left corner. While you may be tempted to use a colorful folder to hold your paper, these often get in the way when a teacher is trying to read and comment on the paper. The best rule to follow as you prepare your final paper is "keep it simple."

Activity

The following paragraph is from an early rough draft of Carla Medina's paper on *The Color Purple*. Carla later dropped this paragraph from her paper since it does not really contribute to her discussion of the novel's voices. Had she used this paragraph, however, she could have improved it by cutting out unnecessary words, varying the choice of words, and correcting errors in punctuation, typing, and documentation. Read the passage carefully, correct the errors, and improve it in any other way you can.

When Alice Walker published <u>The Color Purple</u> in the spring of 1982, some ten years ago, she was a respected, but no particularly well

CHECKLIST 20

Revising and Polishing the Final Draft

Before printing the final paper, make sure you have done the following:

1. Created margins of at least an inch and no more than an inch and a half
2. Made the right margin ragged rather than justified
3. Double-spaced throughout
4. Chosen a typeface (font) that is simple and large enough to be read easily
5. Placed page numbers and headers in the appropriate place
6. Included the required identifying information: name, date, instructor's name, and the name of the course. If your paper is documented according to MLA style, is this information placed flush with the margin at the top of the first page? If you've used APA or CBE style, have you made a separate title page and followed the format illustrated by the sample papers?
7. Double-checked notes, the citations in the list of sources, and the parenthetical documentation to make sure they conform to the requirements of a single style—MLA, APA, or CBE
8. Carefully labeled any tables or figures and placed them in the appropriate part of your text
9. Checked spelling
10. Checked punctuation
11. Read through the paper looking for unnecessary words, ineffective use of passive voice, awkward sentences, and statements that are not clear
12. Incorporated any special instructions your instructor has given you, such as including a title page even though MLA doesn't require it, or using footnotes instead of a list of references

If your instructor allows you to get proofreading help, you may want to ask someone you trust to look over your paper.

known novelist, poet, and essayist. However within a few weeks after this controversial novel was published, it became a best-seller and Alice Walker became well known to people who keep up with popular novels. Awarded the American Book Award and the

```
Pulitzer Prize for literature in 1983, it has been the subject of
much controversy. Even more controversial, however, is the Stephen
Spielberg film based on the novel released in 1985. Pauline Kael,
the critic who reviewed the movie for the December 30 edition of
the New Yorker, condemns both the book and the film, though she
indirectly praises the novel for its "earthy folk style". (Kael,
p. 69)
```

Project Activity

If you are working on a word processor, print double-spaced copies of your paper at least twice before you prepare the final paper—after the first draft and the next to the last draft. Use these printouts or your own handwritten draft and revise as follows:

1. After reading through your first draft, evaluate the organization and mark passages that you want to move.
2. Check your paragraphs. Have you introduced the subject of each paragraph effectively? Are they too long or too short? Would it be better to break up some paragraphs into more than one or move parts of one paragraph elsewhere?
3. Check your sentences. Have you used varied sentence structures? Which sentences are too wordy and can be improved by cutting out unnecessary words.
4. Check your words. Take out any that do not contribute to what you want to say. Notice any words that are unnecessarily obscure and replace them with others that are more easily understood. Make all changes in your file.
5. Using the guidelines in this chapter, check to make sure your sentences are properly punctuated. If you are using a word-processing system that will check your spelling, do that now; if not, circle any words that you have doubts about and look them up.
6. After making the appropriate changes on the computer, reread your improved paper and check once again to make sure that it flows smoothly.
7. Prepare the final copy, proofread it carefully, and make final corrections in black ink.

DOCUMENTING

10

SOURCES USING MLA STYLE

There are different ways to document written reports of research findings, but all have the same purpose: to make the source of such findings perfectly clear to the reader. The differences in documentation styles are mainly small details of capitalization, punctuation, and spacing, but it is important that you use a style that is appropriate for your subject and acceptable to your instructor. It is also important to use only one style for each research paper and to be consistent about the smallest details so that your reader will know exactly what each item means.

Choosing a Documentation Style

The style used in this chapter—known as MLA style since it is recommended by the Modern Language Association—is appropriate for papers in English, philosophy, history, and other disciplines in the humanities; and it will be acceptable to some instructors whatever your topic might be. For his paper on *Rebel Without a Cause,* Michael Gold follows MLA style. He compiles a list of sources and cites all references in an abbreviated form in parentheses in the text of his paper. Carla Medina's papers also use MLA style. Appendix A shows how to document Michael's paper using endnotes.

When necessary, other instructors will direct you to a style commonly used by researchers in the particular subject you are studying. Cherwanda Williams follows APA style (the author/date system recommended by the *Publication Manual of the American Psychological Association*). Cherwanda also provides a complete list of references at the end of her paper—with some

198   Chapter 10: Documenting Sources Using MLA Style

CHECKLIST 21

Planning Ahead for Documentation

To make it easy to assemble your final list of sources, you will want to do the following in advance:

1. As soon as you have chosen a topic, decide which documentation style is appropriate so that you can record the information in the correct form from the beginning. You may want to consult your instructor before making the final decision. For APA style, consult pages 289–97, and for the scientific number system, or CBE style, see pages 315–19.
2. Take down all relevant information—author, title, volume number, publisher, date, page numbers, etc., about each source as you find it in a catalog, index, or bibliography.
3. If you find sources from a computerized index or a CD-ROM that is connected to a printer, print out the citation and then check it against the actual source. Keep in mind that indexes sometimes contain errors.
4. When you locate the actual source, double check the details of the citation.
5. If you photocopy an article, note the publication information on your copy, making sure to record titles of both the periodical and the article, authors, dates, volume and issue numbers, page numbers and sections (for newspapers), and whether the periodical is paginated for each issue or continuously through the volume.
6. Before you return a book you have borrowed from the library, make sure you have correctly recorded all the information you need for documentation.
7. If you are using a computer, keep a file for your list of sources and record them using the correct documentation style.

slight differences of details from those used by Carla and Michael. She identifies the author, the publication date, and, when appropriate, the page number in the text of her paper, using parentheses when needed. Lisa Lee uses the citation-sequence, or number, system recommended by the Council of Biology Editors (CBE) and the National Library of Medicine.

Style manuals sometimes used for other disciplines include:

CHEMISTRY

American Chemical Society. *The ACS Style Guide: Manual for Authors and Editors.* Washington: American Chemical Soc., 1986.

GEOLOGY

United States Geological Survey. *Suggestions to Authors of the Reports of the United States Geological Survey.* 7th ed. Washington: GPO, 1991.

LINGUISTICS

Linguistic Society of America. *LSA Bulletin,* Dec. issue, annually.

PHYSICS

American Institute of Physics. *AIP Style Manual.* 4th ed. New York: American Institute of Physics, 1990.

All four students were careful to be consistent, that is, to cite the same kinds of sources in the same way each time they were used. If you understand the conventions used in all four papers, you will have two valuable skills: the ability to document appropriately any paper you write and the ability to interpret the documentation of articles and books that you read.

Deciding What to Document

As you write your paper, you should keep in mind from the beginning that *literally everything you take from your sources must be documented.* Not only must you make perfectly clear to your readers the exact source of quotations and paraphrases of your sources, but also where you have found ideas, concepts, and the smallest facts. You must give credit for a concept like the relationship of a film to the culture that produced it as well as for a fact such as the particular kind of sports car that James Dean drove. The only material that does not need documentation is information that most people would consider to be general knowledge—widely known facts, such as the fact that Dean was a famous movie actor.

Parenthetical and Textual Documentation

A list of works cited at the end of the paper must be supplemented by references both in the running text of the paper and in parentheses at the ends of sentences and paragraphs. How you cite sources within your paper should be determined by what you want to stress, the need to make your references as clear and concise as possible, and your effort to vary sentence structure to avoid boring repetition. Sometimes you may choose to mention the author's name at the beginning of a sentence or paragraph; at other times, you may place the author's name along with the page number of a source in parentheses at the end of a clause or sentence. When all of the information in a paragraph comes from the same part of a single source, you may place the parenthetical reference at the end of the paragraph.

In every case, your in-text citation should make it clear which source you are citing. For example, if there is only one work in the bibliography by an author, then you need only cite the author's name and a page number. If there are two sources by the same author, however, you must include both the author's name and the title (or shortened title) of the work to which you are referring. For each source you cite, the parenthetical citation combined with any information in the text identifying the source should be as brief and unambiguous as possible, making it perfectly clear to the reader which item in the bibliography is being cited. The first item in a bibliographic citation—author, editor, translator, speaker, performer, director, title, or some other entry—must appear either in the text or in parentheses in order for readers to find it easily.

The following sentences suggest various ways to document your sources within the text of the paper.

Author's Name in Text

> Stephen B. Oates goes even further in exploring the consequences of childhood experiences on Martin Luther King Jr.'s development (1-17).

Note: When there is only one work by an author in the list of works cited, it is not necessary to mention the title in the text.

Title and Author's Name in Text

> In <u>Eleanor and Franklin</u>, his best-selling, Pulitzer Prize-winning biography, Joseph Lash explains Eleanor Roosevelt's role in the League of Women Voters (355).

Note: To stress the importance of a source, use the title in the text.

Author's Name in Text Using More Than One Source by That Author

> Joseph Lash concludes that by 1924 Eleanor Roosevelt was one of the leading politicians of the state of New York (<u>Love, E</u> 86).

Note: When there are two or more sources by the same author in the list of works cited, indicate the title, or an easily understood abbreviation of the title, in the parenthetical reference.

Author's Name in Text Preceding a Quotation

> The film has what Kreidl calls "a disparate smattering of different vocabularies from different sources" (86).

Author's Name in Parenthetical Reference

> Once the actors went to work, the script continued to evolve, with James Dean, in particular, creating as he acted (Kreidl 86).

Author's Name in Parenthetical Reference When There Is More Than One Citation by the Author

> After the publication of her first book, it became clear that Eleanor Roosevelt would have considerable influence on women's efforts to gain political power (Lash, E&F 517).

Author's Name Introducing an Indented Quotation

> Ezra Goodman wrote of the public response to the death of James Dean:
>> The U.S. is currently in the throes of a movie fan craze for a dead man that surpasses in fervor and morbidity even the hysterical mass mourning that attended the death of Rudolph Valentino in the dim past of the movies. The object of this posthumous adulation is James Dean . . . who died at 24 in the wreck of his Porsche sports car a year ago this month. (75)

Volume Number Mentioned in Text

> In the fifth volume of Children of Crisis, Robert Coles tells the story of a young girl who had the habit of staring absently at a cemetery (549).

Volume Number in Parenthetical Reference

> Robert Coles tells the story of a young girl who had the habit of staring absently at a cemetery (5: 548-51).

More Than One Author's Name in Text

> Davidson and Lytle note the difficulty historians have ex-
> plaining the decisions that led to the bombing of Hiroshima
> (353).

Note: For sources with three authors, use all three last names; for more
than three authors, use the last name of the first followed by et al., as in
the list of works cited.

More Than One Author's Name in Parenthetical Reference

> Historians attempting to explain the events leading up to the
> bombing of Hiroshima are faced with a formidable task (Davidson
> and Lytle 319-53).

A Work Listed by Title

> Eleanor Roosevelt took part in the fight before the New York
> State legislature for a forty-eight-hour week for women ("Women
> at Odds").

Note: There is no need to include the page number either for articles
that are only one page long, since the page is included in the bibliography,
or for alphabetized sources, such as dictionaries or encyclopedias.

An Article Listed by Title from a Periodical Mentioned in the Text

> On 16 April of that year, the New York Times reported that she
> had helped win the fight for the right of women to choose their
> own representatives at the state convention ("Democratic Women
> Win").

An Entire Work

> In the first volume of her autobiography, This Is My Story,
> Eleanor Roosevelt explains how she changed her mind about suf-
> frage and became an advocate for women's rights.

Note: To cite an entire work rather than a particular part, it is prefer-
able to use the author's name in the text. In such cases, there is no need
for a parenthetical reference.

More Than One Work in a Single Parenthetical Reference

> In recent years, scholars have examined the place of <u>Rebel With-out a Cause</u> in American film history (Biskind; Cook 427).

Note: Cite each work exactly as if it were cited alone; separate citations with a semicolon.

The List of Sources or Bibliography

The following form for the list of sources—also called the bibliography—is based on the *MLA Handbook* (1995). For advice on using APA style (1994), turn to chapter 13. For the CBE style turn to chapter 14.

What to Include

To decide what to include in a list of sources, sort your bibliography cards into three stacks:

> I. those you actually cited in the text of your paper;
> II. those that helped you understand your topic, but that you did not actually cite;
> III. those that you either did not consult or that were not helpful.

Eliminate the third category. In some cases, you may decide to list only those works you actually cited; and in others you may want to include the second group, whether as part of a single alphabetized list or as a separate list, by dividing your sources into "Works Cited" and "Other Works Consulted."

How to Arrange Your Sources

Sources should be listed alphabetically by the last name of the author or, when there is no author, by the first word of the title, excluding *a, an,* or *the.* When you have more than one work by the same author, give the name in the first entry only. For his or her other works, substitute three hyphens and a period for the name and arrange the titles alphabetically. Occasionally, you may be instructed to separate your sources according to books, articles, and other sources; to arrange them chronologically according to publication date; or to present them in the order that they appear in the text.

Placement and Format

A list of sources is placed at the end of a research paper—after the notes or, for papers that do not have endnotes, immediately after the last page of the text. Begin the list on a new page with a title, "Works Cited," one inch from the top. Skip two lines, and start each entry flush with the left margin. Lines after the first of each entry are indented five spaces or roughly one-half inch, and the entire list is double-spaced. Do not number the items unless you are consistently following the citation-sequence system (see chapter 14).

Using Abbreviations to Refer to Sources

A complete list of sources placed at the end of your paper will allow you to clarify your sources simply by placing a shortened form of the citation—the author's last name, a brief title, or an abbreviation—in parentheses in the appropriate place in the text of your paper.

When you quote frequently from the same text, you may want to use an abbreviation: *S* for *Sula* or *MSND* for *A Midsummer Night's Dream.* Indicate this abbreviation at the end of the bibliographic citation: "Referred to in the text as *MSND.*"

Compiling a List of Sources

Every book in your list of sources should include any of the following information that is available: **author, title, place of publication, publisher,** and **date of publication.** Many sources will require additional information such as multiple or corporate authors, the name of an editor or translator, the edition, the part of a work cited, or other particular information needed to identify the exact source used. In addition to books, you may need to list portions of books, periodicals, other written sources, and nonprint sources as well. The following list of examples should provide you with a model for documenting any item you need to include in your list of sources.

Books

A Book with One Author

> Buell, Lawrence. <u>The Environmental Imagination</u>. Cambridge: Harvard UP, 1995.

Two or More Books by the Same Author

```
Lash, Joseph P. Eleanor and Franklin. New York: Norton, 1971.
---. Love, Eleanor. Garden City: Doubleday, 1982.
```

Note: If the author of one book is also the first of two or more authors of a following book, you must repeat the name, since the three hyphens stand only for the author of the preceding source:

```
Ellmann, Richard. James Joyce. 2nd ed. New York: Oxford UP,
    1982.
---, ed. The New Oxford Book of American Verse. New York: Ox-
    ford UP, 1976.
Ellman, Richard, and Robert O'Clair, eds. The Norton Anthology
    of Modern Poetry. 2nd ed. New York: Norton, 1988.
```

A Book with Two Authors or Editors

```
Ehrlich, Paul R., and Anne H. Ehrlich. Healing the Planet. Read-
    ing: Addison, 1991.
Pryse, Marjorie, and Hortense J. Spillers, eds. Conjuring: Black
    Women, Fiction, and the Literary Tradition. Bloomington:
    Indiana UP, 1985.
```

A Book with Three Authors

```
Kahn, Herman, William Brown, and Leon Martel. The Next 200
    Years. New York: Morrow, 1976.
```

A Book with More Than Three Authors

```
Bailyn, Bernard, et al. The Great Republic: A History of the
    American People. Lexington: Heath, 1977.
```

Note: The abbreviation "et al." stands for "and others." It is also correct to list all of the authors in the order that they are listed on the title page when there are more than three authors.

A Book with a Corporate Author

```
U.S. Department of Energy. An Assessment of Thermal Insulation
    Materials. Washington: GPO, 1978.
```

Note: GPO is an abbreviation for Government Printing Office.

A Book with an Anonymous Author

> <u>Writers' and Artists' Yearbook, 1980</u>. London: Adam and Charles
>   Black, 1980.

A Book with an Author Using a Pseudonym (a Fictitious Name)

> Innes, Michael [J. I. M. Stewart]. <u>Going It Alone</u>. New York:
>   Dodd, 1980.

Note: The author's real name may be supplied in brackets.

A Work Prepared for Publication by an Editor

> Dickens, Charles. <u>Oliver Twist</u>. Ed. Kathleen Tillotson. The
>   Clarendon Dickens. Oxford: Clarendon, 1966.

Note: If the work of the editor is being discussed, this should be cited
as follows:

> Tillotson, Kathleen, ed. <u>Oliver Twist</u>. By Charles Dickens. The
>   Clarendon Dickens. Oxford: Clarendon, 1966.

A Work in a Series

> Reiman, Donald H. <u>Shelley's "The Triumph of Life": A Critical
>   Study</u>. Illinois Studies in Lang. and Lit. 55. Urbana: U of
>   Illinois P, 1965.

*A Single Work Published in More Than One Volume (with Continuous
Pagination)*

> Johnson, Edgar. <u>Sir Walter Scott: The Great Unknown</u>. 2 vols.
>   London: Hamilton, 1970.

A Book That Is Part of a Multivolume Work with a Single Title

> Kettle, Arnold. <u>An Introduction to the English Novel</u>. Vol. 2.
>   London: Hutchinson U Library, 1953. 2 vols.

*A Book That Is Part of a Multivolume Work by One Author When Each Volume
Has a Separate Title*

> Coles, Robert. <u>Privileged Ones</u>. Boston: Little, 1977. Vol. 5 of
>   <u>Children of Crisis</u>. 5 vols. 1967-77.

A Book That Is Part of a Multivolume Work When Each Volume Has a Separate Title and Author

> Stewart, J. I. M. <u>Eight Modern Writers</u>. Oxford: Oxford UP, 1963.
>   Vol. 12 of <u>Oxford History of English Literature</u>. Gen. eds.
>   John Button and Norman Davis. 12 vols. 1945-86.

A Book with Different Authors for Each Chapter and a Single Editor

> Hoffman, Daniel, ed. <u>Harvard Guide to Contemporary American</u>
>   <u>Writing</u>. Cambridge: Harvard UP, 1979.

A Multivolume Work Cited in its Entirety

> Doyle, Arthur Conan. <u>The Annotated Sherlock Holmes</u>. Ed. William
>   S. Baring-Gould. 2 vols. New York: Potter, 1967.

A Multivolume Work Cited in its Entirety Published over a Period of Time

> Haight, Gordon S., ed. <u>The George Eliot Letters</u>. 9 vols. New
>   Haven: Yale UP, 1954-78.

A Republished Book with New Material

> Hurston, Zora Neale. <u>Their Eyes Were Watching God</u>. 1937. Fore-
>   word. Sherley Anne Williams. Urbana: U of Illinois P, 1978.

Note: The date, but not the publisher, of the first edition is given immediately after the title.

A Republished Book

> Gaines, Ernest J. <u>The Autobiography of Miss Jane Pittman</u>. 1971.
>   New York: Bantam, 1972.

A Paperback Reprint of a Hardback Edition

> McKibben, Bill. <u>The End of Nature</u>. 1989. New York: Anchor, 1990.

A Second, Subsequent, or Revised Edition

> Ellmann, Richard. <u>James Joyce</u>. 2nd ed. New York: Oxford UP,
>   1982.

A Revised Version of a Work of Literature

> Fowles, John. <u>The Magus</u>. Rev. version. Boston: Little, 1977.

A Republished Book with Original Publisher Cited

> Lessing, Doris. <u>The Golden Notebook</u>. New York: Simon & Schuster,
>   1962. New York: Bantam, 1973.

Note: Citing the original publisher is not required, but it may come before the original date of publication.

A Translation

> Homer. <u>The Iliad</u>. Trans. Richmond Lattimore. Chicago: U of
>   Chicago P, 1951.

Note: If the work of the translator is being discussed, this should be cited as follows:

> Lattimore, Richmond, trans. <u>The Iliad</u>. By Homer. Chicago: U of
>   Chicago P, 1951.

Sacred Writings

> Bible
> Bible, Revised Standard Version
> Old Testament
> Talmud
> Koran
> Song of Solomon

Note: Sacred writings are neither underlined nor placed in quotation marks. Unless otherwise indicated, references to the Bible or books of the Bible are assumed to refer to the King James Version. Indicate the particular book, chapter, and verse of the Bible in parentheses in the text of your paper:

> (Gen. 20:1-17)

(See pp. 225–27 for abbreviations of biblical works.)

Parts of Books

An Article, Essay, Chapter, or Other Part of a Book with a Single Author

> Oliver, Mary. "Crossing the Swamp." <u>American Primitive</u>. Boston:
>   Little, Brown, 1983. 58-59.

An Introduction, Afterword, Preface, or Foreword to a Book Written by Someone Other Than the Book's Author

> Walker, Alice. Afterword. <u>I Love Myself: A Zora Neale Hurston Reader</u>. Ed. Alice Walker. Old Westbury: The Feminist Press, 1979. 297-313.

A Previously Published Essay or Article from a Collection of Writings by Different Authors

> Said, Edward W. "An Ideology of Difference." <u>Critical Inquiry</u> 12 (1985): 89-107. Rpt. in <u>"Race," Writing, and Difference</u>. Ed. Henry Louis Gates Jr. Chicago: U of Chicago P, 1986. 35-58.

An Essay or Article from a Collection of Works Not Previously Published

> Diedrick, James. "<u>Jane Eyre</u> and <u>A Vindication of the Rights of Woman</u>." <u>Approaches to Teaching Brontë's</u> Jane Eyre. Ed. Diane Long Hoeveler and Beth Lau. New York: The Modern Language Association, 1993. 22-28.

Note: On citing titles within titles, see p. 222.

A Short Story or Poem from an Anthology

> Herbert, George. "The Flower." <u>Seventeenth-Century Prose and Poetics</u>. Ed. Alexander M. Witherspoon and Frank J. Warnke. 2nd ed. New York: Harcourt, 1963. 857.
> Pope, Alexander. "The Rape of the Lock." <u>The Norton Anthology of World Masterpieces</u>. Vol. 2. Ed. Maynard Mack et al. 6th ed. New York: Norton, 1992. 306-26. 2 vols.

A Novel or Play from an Anthology

> Hellman, Lillian. <u>The Little Foxes</u>. <u>The Norton Introduction to Literature</u>. 6th ed. Ed. Carl E. Bain, Jerome Beaty, and J. Paul Hunter. New York: Norton, 1995.

Afterword, Preface, Introduction, or Other Editorial Comment on Individual Pieces in a Collection

> Murfin, Ross C. Introduction to "Darkening the Reader: Reader-Response Criticism and <u>Heart of Darkness</u>." <u>Joseph Conrad</u>, Heart of Darkness: <u>A Case Study in Contemporary Criticism</u>.

```
           Ed. Ross C. Murfin. New York: St. Martin's Press, 1989.
           139-47.
```

An Unsigned Article in a Widely Known Reference Work

```
   "Solar Energy." The Random House Encyclopedia. 1990 ed.
```

A Signed Article in a Widely Known Reference Work

```
   Suber, Howard. "Motion Picture." Encyclopedia Americana. 1981 ed.
```

An Article in a Specialized, Less Familiar Reference Work

```
   Monro, D. H. "William Godwin." The Encyclopedia of Philosophy.
           Ed. Paul Edwards. 8 vols. New York: Macmillan, 1967.
   Roberts, John W. "James Baldwin." Dictionary of Literary Biogra-
           phy. Vol. 33. Ed. Thadious M. Davis and Trudier Harris. Ann
           Arbor: Gale, 1984. 134 vols. to date. 1978-.
```

Note: Since the entries are alphabetical, it is not necessary to provide page numbers.

Periodicals

A Signed Article from a Daily Newspaper Divided into Sections Paginated Separately

```
   Whitney, Craig R. "Under Pressure, France Is Ending Its Nuclear
           Tests." New York Times 30 Jan. 1996: A1+.
```

Note: For newspapers divided into sections with the section designation used as part of the page number, give the page number as it appears on the page (see the example above). For newspapers that are paginated continuously, give date, edition if there is one, and page number (see *A Signed Article from a Daily Newspaper,* below). For newspapers divided into numbered sections, give date followed by a comma, then the abbreviation "sec." and the section number, a colon, and page number (see *An Unsigned Article from a Daily Newspaper,* below).

Note: Use "+" for an article that begins in one part of a periodical and continues elsewhere.

A Signed Article from a Daily Newspaper Paginated Continuously

```
   Passell, Peter. "Czechs Tread Minefield on the Way to Capital-
           ism." New York Times 18 Apr. 1992, natl. ed.: 17+.
```

Note: Some newspapers are published in more than one edition, and the pagination varies from one to another. Indicate the edition if it is specified on the masthead at the top of the first page.

An Unsigned Article from a Daily Newspaper

> "Kevorkian Attends Another Michigan Death." <u>New York Times</u> 30
>   Jan. 1996, natl. ed.: A8.

A Signed Article from a Weekly Magazine or Newspaper

> Bettelheim, Bruno. "Reflections: Freud and the Soul." <u>New Yorker</u>
>   1 Mar. 1982: 52+.
> Lewis, James. "Jobless Reality Fails to Impress Thatcher's Cabi-
>   net." <u>Manchester Guardian Weekly</u> 5 Sept. 1982: 3.

An Unsigned Article from a Weekly Publication

> "Computers." <u>Time</u> 2 Aug. 1982: 72.

A Serialized Article

> Broad, William J. "Science Showmanship: A Deep 'Star Wars'
>   Rift." <u>New York Times</u> 16 Dec. 1985, natl. ed.: 1+. Pt. 2 of
>   a series begun on 15 Dec. 1985.

Note: If author and title are the same for all the articles in the series, give only one citation, indicating the dates and pages at the end. With the same author and different titles, give separate citations, using three hyphens in place of the author's name for all citations after the first. With different authors, give separate citations.

A Signed Editorial

> Smith, Gerard. "Toward Arms Control." Editorial. <u>New York Times</u>
>   29 June 1982: A23.

An Unsigned Editorial

> "Abusing the Nation's Children." Editorial. <u>New York Times</u> 1
>   Jan. 1996, natl. ed.: 20.

An Article from a Monthly Magazine

> Oppenheimer, Todd. "The Rancher Subsidy." <u>Atlantic</u> Jan. 1996:
>   26–28, 36–38.

An Article in a Journal with Pages Numbered Continuously Through Each Volume

> Gelfant, Blanche H. "Mingling and Sharing in American Litera-
> ture: Teaching Ethnic Fiction." <u>College English</u> 43 (1981):
> 763-72.

Note: The numbers after the title of the journal refer to the volume
number, the date, and the pages of the article cited.

An Article in a Journal That Numbers Pages Separately for Each Issue

> Biskind, Peter. "Rebel Without a Cause: Nicholas Ray in the
> Fifties." <u>Film Quarterly</u> 28.5 (1974): 32-38.
> Sprague, Claire. "Dialectic and Counter-Dialectic in the Martha
> Quest Novels." <u>Journal of Commonwealth Literature</u> 14
> (1979): 39-52.

Note: The numbers following the journal title refer to the volume (28)
and issue (5).

Note: Where there is no volume number, treat the issue number as
though it were a volume number.

A Signed Review with a Title

> Dupuy, Marigny. "The Least Worst Land." Rev. of <u>A Handmade</u>
> <u>Wilderness</u> by Don Schueler. <u>New York Times Book Review</u> 28
> Jan. 1996: 18.

A Signed, Untitled Review

> Harrison, John F. C. Rev. of <u>The Age of Capital, 1848-1875</u>, by
> E. J. Hobsbawm. <u>Victorian Studies</u> 20 (1977): 423-25.

An Unsigned, Untitled Review

> Rev. of <u>The French Lieutenant's Woman</u>, by John Fowles. <u>Times</u>
> <u>Literary Supplement</u> 12 June 1969: 629.

A Letter to the Editor

> Murray, Edward. Letter. <u>Audubon</u> Jan.-Feb. 1996: 12.

A Response to a Letter or Letters

> Lemann, Nicholas. Reply to letters of Roger Williams and Vir-
> ginia K. Williams. <u>Atlantic</u> Dec. 1984: 14.

A Speech or Address for a Special Occasion Printed in a Periodical

> Morrison, Toni. "Writers Together." Keynote speech. American
>   Writers Congress. New York, 9 Oct. 1981. <u>Nation</u> 24 Oct.
>   1981: 396+.

An Article from **Dissertation Abstracts** *or* **Dissertation Abstracts**
International

> Webb, John Bryan. "Utopian Fantasy and Social Change,
>   1600-1660." <u>DA</u> 43 (1982): 8214250. State U of New York at
>   Buffalo.

An Article from a Volume of Abstracts

> Johnstone, John W. C. "Who Controls the News?" <u>American Journal</u>
>   <u>of Sociology</u> 87 (1982): 1174-81. Abstract from <u>America:</u>
>   <u>History and Life</u> 20. A (1983): no. 2120.

An Article from a Newsletter

> Cliggott, Douglas. "Proposed Tax Reform Will Have Negative Ef-
>   fect on Capital Investment." <u>Business Executive Expecta-</u>
>   <u>tions</u> Third Quarter 1985: 2.
> "Mathematics Credit for Computer Courses." <u>NCTM News Bulletin</u>
>   22.2 (1985): n. page.
> "Report of Recent Events." <u>American Studies International</u>
>   <u>Newsletter</u> Aug. 1985: 1.

Note: Newsletters may not include volume and issue numbers, dates, or even pagination. Some, like the first item above, are only one sheet, so there is no need to indicate the absence of pagination as in the second citation. In cases where a publication does not employ the usual conventions needed for a citation, adapt what information you have to a form as close as possible to that of a conventional periodical citation, making sure that you provide enough information for readers to find the source. For example, the first citation uses "Third Quarter" to indicate the particular issue since there is no volume number or specific data given.

Government Publications

> Author. <u>Title of the Publication</u>. Number of Congress, session
>   number. The house (S stands for Senate, H and HR for House
>   of Representatives) and type and number of publication.
>   Place of publication: publisher, year of publication.

Lewis, John S. <u>Final Report, National Aeronautics and Space Administration, Planetary Atmospheres Program on a Program of Research on the Origin and Evolution of Planetary Atmospheres</u>. Washington: National Aeronautics and Space Administration, 1992.

If author is unknown:

The name of the government. Branch of government. The name of the agency or committee. <u>Title of publication</u>. Number of Congress, session number. The house. Type of publication. Number of publication. Place of publication: publisher, year of publication.

United States. Cong. Senate. Committee on Appropriations. Subcommittee on Departments of Labor, Health and Human Services, Education, and Related Agencies. <u>Impact of Proposed Budget on Health Research</u>. 99th Cong., 2nd sess. S. Hrg. 99–678. Washington: GPO, 1986.

Georgia. Dept. of Education. <u>Reports of the Survey of the Schools of Chatham County, GA</u>. Atlanta: Dept. of Education, 1932.

United States. Office of the Federal Register. <u>United States Government Manual, 1980–81</u>. Washington: GPO, 1980.

Note: If all of the information called for is not given, provide what is available.

Citing the Congressional Record

<u>Cong. Rec.</u> Date: Page numbers.
<u>Cong. Rec.</u> 9 May 1995: H4604–9.

Other Written Sources

The Published Proceedings of a Conference

<u>Conserving the Historical and Cultural Landscape</u>. Proc. of the Conference of the National Trust for Historic Preservation, Western Region. 2–3 May 1975. Denver. Washington: Preservation Press, 1975.

A Legal Reference

Brown v. Board of Education of Topeka. 347 US 483. US Supr. C. 1954.

A Pamphlet

>Saltman, Jules. <u>Teenagers and Alcohol: Patterns and Dangers</u>. New
>   York: Public Affairs Comm., 1983.

Note: A pamphlet is treated like a book.

A Volume of Published Letters

>Wilson, Elena, ed. <u>Edmund Wilson: Letters on Literature and Pol-
>   itics, 1912-1972</u>. New York: Farrar, 1977.

A Letter Printed in a Volume of Collected Letters

>Wilson, Edmund. "To William Faulkner." 25 Sept. 1956. <u>Letters on
>   Literature and Politics: 1912-1972</u>. Ed. Elena Wilson. New
>   York: Farrar, 1977. 540.

An Unpublished Letter from a Collection

>Stevenson, Adlai E. Letter to Ralph McGill. 11 May 1954. Ralph
>   McGill Papers. Emory University, Atlanta.

Personal Letter

>Lopez, Barry. Letter to the author. 18 Dec. 1995.

A Dissertation, Unpublished

>Gray, Donald Joseph. "Victorian Verse Humor." Diss. Ohio State
>   U, 1956.

Note: A published dissertation is cited as a book.

A Document from an Information Service

>Delker, Paul V. <u>Adult Education--1980 and Beyond</u>. Occasional
>   Paper No. 59. Columbus: Ohio State U, 1979. ERIC ED 189
>   309.

A Manuscript or Typescript

>Crane, Hart. <u>The Bridge</u>, ms. Hart Crane Collection. Columbia
>   University, New York.

Nonprint and Electronic Sources

A Lecture or Publicly Delivered Paper

> Levine, George. "George Eliot's Scientific Ideal: The Hypothesis
>   of Reality." English Institute. Cambridge, MA, 1 Sept. 1979.

A Radio or Television Program

> The Doomsayers. Prod. Brian Capener. PBS Special. 8 Sept. 1982.
>   "Maya Angelou." Narr. Bill Moyers. Creativity. PBS Special.
>   WPBA, Atlanta. 8 Jan. 1982.

Note: When you want to refer to a particular individual (producer, director, narrator, or actor), cite that person's name first:

> Moyers, Bill, narr. "Maya Angelou." Creativity. PBS Special.
>   WPBA, Atlanta. 8 Jan. 1982.

A Performance of Music, Dance, or Drama

> Puccini, Giacomo. La Bohème. Cond. James Levine. With Teresa
>   Stratas. Metropolitan Opera. Metropolitan Opera House, New
>   York. 13 Jan. 1982.

Note: When you want to refer to a particular individual (conductor, director, choreographer), cite that person's name first:

> Levine, James, cond. La Bohème. By Giacomo Puccini. With Teresa
>   Stratas. Metropolitan Opera. Metropolitan Opera House, New
>   York. 13 Jan. 1982.

A Film

> Vietnam: An American Journey. Films Inc., 1979.
> Rebel Without a Cause. Dir. Nicholas Ray. With James Dean, Sal
>   Mineo, and Natalie Wood. Warner Brothers, 1955.

Note: When you want to refer to a particular individual, cite that person's name first:

> Ray, Nicholas, dir. Rebel Without a Cause. With James Dean, Sal
>   Mineo, and Natalie Wood. Warner Brothers, 1955.

A Face-to-Face Interview

> Vitousek, Peter. Personal interview. 21 Jan. 1993.

A Telephone Interview

>Babbitt, Bruce. Telephone interview. 24 Oct. 1995.

A Work of Art

>Cézanne, Paul. <u>A Modern Olympia</u>. Louvre, Paris.

A Work of Art with a Cited Illustration

>Bonnard, Pierre. <u>The Open Window</u>. The Phillips Collection. Washington. Illus. in <u>Master Paintings from the Phillips Collection</u>. By Eleanor Green et al. New York: Penghurst Books, 1981. 71.

A Musical Composition

>Handel, George Frideric. <u>Messiah</u>. Ed. Watkins Shaw. Novello Handel Edition. Sevenoaks, Eng.: Novello, n.d.

Note: Use n.d. (no date) for any undated material.

An Audio Recording

>Pink Floyd. <u>Pulse</u>. Columbia, 1995.

Note: It is not necessary to mention the medium of the recording if it is a compact disc. Indicate any other medium (long-playing record, audiocassette) before the name of the manufacturer as follows:

>Snyder, Gary. <u>The Practice of the Wild</u>. Audiocassette. Audio Press, 1991.

A Song Referred to or Quoted from an Audio Recording

>The Beatles. "Revolution." <u>The Beatles/1967–1970</u>. Capitol, 1973.

An Audio Recording When the Work of the Performer or Performers Is Discussed

>Horne, Marilyn. <u>Orfeo ed Euridice</u>. By Christoph Willibald Gluck. Cond. George Solti. Orchestra and Chorus of the Royal Opera House, Covent Garden. London, 1970.

A Videotape or Recording

><u>The Nuclear Dilemma</u>. Video Recording. BBC-TV. New York: Time-Life Multimedia, 1974.

A Computer Program on Tape or Disk

> Ward, Richard J. <u>The Executive Game</u>. Computer software. Bowling
>   Green State University. Hewlett-Packard. A880-2232A.

Note: Computer programs vary considerably. For this reason, you will have to adapt a citation to the information you have. When possible, you should include an author, title, place of production, company or organization producing the program, identifying number, and date.

A Source from a Database Published Periodically on CD-ROM

> *Source with a Printed Version*
> Author. Title and date of print publication. <u>Title of the data-</u>
>   <u>base</u>. CD-ROM. Name of vendor. Electronic publication date.
> Havermann, Judith. "White House Holding the Line on Medicaid."
>   <u>Washington Post</u> 10 Dec. 1995: A4. <u>Newspaper Abstracts</u>. CD-
>   ROM. UMI. 1995.

A Text Other Than a Periodical Published on CD-ROM

> Author. Title of the part of the work (if necessary). <u>Title of</u>
>   <u>the product</u>. Edition, release, or version (if appropriate).
>   CD-ROM. City of publication: publisher, date of publication.
> Fordham, Mary Weston. "Atlanta Exposition Ode." <u>Database of</u>
>   <u>African-American Poetry, 1760-1900</u>. CD-ROM. Alexandria:
>   Chadwyck-Healy; Electronic Book Technologies, Inc., 1995.

Note: There is no printed version of the above database. In cases where there is a printed version, cite the printed source publication information first.

A Work in More Than One Medium

Note: You may find a book with accompanying CD-ROM, a work that consists of a videocassette and diskette, or any other combination of two or more media. Follow the above model for citing such multimedia publications, but indicate all the media forms immediately after the title as follows: CD-ROM, videocassette; print version, CD-ROM; diskette, videocassette, print version.

A Publication on Diskette

> Author. "Title of the part of the work." <u>Title of the product</u>.
>   Edition, release, or version. Diskette. City of publica-
>   tion: publisher, year of publication.

Alpha, Tau Rho. <u>The Northridge, California, Earthquake of Janu-</u>
<u>ary 1994</u>. Diskette. Menlo Park, CA: U.S. Dept. of the Inte-
rior, 1994.

A Publication on Magnetic Tape

Author. "Title of the part of the work." <u>Title of the product</u>.
Edition, release, or version. Magnetic tape. City of publication: publisher, year of publication.

United States. Internal Revenue Service. <u>Form 941, Employers</u>
<u>Quarterly Federal Tax Return</u>. Magnetic tape. Washington:
Department of the Treasury, Internal Revenue Service, 1985.

Material from an Online Full-Text Database

Sources with Print Versions

Author. Title. Date of print publication. <u>Database</u>. Online. Name
of computer service. Date of access.

"Addiction is a Family Problem, Too." <u>New York Times</u> 20 March
1988, late ed., sec. 1:50. <u>Nexis</u>. Online. 18 Dec. 1995.

Sources without Print Versions

Note: Cite sources without print versions as follows:

Author. "Title of the Material Accessed." Date of the material.
<u>Title of the Database</u>. Online. Name of Computer Service.
Date of access.

Material (Electronic Journals, Newsletters, and Conferences) from a Computer Network

Author. "Title of the article or document." <u>Title of Journal,</u>
<u>Newsletter, or Conference</u>. Volume, issue, or other numbers
(year or date of publication): number of pages or paragraphs or n. pag. Online. Name of computer network. Address
Date of access.

Note: Because punctuation is an important part of Internet addresses,
do not add punctuation between an address and the date of retrieval.

Beerman, Dave. "Galapagos: An Adventure in Nature." <u>A Sense of</u>
<u>Place</u> 5.1 (1994): 7 pars. Online. Retrieved from Dartmouth
Home Page. World Wide Web. http://www.dartmouth.edu/ (8
Jan. 1996).

An Electronic Personal Communication (E-Mail)

> Author of the letter. "Title" or description of the letter.
>   Date.
> Cattier, Alan. "The World Wide Web." E-mail to Melissa Walker. 4
>   Dec. 1995.

Material from an Electronic Text Retrieved from the Internet

> Author. <u>Title of text</u>. Place of publication: publisher, date of
>   publication. Online. Place where the text is held. Name of
>   computer network. Date of access.
> Twain, Mark. <u>Adventures of Huckleberry Finn</u>. New York: Harper &
>   Bros., 1886. Online. Literature and Publications Gopher.
>   Internet. 4 Jan. 1996.
> Swift, Jonathan. <u>An Argument Against the Abolishing of Chris-
>   tianity</u>. Online. English and Literature Gopher. U of Penn-
>   sylvania Literature and Publications Gopher. Internet. 4
>   Jan. 1996.
> Clinton, William Jefferson. <u>Inaugural Presidential Address</u>. 20
>   Jan. 1993. Online. Literature and Publications Gopher. In-
>   ternet. 14 Dec. 1995.

Note: Include information about the printed source when it is provided.

Mailing List (Newsgroup or Listserve)

> Sierra Club. "Reach Out for Earth Day." Online. Retrieved e-
>   mail: Sf.moderator@sfsierra.sierra (1 April 1996).

FTP Site

> Newscorp Project. "Newscorp FTP file on Curtis B. Dall."
>   ftp://ftp.almanac.bc.ca/pub/fascism/dossier/dall (4 January
>   1996).

Gopher Site

> World Bank. "Bolivia: Poverty, Equity, Income." 2 February 1996.
>   Internet Gopher Server. gopher://gopher.workbank.
>   org/11/PIC/eco/eco/15272. Retrieved 9 May 1996.

Telnet Site

> University of North Carolina. <u>Grants and Funding Index</u>. Inter-
>   net. telnet://info.acs.unc.edu (Retrieved 9 April 1996).

USENET Newsgroup

> Litt, J. "Indian Wars." Discussion. Internet. Retrieved e-mail:
>   USENET Newsgroup: alt.revisionism (11 April 1996).

World Wide Web Site

> Rainforest Action Network. "Global Rates of Destruction."
>   http://www.ran.org/info_center/products.html (Retrieved 9
>   May 1996).

Special Cases

You will occasionally find sources that are different from any of the sample citations in this chapter. You may find, for example, a book with no date that has an author, an editor, and a translator. Privately printed material or books published in the seventeenth century may not include any publication information. To cite unusual or one-of-a-kind sources, you may have to devise your own citation, adapting the order suggested by the models above: author, title, editor, translator, place of publication, publisher, and date.

Citing Material from a Secondary Source

There may be times when you will want to cite material from a book or an article that you have found in a secondary source rather than in the original. Generally, it is best to locate the original and to cite it directly; but in cases when the original is not available, you must cite the source you actually use.

For Citing the Source of Information Found in a Second Source

> Squire, James R. The Responses of Adolescents While Reading Four
>   Short Stories. Urbana: NCTE, 1964. In David Bleich, Subjec-
>   tive Criticism. Baltimore: Johns Hopkins UP, 1978. 101.

For Citing a Quotation from a Source Other Than the Original When You Want to Call Attention to the Original

> Fish, Stanley E. "Literature in the Reader: Affective Stylis-
>   tics." New Literary History 2 (1970): 140. As quoted in
>   David Bleich, Subjective Criticism. Baltimore: Johns Hop-
>   kins UP, 1978. 122.

For Citing a Quotation or Paraphrase of a Quotation When You Have No Access to the Original

> Branch, Taylor. <u>Parting the Waters: America in the King Years,</u>
>   <u>1954-63</u>. New York: Simon, 1988.

Note: Indicate the source of a quotation or paraphrase of a quotation in parentheses in your paper as follows:

> (qtd. in Branch 922).

Citing Titles within Titles

When the title of one work is part of the title of another, you may be confused by what to underline and what to enclose in single or double quotation marks.

Any Titles Normally Underlined (Books, Plays, Films) That Are Part of the Titles of Articles Are Still Underlined

> <u>The Duchess of Malfi</u>
> "Sexual and Social Mobility in <u>The Duchess of Malfi</u>"

Omit Underlining of Titles That Would Normally Be Underlined but That Are Part of a Book Title

> <u>Paradise Lost</u>
> <u>Surprised by Sin: The Reader in</u> Paradise Lost

Underline the Titles of Books That Include Other Titles Normally Enclosed Within Quotation Marks

> "Michael"
> <u>Ten Interpretations of Wordsworth's "Michael"</u>

Use Single Quotation Marks for Titles Normally Enclosed in Quotation Marks That Are Part of the Title of an Article

> "The Drowned Man of Esthwaite"
> "The Illusion of Mastery: Wordsworth's Revisions of 'The Drowned
>   Man of Esthwaite' "

Citing Tables and Illustrations

A table or illustration should follow as closely as possible that part of the paper that it illustrates. Double-space before, after, and within tables, making ruled lines when necessary to clarify the material. Type any heading or caption at the top of the table or illustration flush with the left margin: Table 1; Fig. 1. Give the source at the bottom, also flush with the left margin:

> Source: Harriet Kramer Linkin. "The Current Canon in British Romantic Studies." <u>College English</u> 53 (1991): 554.

Making an Annotated Bibliography

Occasionally an instructor will ask you to make an annotated bibliography. To do this, you simply add a brief descriptive note after the appropriate bibliographic entry. Consider the following examples:

> Hareven, Tamara. "Social and Political Apprenticeship, 1920-1933." <u>Eleanor Roosevelt: An American Conscience</u>. Chicago: Quadrangle, 1968. 21-47. This chapter is about Eleanor Roosevelt's initial work with social reform and labor groups. It outlines her development and increasing influence in politics and women's rights. A good, concise overview of these years.
>
> Lash, Joseph P. <u>Eleanor and Franklin</u>. New York: Norton, 1971. A broad, reliable basis for further study, this book is a good place to begin a study of the Roosevelts. Lash explores the environments in which they were raised and covers their lives up until Franklin's death.
>
> Rice, Diana. "Mrs. Roosevelt Takes on Another Task." <u>New York Times</u> 2 Dec. 1928, sec. 5: 5. This article is based on an interview with Eleanor Roosevelt in which she discusses her coming role as First Lady of New York State. Her views on women in politics are particularly interesting and are reported in her own words.

Using and Interpreting Abbreviations

These designations are almost always indicated in abbreviated form:

AD (A.D.)   *anno Domini*, meaning "in the year of our Lord," as in AD 169

a.m.   *ante meridiem,* meaning "before noon"
BC (B.C.)   before Christ, as in 400 BC
BCE (B.C.E.)   before Common Era
CE (C.E.)   Common Era
p.m.   *post meridiem,* meaning "after noon"

States

Spell out in the text of a research paper, but for documentation use the two-letter abbreviations recommended by the postal service.

AL	Alabama	MT	Montana
AK	Alaska	NB	Nebraska
AZ	Arizona	NV	Nevada
AR	Arkansas	NH	New Hampshire
CA	California	NJ	New Jersey
CO	Colorado	NM	New Mexico
CT	Connecticut	NY	New York
DE	Delaware	NC	North Carolina
DC	District of Columbia	ND	North Dakota
FL	Florida	OH	Ohio
GA	Georgia	OK	Oklahoma
GU	Guam	OR	Oregon
HI	Hawaii	PA	Pennsylvania
ID	Idaho	PR	Puerto Rico
IL	Illinois	RI	Rhode Island
IN	Indiana	SC	South Carolina
IA	Iowa	SD	South Dakota
KS	Kansas	TN	Tennessee
KY	Kentucky	TX	Texas
LA	Louisiana	UT	Utah
ME	Maine	VT	Vermont
MD	Maryland	VA	Virginia
MA	Massachusetts	VI	Virgin Islands
MI	Michigan	WA	Washington
MN	Minnesota	WV	West Virginia
MS	Mississippi	WI	Wisconsin
MO	Missouri	WY	Wyoming

Publishers' Names

The MLA recommends that in documentation you indicate publishers' names with appropriate abbreviations. Use the following samples as models:

Farrar	Farrar, Straus & Giroux
Knopf	Alfred A. Knopf, Inc.
MIT P	The MIT Press
MLA	Modern Language Association of America
NAL	New American Library, Inc.
Norton	W. W. Norton and Co., Inc.
Oxford UP	Oxford University Press, Inc.
Pocket	Pocket Books
Random	Random House, Inc.
U of Chicago P	University of Chicago Press
UP of Florida	University Presses of Florida
Viking	Viking Press, Inc.

The Bible

Old Testament (OT)

Gen.	Genesis
Exod.	Exodus
Lev.	Leviticus
Num.	Numbers
Deut.	Deuteronomy
Josh.	Joshua
Judg.	Judges
Ruth	Ruth
1 Sam.	1 Samuel
2 Sam.	2 Samuel
1 Kings	1 Kings
2 Kings	2 Kings
1 Chron.	1 Chronicles
2 Chron.	2 Chronicles
Ezra	Ezra
Neh.	Nehemiah
Esth.	Esther
Job	Job
Ps.	Psalms
Prov.	Proverbs
Eccles.	Ecclesiastes
Song Sol. (also Cant.)	Song of Solomon (also Canticles)
Isa.	Isaiah
Jer.	Jeremiah
Lam.	Lamentations

Ezek.	Ezekiel
Dan.	Daniel
Hos.	Hosea
Joel	Joel
Amos	Amos
Obad.	Obadiah
Jon.	Jonah
Mic.	Micah
Nah.	Nahum
Hab.	Habakkuk
Zeph.	Zephaniah
Hag.	Haggai
Zech.	Zechariah
Mal.	Malachi

New Testament (NT)

Matt.	Matthew
Mark	Mark
Luke	Luke
John	John
Acts	Acts
Rom.	Romans
1 Cor.	1 Corinthians
2 Cor.	2 Corinthians
Gal.	Galatians
Eph.	Ephesians
Phil.	Philippians
Col.	Colossians
1 Thess.	1 Thessalonians
2 Thess.	2 Thessalonians
1 Tim.	1 Timothy
2 Tim.	2 Timothy
Tit.	Titus
Philem.	Philemon
Heb.	Hebrews
Jas.	James
1 Pet.	1 Peter
2 Pet.	2 Peter
1 John	1 John
2 John	2 John
3 John	3 John
Jude	Jude

Rev. (also	Revelation
Apoc.)	(also Apocalypse)

General

Some of the following abbreviations are occasionally used in writing using the new streamlined MLA style; you may encounter others in your reading. It is best to refer first to the sample citations in this chapter to document your own work and to use this list for clarification and for interpreting your sources. In general, use appropriate abbreviations in documentation and brief qualifying parenthetical asides (i.e., cf., etc.). Spell out most words in the text of your paper.

abbr.	abbreviation, abbreviated
abr.	abridged, abridgment
adapt.	adapted by, adaptation
anon.	anonymous
app.	appendix
assn.	association
assoc.	associate, associated
attrib.	attributed to
b.	born
bibliog.	bibliography, bibliographer, bibliographic
biog.	biography, biographer, biographical
bk.	book
bull.	bulletin
c. (ca.)	*circa,* meaning "about" (commonly used to indicate approximate dates, as c. 1840)
cf.	*confer,* meaning "compare"
ch., chs. (chap., chaps.)	chapter, chapters
col.	column
colloq.	colloquial (indicates informal speech)
comp.	compiled by, compiler
cond.	conducted by, conductor
cont.	contents, continued
(contd.)	continued
d.	died
dept.	department
dev.	developed by, development
dir.	directed by, director
diss.	dissertation
distr.	distributed by, distributor

div.	division
doc.	document
ed.	edited by, editor, edition
educ.	education, educational
e.g.	*exempli gratia,* meaning "for example"
esp.	especially
et al.	*et alii,* meaning "and others" (used in citing works with more than three authors)
etc.	*et cetera,* meaning "and so forth" (Avoid using this and most other abbreviations in the text of a paper.)
ex.	example
fac.	faculty
fig.	figure
fl.	*floruit,* meaning "flourished" (commonly used to indicate the approximate time that a person lived—usually the period of highest achievement—when birth and death dates are unknown)
fwd.	foreward, forward by
govt.	government
hist.	history, historian, historical
ibid.	*ibidem,* meaning "in the same place" (Though no longer recommended by the MLA or the APA style, this abbreviation was once commonly used in endnotes to indicate that a source is the same as the preceding one.)
i.e.	*id est,* meaning "that is" (Like "e.g." and "etc.," this abbreviation should be confined to parenthetical references and notes and avoided in the running text.)
illus.	illustrated by, illustrator, illustration
inst.	institute, institution
intl.	international
introd.	introduced by, introduction
jour.	journal
l., ll.	line, lines
lang.	language
legis.	legislation, legislative, legislature, legislator
mag.	magazine
misc.	miscellaneous
ms., mss.	manuscript, manuscripts
narr.	narrated by, narrator
natl.	national
n.d.	no date (of publication)

no.	number
n.p.	no place (of publication), no publisher
obs.	obsolete
P	Press (Note UP in documentation to refer to University Press, as Oxford UP.)
p., pp.	page, pages
pref.	preface, preface by
proc.	proceedings
prod.	produced by, producer
pseud.	pseudonym
pt.	part
pub. (publ.)	published by, publisher, publication
qtd.	quoted
rev.	revised by, revision; or review
rpt.	reprinted, by reprint
sc.	scene (used in citing passages from plays, omitted when scene and act are cited together: *Hamlet* 2.1)
sec. (sect.)	section
ser.	series
sic	"thus, so" (used in brackets within a quotation, or in parentheses following a quotation to indicate that an error in spelling, punctuation, grammar, logic, or fact is reproduced faithfully from the original)
soc.	society
st.	stanza
supp.	supplement
trans. (tr.)	translated by, translator, translation
U	University (Note UP in documentation to indicate University Press, as Oxford UP.)
UP	University Press, in documentation, as Oxford UP.
v., vv.	verse, verses (vs. and vss. also used)
viz.	*videlicet,* meaning "that is" or "namely"
vol., vols.	volume, volumes
vs. (v.)	versus or against (In titles of legal cases, v. is commonly used.)

Content Notes

Occasionally you may want to use a note to give information that would be distracting if you included it in the text of your paper. Michael Gold, for example, notes that new technology may well change the approach of future papers on his subject.

A content note is also useful to point the reader to several sources—perhaps not included in the bibliography—where he or she can find a full discussion of a topic. Whether it occurs at the foot of a page or the end of a paper, chapter, or book, a content note is simply a note that gives information or makes a comment instead of or in addition to a normal source citation. *Warning:* Content notes should only give significant information; avoid the temptation to include interesting but irrelevant facts in notes.

Activities

A. Using as a guide the MLA style represented by the examples in this chapter, write bibliographic citation for the sources below:

1. A book by Barry Lopez entitled *Field Notes* published in 1994 by Alfred A. Knopf in New York.

2. An article by Leon Jaroff in the 1 April 1996 *Time* entitled "The Man's Cancer" and running continually from pages 58 to 65.

3. A book by Adrian Forsyth and Ken Miyata entitled *Tropical Nature,* published in 1984 by Charles Scribner's Sons in New York.

4. A poem by Adrienne Rich entitled "Darklight," on pages 55–56 of her book *An Atlas of the Difficult World,* published in 1991 by W. W. Norton & Company in New York.

5. An essay by Gregory S. Jay entitled "The End of 'American' Literature: Toward a Multicultural Practice," published on pages 264–79 of the third number of volume 53 of the journal *College English* (March 1991). The pages of this journal are numbered continuously through each volume.

6. A video recording entitled *Shakespeare of Stratford and London,* produced in 1978 by the National Geographic Society in Washington, D.C.

7. An article by Malcolm W. Browne in the *New York Times* of 21 January 1992 entitled "Galapagos Mystery Solved: Fauna Evolved on Vanished Islands." The article begins on page 5 of section B and is continued on page 8.

8. A book entitled *The Second Sex,* written by Simone de Beauvoir, originally published in 1949, translated by H. M. Parshley, and published in 1975 by Alfred A. Knopf in New York.

9. An article called "Waste Disposal, Chemical" in the 1990 edition of the *Random House Encyclopedia* published by Random House in New York.

10. An article entitled "Ishmael Reed" by Henry Louis Gates Jr. in volume 33 of the multivolume *Dictionary of Literary Biography*. Published in Ann Arbor by Gale Research Company in 1984, volume 33, entitled *Afro-American Fiction Writers After 1955*. Entries are alphabetical. This volume is edited by Thadious M. Davis and Trudier Harris. There are 134 volumes in the series.

B. Write a bibliographic citation according to the APA style for the following:

1. A book by William Cronon entitled *Nature's Metropolis: Chicago and the Great West* published in New York by W. W. Norton in 1991.

2. A book by Joseph M. Hawes and N. Ray Hiner called *Children in Historical and Comparative Perspective: An International Handbook and Research Guide* published in 1991 by Greenwood Press in New York.

3. An article on pages 8 & 10 of the November 1989 periodical *Natural History*. The author is Michael Fobes Brown, and the title is "Dark Side of the Shaman: The Traditional Healer's Art Has Its Perils."

4. An article by C. A. Taube, B. J. Burns, and L. Kessler entitled "Patients of Psychiatrists and Psychologists in Office-based Practice: 1980." The article is on pages 1435–47 of volume 39 of *American Psychologist* published in 1984.

5. An article by L. J. Weitzman and three other authors entitled "Sex-Role Socialization in Picture Books for Preschool Children," published on pages 1125–50 of volume 77 of *American Journal of Sociology* in 1972. The other authors are D. Eifler, E. Hokada, and C. Ross.

C. Write bibliographic citations for the following based on the CBE style in chapter 13:

1. "Man as an Agent in the Spread of Organisms," a paper by Marston Bates presented at a symposium held from June 16 to 22 in 1955 at Princeton and published on pages 788–804 of a volume with the other papers presented at the symposium by the University of Chicago Press in 1956. Entitled *Man's Role in Changing the Face of the Earth* with the subtitle, *An International Symposium,* the volume is edited by William L. Thomas Jr.

2. A book of essays with 450 pages edited by Stephen R. Killert and Edward O. Wilson entitled *The Biophilia Hypothesis* published in 1993 by Island Press in Washington, D.C.

3. An article entitled "Plant Reproductive Characteristics During Secondary Succession in Neotropical Lowland Forest Ecosystems," by P. A. Opler, H. G. Baker, and G. W. Frankie, published in 1980 on pages 40–46 of volume 12 of *Biotropica*. This journal is paginated continuously throughout the volume.

WRITING RESEARCH PAPERS IN THE HUMANITIES

11

Approaches to Research in the Humanities

The humanities include those academic disciplines that explore human beings and their cultures: art, history, literature, music, and philosophy. Each of these disciplines is subdivided into a number of categories; the visual arts, for example, include motion pictures, graphics, painting, photography, and sculpture. There is some overlap between the humanities and the social sciences: in recent years some historians have applied the methods of social science to historical topics by doing very detailed quantitative studies with the help of computers, while some literary texts are examined as sociological documents. There are many kinds of investigations that students can pursue in the humanities involving both primary and secondary materials. Doing primary research in literature, history, or philosophy involves examining original documents in these fields: in literature, for example, studying the text of a novel, letters written to and by the author, manuscripts or facsimiles of manuscripts of the literary text, or other writings by the author referring to the text. Secondary research related to the same novel would include the study of critical essays, book reviews, or other materials about the text or author written by others.

Art

Since production of visual art predates written history, students have a vast array of material to explore spanning many centuries, ranging from the cave drawings at Lascaux in southwestern France to the subway graffiti of the 1980s. To do primary research in the visual arts you would study works themselves, usually in museums. To do secondary research, you would examine reproductions of the art (printed photographs or slides), as well as books and articles written about artists and their work. You might research the career of an individual artist—Velásquez, Vermeer, Van Gogh; the influence of an artist on others—Caravaggio on Ribera and Rembrandt; the relationship of an artist to a patron—Goya to Charles IV; an artist's treatment of a particular subject—Mary Cassatt's paintings and drawings of children; or even a single painting—Picasso's *Guernica.*

History

History, in some ways the broadest of disciplines since it comments on all others—the history of science, of economics, of art, literature, and ideas—involves using a great variety of resources to reconstruct the past of human experience. There are three different kinds of materials available to professional historians and student researchers: primary sources generated by events themselves—letters, government reports, newspaper accounts, video or audio tapes of events; secondary sources—books and articles produced by historians who have studied the primary materials; and tertiary sources—encyclopedia articles, textbooks, or popular histories based on the secondary sources.

Literature

Ideas about what constitutes literature are changing to include much more than poetry, drama, and fiction written by established writers. Literary scholars now do serious research that involves examining essays, memoirs, diaries, and letters, as well as popular novels, film scripts, and even television scripts. Although writing about literature in some courses may simply involve examining and analyzing a novel, poem, or play without reference to any other sources, you may have an opportunity to do some original research. Teachers of literature who assign research projects, like instructors of other disciplines, usually are very specific about the kind of research they want students to pursue. Possibilities include synthesizing various interpretations of a work by reading and evaluating critical essays about it, researching the critical reception of a book by reading the original reviews published in periodicals and newspapers, studying published letters to discover an author's intentions in writing a work, or reading a biography to find out how a particular work relates to the author's life. In some cases, you may be asked to research some aspect of the social context in which a work was written. In a course on Victorian literature, for example, you might be asked to research child labor practices in the period and to show how particular writers—Elizabeth Barrett Browning and Charles Dickens—used their works to protest those practices.

Music

There are many interesting research projects for students to pursue in the area of music, ranging from the life and works of one of the great classical composers to the role of music in a first-grade classroom. In a course in music theory, for example, you might study the ideas of the classical theorists and perhaps compare Plato's and Aristotle's theories of the relationship between musical tones and emotional states. In a course that relates music criticism to composition, you might research the relationship of the critical writings of Robert Schumann to the music produced in the mid-nineteenth century, focusing perhaps on the work of Johannes Brahms. In another context, you might examine the historical and critical issues surrounding Mozart's *Requiem* and its place in the development of church music. If you are studying popular culture and contemporary music, you might want to explore the public demand for censorship of lyrics of rock and roll songs.

Philosophy

There is enormous variety among the works of philosophers who reflect on and discuss the nature and meaning of human existence. As a student of philosophy, you might be asked to research the historical foundations of a school of thought—the development of utilitarianism; to research perennial themes such as perception and reality, the nature of the moral life, or the interplay between justice and freedom; or to examine the influence of a particular philosopher on some aspect of a culture, perhaps the influence of Kant on German education or Simone de Beauvoir on American feminism.

A Sample Paper in the Humanities Using MLA Style

MICHAEL GOLD

When Michael's freshman English teacher asked the class to choose a topic and write a research paper in one of the disciplines within the humanities, he chose film studies since he has always been interested in movies. His paper on *Rebel Without a Cause* draws on a variety of sources, including contemporary reviews, the book that originally inspired the film, books about the director and the actors, articles in popular magazines, and critical essays in film journals. The paper is documented with parenthetical references in the text and a list of sources at the end, the style recommended by the Modern Language Association, which is the style most commonly used in college courses in the humanities.

Steps Leading to Michael's Paper

1. Develops an existing interest and focuses his subject (p. 21)
   - Is surprised to discover academic courses in film
   - Goes to the library and reads an *Encyclopedia Americana* article on the history of motion pictures
   - Concludes that the best way to approach the subject is to break it down into different types of movies
   - Visits a bookstore and studies textbooks used in film courses
   - Talks to a film student about cult movies
   - Jots down ideas and consolidates his list
   - Chooses to study *Rebel Without a Cause*
2. Identifies his sources (p. 32)
   - Talks with the reference librarian
   - Consults appropriate indexes in the library and collects relevant articles and books
3. Plans his strategy (p. 70)
4. Writes a letter to the film's distributor asking how often *Rebel* is shown (p. 100)
5. Takes notes—quoting, paraphrasing (p. 124), and interpreting (p. 127) his sources
6. Sorts and classifies his note cards (p. 140)
7. Writes out a preliminary thesis statement (p. 142)
8. Writes a thesis statement setting up his argument (p. 143)
9. Outlines, drafts, and revises his paper (p. 150)
10. Prepares a list of works cited, checks spelling and punctuation, and prints out the finished version of his paper

Introductory paragraphs catch reader's
attention and lead to thesis statement.

Gold 1

Michael Gold
Professor Levine
English 102
13 March 1995

Conflict and Cooperation:

The Making of Rebel Without a Cause

In the 1950s movies were very different from what they are
today. The most popular were musicals, Westerns, and comedies; and
most were intended for family entertainment. Only a few were
produced primarily for a teenage audience. Young people referred to
them as movies, adults as picture shows and hardly anyone thought
of going to a film—which is what movies or picture shows are called
when they are taken seriously. Occasionally a film was made in those
days that influenced future films and that affected the way people
behaved. Such a film was Rebel Without a Cause.

Most people who remember Rebel associate it with one person,
James Dean--his life, his death, and the cult that developed among
some of his more ardent fans. A few may recall that Rebel was also
the film that made Sal Mineo and Natalie Wood famous. Perhaps
because of the premature deaths of all three of its stars, Rebel feeds a
kind of nostalgia among people who first saw it in their teens, and it
continues to attract young audiences in colleges across the country
(Lusk). The association of Rebel with the sudden death of young
people began when James Dean was killed--clearly because of his
own recklessness--in an automobile accident before the film was

Source indicated in parentheses; details
given in bibliography.

No comma between source and page
number.

Gold 2

released in 1955. It continued in 1976 when Sal Mineo was stabbed
by an unknown assailant and again in 1981 when Natalie Wood
drowned under somewhat mysterious circumstances.

Immediately after James Dean's death, a large number of young
people became obsessed with keeping his memory alive, their efforts
soon reaching the intensity of hysteria. For some, grief developed
into a kind of death cult. According to Life magazine, thousands of
fans wrote letters to Dean every month in which they insisted either
that he was not dead or that he was immortal (Goodman 75). In 1957,
Sam Astrachan reported in the New Republic that a whole generation
of young people had adopted the jacket, gestures, and expressions
that were part of Dean's image in Rebel (17). The Dean mania
became a profitable business: some fans were willing to pay up to
two hundred dollars for poorly done oil paintings of Dean (Mitgang
114); others purchased life-sized casts of Dean's head, records of
ballads about his death, and pieces of old Porsche aluminum
purported to be part of his car (Goodman 78). What Life magazine
referred to as the "Delirium over Dead Star" lasted a long time. As
late as 1969, a reporter for the New Yorker interviewed fifty-seven-
year-old Mrs. Therese J. Brandes, the founder of the James Dean
Memory Club. Mrs. Brandes, who had been in her mid-forties when
Dean died, explained that while teenagers may have had a romantic
attachment to Dean, she and her contemporaries "loved him as a
son." Mrs. Brandes showed the reporter two closets full of recent
letters as evidence of Dean's continuing popularity ("Fan" 22).

Brief quoted phrase integrated
into sentence.

Several sources are used in this paragraph;
each requires separate citation.

Quotation from a personal letter

Gold 3

The Dean mania has subsided somewhat, but the film remains a favorite. It periodically plays in commercial theaters that book classic or cult films. According to Jack Lusk, who distributes the film to colleges, churches, and other nonprofit institutions, Rebel "is a perennially popular title" with a "steady booking pattern." It is "one of the few cult films, like Casablanca, that people see over and over again" (Lusk).

It is of course impossible to know what our perceptions of Rebel Without a Cause would be if it were not for James Dean's untimely death, but it is obvious that the Dean mania has obscured the real story of how Rebel Without a Cause came to be. James Dean made an important contribution to Rebel, but he was only one of many people who helped to make this film memorable. Rebel was really the product of the imagination, the creative energy, and the plain hard work of a group of people--the producer, director, writers, actors, and technical experts--who compose the community of a film. More than any other work of art, a film is a collaborative effort requiring cooperation and compromise. Some films--and Rebel is one--grow not only from the minds of the collaborators but also out of existing social concerns and the demands of the movie-going public. Once films are released, they go back into society, influencing the feelings, behavior, and ideas of their audiences. And finally they become subjects for interpretation, for critics and historians who try to understand what films mean.

The story of Rebel Without a Cause began in 1944 when a

Thesis statement or controlling idea

Name of author is used to introduce
quotation.

Gold 4

young psychologist named Robert Lindner published a book entitled
<u>Rebel Without a Cause . . . The Hypnoanalysis of a Criminal
Psychopath</u>, which was widely read. George Mayberry, writing in the
<u>New Republic</u>, referred to it as a "deeply and tragically human" story
(108); and Edwin J. Lukas, in the <u>Annals of the American Academy
of Political and Social Science</u>, hailed it as essential reading for
professionals concerned with the criminal personality (216). In 1947,
Warner Brothers purchased the right to make a movie based on
Lindner's book and signed the young Marlon Brando to star; when
Brando's contract expired, the project was temporarily abandoned.
Juvenile delinquency, however, was a serious social concern, spurring
Columbia Pictures to make a successful film on the subject, <u>The Wild
One</u>, starring--a popular choice for the role of delinquent--Marlon
Brando. When Nicholas Ray became a director for Warner Brothers
in 1954, he too wanted to make a film about juvenile delinquency, and
as a consequence the <u>Rebel</u> project was revived (Kreidl 91). But the
film Ray wanted to do had little in common with the content of
Robert Lindner's professional case history.

     Some of Lindner's material was used in the film, from the title--
which would catch the imagination of a generation of teenagers--to
the suggestion that problems within a family are the cause of
antisocial behavior among the young. Lindner's study reveals how
family conflicts lead young Harold to chronic criminal behavior; in
the film unhappy homes provoke Jim, Judy, and Plato to pranks and
illegal acts that have serious consequences. But the details are very

Michael's own conclusions—no citation
needed.

Movie titles underlined.

Gold 5

different. Lindner's sullen Harold, based on an actual case history, is from an immigrant-laborer home with few material comforts. He engages in criminal behavior from the age of twelve, drops out of school, is periodically arrested, put on probation, sentenced to jail, and finally committed to a penitentiary. Jim Stark (James Dean) is one of a group of indulged but unhappy, privileged but rebellious teenagers who argue with their parents, drink, and sometimes steal cars. Their escapades end in the deaths of Buzz (Corey Allen) in a car accident and of Plato (Sal Mineo) in a shootout with the police, who mistakenly assume that he is armed. For Jim Stark, however, the day ends positively, as he gets the pretty girl (Natalie Wood) and is reconciled with his parents.

When Nicholas Ray's proposal to make a film about affluent suburban kids was merged with the studio's plan to make a movie called Rebel Without a Cause, there was no script and no real vision of how the differences between the original book and Ray's intentions could be resolved. In fact, the seeds that would flower in the final film were scattered in the minds of many different people. Nicholas Ray brought them together. He chose Dave Weisbart for the producer because Weisbart had two teenage children, and Ray thought that he would have a special sympathy with the project (Ray 70). Leonard Rosenman, the musical director, was a good choice because he had already worked with Dean in East of Eden (Kreidl 94).

Finding a screenwriter was more difficult. According to Ray,

Source is noted at the end when all
information in a paragraph is from a
single source.

Gold 6

there is often animosity between a writer and a director, since each is
dependent on the other and yet each wants to make final decisions.
Famous writers present additional problems, since they often want to
follow their own ideas, while the studio requires that they cooperate
with the needs of a production. Sometimes a studio will insist that a
director use a writer who is already under contract to the studio, even
though the writer is not suited to the project (Ray 71–72).

Ray originally approached Clifford Odets, a friend, to do the
script; but Warner Brothers had other ideas since Leon Uris, a best-
selling author and successful scriptwriter, was already under contract
to them (Dalton 225). Ray agreed to Uris's joining the project since
he was interested in the subject, had experience working with
teenage boys, and was willing to do research. But when Uris
produced a sketch of a small town plagued by juvenile delinquency,
Nicholas Ray did not like it, and Uris had to be replaced. Ray's
account of his experience with Uris suggests that studying and finally
rejecting Uris's work allowed Ray to refine and clarify his own
intentions. By seeing what he did not want, he perhaps came closer to
knowing what he did want (Ray 73).

The next writer to work with the <u>Rebel</u> crew was Irving
Shulman, a novelist and scriptwriter who had been a high school
teacher and who loved sports cars, something that Ray hoped would
provide a bond with the moody James Dean. Although an affinity
with Dean never developed and his vision of the film proved
incompatible with that of Nicholas Ray, Irving Shulman was directly

Gold 7

responsible for significant features of the film. His discovery of a newspaper article about a teenage boy who plunged to his death off the Pacific Palisades when he failed to jump free in a "chickie run" became the famous scene in which Buzz accidentally drives his car off a cliff because his sleeve is caught and he cannot open the car door to escape. Shulman also helped develop the character of Plato; Plato's luxurious house, self-indulgent mother, and absent father were all his ideas. It was finally a disagreement about the character of Plato, however, that led to Ray's decision that he needed still another writer (Ray 73).

Leonard Rosenman, the musical director of Rebel, suggested the thirty-one-year-old Stewart Stern, who worked with Ray until the film was finished, bringing together the ideas of previous writers with his own (Kreidl 93). But even Stern did not produce a final, definitive screenplay. Although he wrote at least three different versions, none reflects completely the dialogue and the action of the final film. Once the actors went to work, the script continued to evolve, with James Dean, in particular, creating as he acted (Kreidl 86).

"Please let me do something here. Let me play with it. Just roll it." When Dean asked to be allowed to play a scene his way, Ray said yes (Dalton 236). It is difficult to know what subtle character traits contribute to a successful collaboration between an actor and a director, but we do know that Nicholas Ray trusted James Dean's instincts. From the beginning, Ray followed the advice of Elia

Note use of direct quotation.

Ellipsis dots are used to indicate words omitted.

Kazan, who insisted that a good director never tries to direct a natural actor. Ray's version of Kazan's rule was this: "A director shows the way. He does not manipulate his actors" (Dalton 232). Two of the more famous scenes in the film--the opening scene with Dean lying drunk in the street playing with a toy monkey and the scene after the fatal car accident with Dean taking a bottle of milk and slowly pressing it to his face--were the actor's spontaneous performances (Dalton 236, 253). The milk bottle scene was planned one night at Ray's house with Dean thinking through the situation and Ray playing the father (Houston and Gillett 184).

Nicholas Ray encouraged the other young actors to develop their own parts. Looking back on the experience, Natalie Wood observed: "Nick gave me a career . . . with <u>Rebel</u>. . . . Because he regarded me as an actress with a meaningful contribution to make, I felt better of myself and better of my work. . . . I think he did that for a lot of people" (Kreidl 208). Steffi Sidney, who played one of the gang members, has also testified to Nicholas Ray's freeing his actors to develop the character of a gang: "He wanted the movie to come from <u>us,</u> rather than from his direction." When Ray felt that they were still acting as individuals rather than as a gang, he urged them to go out together and to do things as a group--to go to the beach and prowl around deserted buildings at night (Dalton 230).

The evidence is abundant: from the very beginning, Nicholas Ray recognized that the kind of film he wanted to make would be a community effort requiring the cooperation of many people. He wanted to make a film shot through with "conflict" (Thomson 15), and he achieved that through the conflict of real people--the producer, the director, the writers, the actors, and others. The conflicts among young people trying to grow up, between the young and their baffled parents, and between the young and the forces of authority--all are portrayed convincingly. Ray brought together the fragments of many people's experiences: Uris's talks with juvenile authorities and delinquents (Kreidl 77), the newspaper article about a chicken run, Shulman's work as a high school teacher (Ray 74), Sal Mineo's actual idolizing of Dean (Kreidl 82), and the ganglike, semidelinquent behavior of many of the young actors (Dalton 227). Perhaps Ray achieved a kind of authenticity and unity because he was able to fuse the experiences of so many real people struggling to say something about the eternal conflicts between the young and the old.

Although there are probably very few people who would insist today that James Dean lives, Rebel Without a Cause is still alive in the minds of people who study the history of film. In recent years, scholars have tried to judge the film as a whole, rather than as a showcase for the magic that Dean created. They are studying its values, its art, and its place in American film history. Peter Biskind, writing in Film Quarterly, sees Rebel as a reflection of the conservative values of mid-fifties America. He argues that the young characters condemn their parents' weaknesses, but that in the end the film affirms traditional family values and remains "a profoundly

Note how Michael uses the names of authors he quotes; he then does not need to repeat name in the parenthetical citation.

Note how Michael uses the names of
authors he quotes; he then does not need
to repeat name in the parenthetical
citation.

Gold 10

conservative film" (37). David Cook, on the other hand, in his
History of Narrative Film, sees the film as "a definitive statement of
the spiritual and emotional ills that beset America during the period"
(500). Douglas McVay considers Rebel to be Nicholas Ray's
masterpiece and one of the four best films of the fifties (24). David
Thomson, who thinks of Rebel as the work of a director who was
both a serious social critic and a "great romantic" producing great
art (15), warns of the difficulty of ever recreating that initial
response:

> So Rebel is vibrant with yearning aspirations, and Ray's
> beautiful and brave venturing with space, decor, and
> faces lost in a night wilderness of screen. We can never
> regain the view we had of the film in 1955, when its
> rueful passion swept so many of us away. (16)

Even though almost thirty years have passed since audiences
first settled down to watch Rebel Without a Cause, evaluating its
place both in film history and in American society is still not easy. A
profoundly conservative film, a tragedy in the classical sense, a high
romance, or scathing social comment--which is the appropriate
category for this still controversial film? When we consider the many
different people who contributed to its creation, we may conclude
that it is all of these. It is certainly not surprising to discover that the
film that has what Kreidl calls "a disparate smattering of different
vocabularies from different sources" should evoke such varied
responses (86).

Long quotation is indented ten spaces or
approximately one inch; double-spaced
before, throughout, and after quotation.

Concluding paragraph echoes thesis
statement: note repeated ideas *community,*
compromise, cooperate.

Gold 11

Rebel Without a Cause was generated through conflict; it was finally realized when the community of people who wanted to bring it about discovered ways to compromise and cooperate. But the conflict that created Rebel is still alive in the minds of people who interpret it. A film more than a book exists in the minds of its viewers. Although some may have a videotape of the film, which they can study at their leisure, most people must rely on memory.[1] The community of interpreters--those who remember, study, and talk and write about Rebel--will probably always be fraught with conflict both because memories are highly personal and because the struggle between generations that Rebel explores is constantly being renewed.

Note

[1]The availability of videotape for purchase or rental makes it possible to study films the way scholars study written works of literature. Future responses to Rebel may be based more on careful critical analysis than on emotional response.

Content note offers a thought of Michael's
that is interesting and relevant but that
would distract from the main point if
included in the text of his paper.

Items in bibliography are alphabetized by last name of author.

When there is no author, item is alphabetized by first word of title (excluding *a, an,* or *the*).

Gold 12

Works Cited

Astrachan, Sam. "The New Lost Generation." <u>New Republic</u> 4 Feb.
    1957: 17–18.

Biskind, Peter. "Rebel Without a Cause: Nicholas Ray in the Fifties."
    <u>Film Quarterly</u> 28.5 (1974): 32–38.

Cook, David A. <u>A History of Narrative Film</u>. 2nd ed. New York:
    Norton, 1991.

"Correspondence." <u>The New Republic</u> 18 Feb. 1957: 22–23.

Dalton, David. <u>James Dean: The Mutant King</u>. San Francisco:
    Straight Arrow, 1974.

"Fan." "The Talk of the Town." <u>New Yorker</u> 2 Aug. 1969: 21–23.

Goodman, Ezra. "Delirium over Dead Star." <u>Life</u> 24 Sept. 1956:
    75–76.

Houston, Penelope, and John Gillett. "Conversations with Nicholas
    Ray and Joseph Losey." <u>Sight and Sound</u> 3 (1961): 182–87.

Kreidl, John Francis. <u>Nicholas Ray</u>. Twayne's Theatrical Arts Series.
    Boston: Twayne, 1977.

Lindner, Robert M. <u>Rebel Without a Cause . . . The Hypnoanalysis of
    a Criminal Psychopath</u>. New York: Grune, 1944.

Lukas, Edwin J. Rev. of <u>Rebel Without a Cause . . . The
    Hypnoanalysis of a Criminal Psychopath</u>, by Robert M.
    Lindner. <u>The Annals of the American Academy of Political and
    Social Science</u> 236 (1944): 215–16.

Lusk, Jack. Swank Motion Pictures, Inc. Letter to the author. 28 Feb.
    1995.

Indent second and subsequent lines of bibliographic citations approximately five spaces or one-half inch from left margin.

Gold 13

Mayberry, George. "Alternatives to the Novel." <u>New Republic</u> 24
  July 1944: 108.

McVay, Douglas. "Rebel Without a Cause." <u>Films and Filming</u> 23.2
  (1979): 16–24.

Mitgang, Herbert. "The Strange James Dean Death Cult." <u>Coronet</u>
  Nov. 1956: 110–15.

Ray, Nicholas. "Story into Script." <u>Sight and Sound</u> 26 (1956):
  70–74.

Thomson, David. "Rebel Without a Cause." <u>Take One</u> Mar. 1979:
  15–16.

WRITING RESEARCH PAPERS ABOUT LITERATURE

12

Kinds of Research

Research about literature may involve study, analysis, or interpretations of individual poems, stories, plays, and novels. Once you become interested in a particular work, you may want to investigate the method of composition, its reception by reviewers and the general public, or wider issues such as its place in the author's work as a whole or in its cultural or social setting. Among the topics that students might want to investigate are the following:

1. How the work was written
2. How the work was received by the public (reviews, letters, private journals)
3. How critics have interpreted the work (professional journals and books)
4. How the critical reception/interpretation of the work has changed through the years
5. How the work relates to time and place of publication, for example the geographical, historical, or cultural context
6. How a work relates to other literary works published at the same time
7. How a work relates to the literary tradition
8. How a work relates to others by the same author
9. How a work relates to philosophical, political, religious, or social values

10. How a work relates to events of the author's life
11. How a work relates to author's character or psychological makeup
12. How the work is illuminated by particular critical methods, such as formalism, reader response, or the new historicism

The first step in studying a literary work is always to read the text carefully and to identify the other works it reminds you of, questions it raises about background, or other areas you would like to know more about. Particular works of literature raise certain kinds of questions that might lead to meaningful research. For example, a student reading Ernest Hemingway's *For Whom the Bell Tolls* may find out about the Spanish Civil War, while someone studying Willa Cather's *My Ántonia* may want to investigate the history of the railroad or pioneer life in Nebraska. Works by writers using myth or folklore in unconventional ways (William Butler Yeats, William Blake, Toni Morrison) may attract students to explore the sources of such works; those by authors with large public reputations (William Faulkner, Tennessee Williams, or Lillian Hellman) encourage detailed studies of the authors' lives. The list below gives examples of kinds of research that may illuminate works of literature:

1. Charlotte Brontë's *Jane Eyre* and the role of the governess in the nineteenth century
2. Joseph Conrad's *Heart of Darkness* and colonialism and racism in the nineteenth century
3. Charles Dickens's *Tale of Two Cities* and the French Revolution
4. F. Scott Fitzgerald's *The Great Gatsby* and the 1919 World Series
5. Bobbie Anne Mason's *In Country* and the Vietnam veterans
6. Herman Melville's *Billy Budd* and the United States Navy
7. Toni Morrison's *Beloved* and the Underground Railway
8. Tim O'Brien's *Going After Cacciato* and the Vietnam War
9. William Shakespeare's *Othello* and Africans in Renaissance Europe; *The Merchant of Venice* and antisemitism.
10. Leslie Marmon Silko's *Ceremony* and problems of retaining Native American traditions
11. Kurt Vonnegut's *Slaughterhouse-Five* and the bombing of Dresden
12. Virginia Woolf's *Orlando* and Vita Sackville-West

You may be asked to research some aspect of an author's general concerns. The following list suggests broad topics that need to be narrowed and focused. For example, a paper on Faulkner's use of the grotesque might focus on humor and pathos in "Spotted Horses."

1. Jorge Luis Borges: narrative techniques, the story within the story
2. Willa Cather: the American Midwest
3. George Eliot: marriage
4. William Faulkner: the grotesque
5. Gabriel García Márquez: magical realism
6. Nadine Gordimer: apartheid in South Africa
7. Nathaniel Hawthorne: Puritanism
8. Zora Neale Hurston: African folk tales
9. Maxine Hong Kingston: Chinese traditions
10. Wole Soyinka: Yoruba ritual and religion
11. Harriet Beecher Stowe: the abolitionist movement
12. Tennessee Williams: the southern aristocracy
13. Richard Wright: the Communist Party
14. William Butler Yeats: the Irish independence movement

Sample Papers in Literature Using MLA Style

CARLA MEDINA

Carla decided to write her paper on Alice Walker's *The Color Purple* in order to fulfill one part of her class assignment to research two controversial literary works. After discovering that secondary material on the work concentrated largely on the character Celie's voice, she chose to focus her subject on the voices of *The Color Purple*.

Steps Leading to Carla's Paper

1. Instructor assigns two research papers on controversial literary works, and she chooses to write her first on *The Color Purple* (p. 25)
2. Identifies her sources (p. 46)
   - Makes an appointment with the reference librarian
   - Performs a computer search in two indices, the *MLA International Bibliography* and *InfoTrac*
   - Consults the *Book Review Index* and the *New York Times Index* for more references

- Locates the articles in her library
- Reads through several articles, photocopying three and taking notes from others

3. Focuses her topic on the voices of the novel, and makes source cards for articles that treat this issue (pp. 77, 115)
4. Calls professor and interviews her over the phone (p. 102)
5. Organizes her paper, writes a first draft, and prepares a list of references (p. 166)
6. Prepares her final paper

Carla's main idea or thesis statement

Medina 1

Carla Medina
Professor Walker
English 110
28 February 1995

The Voices of The Color Purple

Alice Walker's The Color Purple, winner of the
American Book Award and the Pulitzer Prize for
literature, was a best-seller in 1982. It has
received considerable attention both in the popular
press and in scholarly publications. The novel's
success is in part due to the voice of its ignorant,
poor, but appealing heroine, Celie, and the lively
group of characters to whom she gives a voice.
Equally compelling is the novel's vision of people
as constantly in flux and therefore capable of being
transformed for the better. Such change takes place
through human interaction as the characters speak
and listen to each other.

An epistolary novel, The Color Purple consists
of letters: from Celie to God; from Celie to her
sister, Nettie, a missionary in Africa; and from
Nettie to Celie. Celie writes about being raped,
about having her children taken from her, and
eventually about being transformed from a woman who
passively accepts her lot to one who sets the terms
of her own life. The more educated Nettie tells of
her harsh life among the Olinka, an African tribe
devastated by British rubber planters; of the

A description of the novel to help readers
unfamiliar with it

Carla indicates the focus of her paper.

Medina 2

conflicts she and the other two missionaries have
with the Africans; and of her own disappointment
over their failure to help the Olinka. Though Nettie
too gives voice to others, this paper will focus on
the more lively and immediate voices of Celie's
letters to God and to Nettie.

In an article that came out just as the novel
was published in 1982, Gloria Steinem calls Alice
Walker a "necessary" and "major" writer (35); and
she praises the novel for its "storytelling style,"
particularly Celie's voice as she "writes her heart
out" in letters first to God and then to her sister,
using the powerful rhythms of her own "black folk
English" (89). Steinem also admires Nettie's letters
to Celie for their "blow-by-blow" accounts of the
devastating consequences of British colonialism,
which say more about that subject "in a few pages
than do many academic tomes" (90). But most
reviewers of the novel either ignore or criticize
Nettie's letters and single out Celie's language for
praise. The New Yorker reviewer feels that Celie's
letters "burst with a kind of poetry," and Dinitia
Smith in the Nation commends the novel's "vivid
figures of speech" and its "black folk idiom" (182).
Similarly, Mel Watkins, writing for the New York
Times, applauds the "lyrical cadence" of Celie's
"intensely subjective voice" (7). Trudier Harris,
who has serious reservations about the novel's

Name of author used to introduce
quotation.

Gates's words

Medina 3

merit, considers Celie's voice to be "powerful,
subtly humorous" and "perfectly suited to the
character" (156).

 Some of the more memorable passages of the
novel are those in which Celie recounts in letters
to God private experiences that she has never told
to anyone else. In the early parts of the novel, she
often compares herself and others to trees or
inanimate objects rather than to other people. When
her husband beats her, Celie writes that she talks
to herself: "I say to myself, Celie, you a tree.
That's how I come to know trees fear men" (30). She
feels so little for her stepchildren that patting
them is like patting a piece of wood: "Not a living
tree, but a table" (37). And when she first sees
Shug Avery, Celie projects her response onto the
trees: "The trees all round the house draw themself
up tall for a better look" (50).

 The power of the novel lies not just in Celie's
account of her own subjective experiences, but in
the way she consumes and then recounts the stories
of others. Henry Louis Gates Jr., points out that
Celie's growth "in self-awareness" is revealed as
she finds her voice in part by giving voice to other
characters, including her sister, Nettie (250).
Nettie lives not just in her own speaking, but in
Celie's accounts of her. Celie lives--and grows and
develops--as she absorbs the voices of Nettie and

Medina 4

others. Celie's unique character is the consequence of the particular voices she absorbs. She grows by the discovery not of her true inner self, but of an evolving self, a self constantly recreated by the voices she encounters.

There are four distinct ways that Celie gives voice to others: she relates the speech of others and calls attention to her own silence; she recounts a dialogue between herself and one other person; she relates a conversation between two or more other characters; and she recounts a discussion she has had with someone about what someone else has told her. Though toward the end of the novel Celie conveys the transformed voice of the once abusive Albert, most of the strong voices are those of women. Mae Henderson proposes that Walker signs the novel at the end "A.W., author and medium" to suggest that her intention has been "to give voice and representation to these same women who have been silenced and confined in life as well as literature" (14). While Celie herself has been silenced by abuse, fear, and ignorance, she learns to speak by listening to and reporting the words of those who have not.

At first Celie is even silent about how she perceives the world. When they are growing up, the man they know as "Pa" tells Celie that she is "dumb" and that Nettie is "the clever one" (19). Being told

Note short quotation integrated into paraphrase.

by an adult that she is not smart seems to have more
power over Celie than anything her sister does to
counter it. Though Nettie attempts to help her with
her lessons, Celie does not learn:

> I feel bad sometime Nettie done pass me in
> learnin. But look like nothing she say can
> git in my brain and stay. She try to tell
> me something about the ground not being
> flat. I just say, Yeah, like I know it. I
> never tell her how flat it look to me.
> (20)

Celie's world at this point is flat, and she
cannot see beyond what is immediately in front of
her.

When she is first married to Albert, whom she
calls Mr. _____, Celie cannot imagine a life for
herself except one of mistreatment, deprivation, and
loneliness. It is not until other people enter her
world--and talk to her--that the possibility of a
better life even occurs to her. Kate, her husband's
sister, chides her brother for letting Celie wear
rags and takes her to be fitted for a new dress.
Celie is so moved that she stutters trying to
explain what it means to her to "be the first one in
my own dress." By first listening to Kate, a woman
who stands up for other women, and then giving voice
to Kate's position, Celie grows. When Kate tells her
that she deserves "more than this," Celie seems to

**References that are clearly from the book
don't require the author's name.**

Medina 6

hear: "Maybe so. I think" (28). That silent, but
nevertheless thought and recorded, "maybe so" is a
first step in discovering new possibilities for
herself.

At other times Celie writes about conversations
she has listened to and then rejected. When her
brother-in-law argues that certain views of women
are hard to "prove to the world," Celie silently
disagrees: "What the world got to do with anything,
I think" (61). Because she remains in an isolated,
private world, it will be a long time before Celie
grows in her understanding of what the world has to
do with things. It will also be a long time before
she speaks out and gives voice in the world to her
own thoughts. Typically, her letters to God relate
how people from Celie's world gather together to
have fun, to fight, to argue, or to solve problems.
An example is the scene in which Sophia's friends
and family sit down after supper to discuss how they
might get Sophia out of jail. Celie reports the
conversation with so much detail that it is clear
she is listening carefully, but she also points out
that she "don't say nothing" (90).

Eventually Celie becomes a full participant in
such gatherings, and her voice becomes strong and
persuasive. Two events seem to lead Celie to
discover her voice. First, Shug Avery encourages her
to talk about her early sexual experiences, and for

the first time, Celie tells another human being about the horrible details of the repeated rapes she endured as an adolescent. The second event is the discovery of Nettie's letters, which her husband has been hiding from her for years. Shug gives Celie the support she needs to talk about her pain; Nettie's letters provide her with the information she needs to confront those who have abused her.

In one of her early letters, Nettie explains to her sister that even though she knows Celie is not receiving the letters, writing them keeps her from feeling "locked up in myself and choking on my own heart" (122). Nettie's letters give Celie the courage to speak out. One of her first acts after reading the long-hidden letters is to visit the man who raped her and to let him know that she knows he is not her father but her stepfather. Shortly afterward, the long-silent Celie confronts Albert, tells him she is leaving, and warns him that she will kill him if he tries to stop her: "You a lowdown dog is what's wrong, I say. It's time to leave you and enter into the Creation. And your dead body just the welcome mat I need" (181).

In her letters to Nettie, unlike the earlier ones to God, Celie increasingly plays a dominant role in the conversations she reports. Rather than silently agreeing or disagreeing with what others say, she often sets the terms of the dialogue,

challenging what others say and letting her voice be
heard. When Celie curses her husband, he attempts to
dismiss her: "You can't curse nobody. Look at you.
You black, you pore, you ugly, you a woman. Goddam,
he say, you nothing at all" (187). But Celie gets
the last word: "I'm pore, I'm black, I may be ugly
and can't cook, a voice say to everything listening.
But I'm here" (187). What is new about the way Celie
reports this conversation is that she recognizes her
voice as powerful and she perceives that others are
listening. Celie has heard her own voice.

 With the help of Shug Avery, Celie soon turns
her life around, and the talk about being poor,
black, and ugly is transformed in the opening words
of a letter to Nettie: "I am so happy. I got love. I
got work. I got money, friends, and time" (193).
When Shug temporarily abandons her, Celie is sad and
loses some of her confidence. But in her longest
letter to Nettie (229-41), Celie reveals that she
now has many resources to get her through a hard
time: the conversations of her friends, a letter
from Shug, and a letter from Nettie. Celie even
assumes the role of teacher, and she writes to
Nettie about how she is teaching Albert about
African customs and beliefs, information which of
course she received in a letter from Nettie.

 By the end of the novel, Celie has become an
accomplished storyteller, who not only recounts her

Quotations longer than four lines are
indented ten spaces and double-spaced
before, throughout, and after.

Medina 9

own personal experience but takes the stories of
others and remakes them, giving them voice and new
functions in the lives of others. Albert knows
Nettie because Celie recreated her voice. If Nettie
were to receive that letter, she would know Albert
through Celie's recapitulation of the conversation
she had with him about the letter Nettie wrote to
her. The many voices of The Color Purple live not
just in the moment that they speak (or write), but
as others hear them, respond to them, and in the
process transform their lives.

Celie even finds the words to speak of the
transformation of her relationship with Albert:

> Then the old devil put his arms around me
> and just stood there on the porch with me
> real quiet. Way after while I bent my
> stiff neck onto his shoulder. Here us is,
> I thought, two old fools left over from
> love, keeping each other company under the
> stars. (238)

The man that Celie describes here is quite
different from the one readers meet in the opening
passages of the novel.

In an essay entitled "Writing The Color
Purple," Walker recounts the process of creating
this enormously popular book. In quiet moments in
the country, in California, where she was living,
"Celie, Shug, Albert, Sophia, or Harp would come for

Use shortened title in parentheses when
there is more than one source by the same
author. (No page number is needed here
since the article is only one page.)

a visit" (359). By listening to the characters as
individuals, Walker was able to recreate them in
Celie's letters, giving them the authority of voices
that she has listened to and heard. In an interview
published in <u>Newsweek</u>, Walker refers to the
characters as real people and expresses her concern
whether readers will be able to hear what they have
to say: "Let's hope people can hear Celie's voice.
There are so many people like Celie who make it, who
come out of nothing. People who triumph"
("Characters in Search of a Book"). At the time that
Walker expressed this hope, it was still not clear
how important <u>The Color Purple</u> would become. Today
we know Celie and her friends have been heard.

If a review is neither titled nor signed,
begin entry with "Rev. of" and
alphabetize under title of work reviewed.

Medina 11

Works Cited

Rev. of The Color Purple, by Alice Walker. New
        Yorker 6 Sept. 1982: 106.

Gates, Henry Louis Jr. The Signifying Monkey: A
        Theory of Afro-American Literary Criticism. New
        York: Oxford UP, 1988.

Harris, Trudier. "On The Color Purple, Stereotypes,
        and Silence." Black American Literature Forum
        18 (1984): 155-61.

Henderson, Mae G. "The Color Purple: Revisions and
        Redefinitions." SAGE: A Scholarly Journal on
        Black Women 2 (1985): 14-18.

Smith, Dinitia. "Celie, You a Tree." Rev. of The
        Color Purple, by Alice Walker. The Nation 4
        Sept. 1982: 181-83.

Steinem, Gloria. "Do You Know This Woman?" Ms. June
        1982: 35+.

Walker, Alice. "Characters in Search of a Book."
        Interview with Ray Anello and Pamela Abramson.
        Newsweek 21 June 1982: 67.

---. The Color Purple. New York: Harcourt, 1982.

---. "Writing The Color Purple." In Search of Our
        Mothers' Gardens. New York: Harcourt, 1983.
        355-60.

Watkins, Mel. "Some Letters Went to God." Rev. of
        The Color Purple, by Alice Walker. New York
        Times 25 July 1982: 7.

Use three hyphens followed by a period for
additional books by the same author.

CARLA'S PAPER ON *ADVENTURES OF HUCKLEBERRY FINN*

While Carla is researching the paper on *The Color Purple,* she finds an article by Leland Krauth comparing Walker's novel to Mark Twain's *Adventures of Huckleberry Finn.* Though she does not use Krauth's essay, reading it gives her the idea of doing her major research paper on Twain's most famous novel. When Carla takes the novel home with her for the weekend, her mother explains that *Huck Finn* was banned in her high school in the 1960s mainly because Huck uses racist language. Browsing through the essays at the end of the edition she is reading, Carla learns that there were people who objected to this novel from the time it was first published, and so she decides to investigate the controversy that has led to censorship, bannings, and much argument.

Search Strategy

To do research on one of the most popular novels of all times can involve overwhelming amounts of material. Carla makes another appointment with the same reference librarian who helped her before and who explains that to research a topic about a book that is more than a century old will be more complicated than researching one published just over a decade ago. She recommends that Carla look for articles by searching the following:

1. *MLA International Bibliography*
2. Appropriate databases in *InfoTrac*
3. *ERIC*
4. *New York Times Index*

Carla is able to search the first three indexes very rapidly on CD-ROM, but she finds that she must experiment somewhat to locate what she needs. This is how Carla finds her first sources:

1. After loading the MLA CD-ROM, using the "browse" mode, Carla keys in "Samuel Clemens" and finds 771 articles under that heading. To narrow the search to a more manageable number, she uses the "Wilsearch" mode and requests articles that are about both

Samuel Clemens and *Adventures of Huckleberry Finn.* This time she finds only 51 articles. After scanning these, she identifies 9 that seem relevant. When Carla asks for *Adventures of Huckleberry Finn* and ''censorship,'' she finds 6 articles. All seem relevant.

2. To search *InfoTrac,* or the *General Periodicals Index,* Carla finds that the appropriate heading is "Twain," rather than "Clemens," and that subheadings appear under this. This index produces a number of different articles under the subheading "Criticism and interpretation."

3. To search the *ERIC* CD-ROM, Carla uses the headings *"Huckleberry Finn"* and "censorship" to locate 11 more articles. Because the *ERIC* index includes brief summaries (abstracts) of the articles, she is able to identify 3 to add to her list of sources.

4. To search the *New York Times Index* for accounts of bannings, Carla uses the bound volumes. To find news articles about the ongoing controversy, Carla discovers that "Samuel Clemens" is the appropriate heading, which directs her to another heading, "books and literature." In less than an hour she is able to find some 13 articles about the censorship of *Huck Finn* published in the *Times* since 1957.

5. To find books that deal with the subject, Carla begins with the library's online catalog and identifies several books that seem to be about *Huck* or about Twain and *Huck.* After getting the call numbers (Carla's library's computerized catalog prints out the bibliographic information of each book), she goes directly to the stacks to look for books that seem relevant to her topic. Carla finds several books, but others are not on the shelf. Browsing through the many books about Twain and his work, she selects a couple of others that interest her.

6. Carla's next step is to check out the books she has found and to recall the relevant books that have been checked out. She also requests from interlibrary loan those articles that her library does not have. With the help of electronic indexes, Carla is able to complete this part of her search in an afternoon.

Collecting Sources

After browsing through the books and carefully studying the bibliographies in search of more material, Carla goes back to the library to begin collecting sources. She plans to stay long enough to determine which articles are worthwhile. Some journal articles she reads and discards as not useful, and others she photocopies to consult later.

She reads newspaper articles on microfilm readers and photocopies several.

Alternative Search Strategies

Students using libraries that do not have the CD-ROM indexes or online computers that Carla uses may find the same sources by using the bound volumes of the *MLA Bibliography, ERIC,* the *Readers' Guide to Periodical Literature,* and *America: History and Life.* Other relevant material may be found in the bound volumes of the *New York Times Index,* which Carla uses, and in *Essay and General Literature Index.* For books others may use a card catalog rather than the online catalog.

Getting Started

After two more sessions in the library collecting, reading, taking notes from, and photocopying materials, Carla is ready to plan her paper. Because Carla has photocopied so many articles, she is able to sort her sources into two categories: those that deal with the opposition to *Huck Finn* and those concerned with its defense. She decides to trace the two main parts of the controversy, with each organized chronologically from the time of the book's publication to recent episodes in the battle between those who attack and those who champion the novel.

By the time Carla is ready to write her paper she has many notecards, books, and photocopies of articles—more than she can handle on a small desk. She then divides them into three categories: those she intends to use, those she might use, and those that are irrelevant. Using her bed as well as her desktop, she sorts the ones she intends to use into two groups: those dealing with the controversy during Twain's time and those concerned with the more recent controversy. After subdividing her sources within the two groups, Carla is able to make a rough plan for her paper:

```
    I. Introduction: the Huck Finn debate
       A. History's interpretation
       B. The novel's provocation
   II. The prepublication uproar
```

    A. The obscene drawing
    B. The <u>Century</u> magazine excerpts
       1. Deletions
       2. Debates about race
III. Reactions to publication
    A. Reviews and commentary
    B. Concord library ban
    C. Twain's rebuttal
    D. Other defenders
    E. Lull
 IV. <u>Huck</u> in the schools
    A. The New York ban
    B. Other bans
  V. <u>Huck</u>'s public defenders
    A. Early praise
    B. Famous writers of mid-twentieth century
 VI. Recent defenders
    A. Scholars
    B. Journalists
VII. Resolution: Controversy inherent in the novel

Composing and Taking a Position

Using this plan, Carla composes this paper directly on the computer. As she is drafting her introduction, she becomes clear about what position she intends to take: that the terms of the debate about the novel are determined by moral and social values of a given time, but that the debate itself is inherent in the provocative nature of the story. As she continues drafting her paper, she often stops to reread parts of books and articles, discovering as she goes more and more evidence of the ways the issues of the *Huck Finn* controversy are both provoked by the novel and dictated by their times.

As she writes her paper, Carla enters her references into the bibliography, following MLA parenthetical style of documentation.

Introduction to long quotation (note name
of author).

Medina 1

Carla Medina

Professor Walker

English 210

9 April 1995

Always Trouble: <u>Huck Finn</u> and American Social Values

Students of Mark Twain's <u>Adventures of
Huckleberry Finn</u> who want to find out how the book
has been reviewed, interpreted, and criticized will
find an enormous number of books, essays, and
newspaper articles that discuss this most talked-
about and written-about American novel. Fifty years
ago there was already so much written about this
novel that Kenneth Burke described it as a complex
cultural conversation:

> Imagine that you enter a parlor. You come
> late. When you arrive, others have long
> preceded you, and they are engaged in a
> heated discussion, a discussion too heated
> for them to pause and tell you exactly
> what it is about. . . . You listen for a
> while, until you decide that you have
> caught the tenor of the argument; then you
> put in your oar. Someone answers; you
> answer him; another comes to your defense;
> another aligns himself against you, to
> either the embarrassment or gratification
> of your opponent, depending upon the
> quality of your ally's assistance.

Quotation of more than four lines is set off
and indented ten spaces.

Thesis statement

Medina 2

However, the discussion is interminable.
The hour grows late, you must depart. And
you do depart, with the discussion still
vigorously in progress. (Mailloux 107)

Burke published these words in 1941, fifty-six
years after the novel came out. Another half century
has passed since then, and the "heated discussion"
he describes has gone on and on, growing louder and
louder. With the help of indexes, bibliographies,
and even a computer search, it is now possible to
sort out some of the major topics that the
participants continue to debate and the sides they
take.

This paper will trace two currents within the
discussion about the ultimate value of <u>Huckleberry
Finn</u>, and it will demonstrate that the controversy
is larger than the book. The terms of the debate are
dictated by moral and political concerns of a
particular time in history, but the energy that
fuels the battles comes from the provocative nature
of the novel. Readers will never be neutral about
this book in which a poor white boy uses the most
offensive racial epithets to refer to a black man
who risks his life to help him. The very fact that
the controversy rages as strong as ever suggests
that the book is capable of offending and pleasing
with equal intensity. Perhaps the greatest value of
the novel lies in its ability to create controversy

Carla sets up her argument.

Abbreviated title underlined.

Medina 3

and discussion about larger social issues, keeping
those issues alive in the process. It is not so much
that one side is wrong and the other right, but that
each side is responding to aspects of the novel that
seem to reinforce or challenge its own values.

One side of the debate is concerned with what
is wrong with the novel and why people, particularly
young people, should not read it. The other is about
why <u>Huck Finn</u> is one of our most important, if not
<u>the</u> most important, American novel. As in any
debate, the persistence of one side sustains the
other.

Mark Twain's <u>Adventures of Huckleberry Finn</u>
itself aroused controversy before it was ever
published as a book. <u>Huck Finn</u>'s bad reputation may
have begun with pictures, rather than words. One of
the illustrations was altered at the printers,
presumably as a joke, to show Uncle Silas "in a
flagrant act of indecent exposure" (David 269). The
obscene picture was corrected, but a New York
newspaper published the story, creating undesirable
publicity and perhaps starting the idea that the
book was improper and inappropriate for children
(Egan 9). Publication was delayed and the Christmas
season was missed (Blair 366-70).

When the editor of <u>Century</u> magazine published
extracts from the novel in December, January, and
February of 1884-85, he must have anticipated

Medina 4

trouble because he omitted some 18 percent of the
passages he selected. For example, he took out all
references to nakedness and deleted such expressions
as "to be in a sweat" (Rule 9). Even so, a school
superintendent, who objected even to the expurgated
magazine excerpts, wrote an angry letter complaining
to the editor of <u>Century</u> (Scott 356-58).

Though the deletions did not have to do with
race, <u>Huck</u> was from the beginning surrounded by
discussions of racial issues. The January 1885 issue
of <u>Century</u> magazine that contained excerpts from
<u>Huck Finn</u> also ran an article by George Washington
Cable, who challenged southern notions of white
supremacy. Cable's arguments stimulated more
controversy, and in April, two months after <u>Huck</u>
appeared in book form, <u>Century</u> published an article
by Henry Grady, the editor of the <u>Atlanta
Constitution</u>, who countered Cable's position by
arguing for separation of the races and for white
supremacy. In a recent essay, Stephen Mailloux has
pointed out that <u>Adventures of Huckleberry Finn</u>
entered the world in the context of "this highly
charged and polarized argument" (112). Furthermore,
he notes that Twain and Cable had teamed up for a
much-publicized reading tour, thus further
associating Huck and Jim with the public
conversation about race (110). According to
Mailloux, Twain reinforced the connection by reading

**When an author's name is used or implied
in sentence, it isn't necessary to use name
in parenthetical citation.**

Medina 5

passages from the novel that made fun of white supremacy (112). But it would be more than seventy years before the race issue would become the focus of <u>Huck</u>'s detractors, and then not because Twain was critical of white racist attitudes, but because the book was perceived to be racist.

The publication of <u>Adventures of Huckleberry Finn</u> in February 1885 was greeted by a moderate number of reviews compared to the fifty-odd reviews received by earlier works, <u>The Innocents Abroad</u> and <u>The Gilded Age</u>. In a recent study of the way <u>Huck</u> was received in the months following publication, Victor Fisher found some twenty reviews, but more than a hundred editorials and articles that reported the goings-on following the novel's appearance (2). The public argument was launched in March 1885 when the Concord Free Public Library in Massachusetts banned it from circulation, an event that has been widely discussed in and out of print, and the argument has gone on ever since. There are a number of published articles and essays that include an account of the story of this first of many public bans of <u>Huckleberry Finn</u> (see Fischer 16-32; Stanek 19-20; Gerson 1655-56), not just because it was first, but because of the prestige of the people who served on the committee. Ralph Waldo Emerson's son was a member, having taken the place his father held until his death three years before (Gerson 1656). But the

All three sources in parentheses.

Both quotes come from same page in article.

Medina 6

Concord ban was also important because of the enormous public response that followed in its wake. Fisher's article includes excerpts from many newspapers that took a stand either for or against the censorship of <u>Huck Finn</u>.

The Concord committee was clear that the novel was "the veriest trash . . . more suited to the slums than to intelligent, respectable people." At the same time, Louisa May Alcott condemned the book and chided Twain, suggesting that if he "cannot think of something better to tell our pure-minded lads and lasses, he had better stop writing for them" (Gerson 1656). These frequently quoted scoldings reveal the primary concerns of those who first disapproved of Huck. The boy was simply not nice, he spoke poor English, he behaved badly, and he was in every way a poor role model for nice boys and girls. Twenty years later, when <u>Huckleberry Finn</u> was banned from the Brooklyn Public Library in 1905, Twain, fed up, responded with sarcasm, insisting that he never intended the book to be read by children:

> I wrote <u>Tom Sawyer</u> and <u>Huck Finn</u> for adults exclusively, and it always distresses me when I find that boys and girls have been allowed access to them. The mind that becomes soiled in youth can never again be washed clean. I know this

Journal title is not necessary; used here for
emphasis.

Medina 7

by my own experience, and to this day I
cherish unappeasable bitterness against
the unfaithful guardians of my young life,
who not only permitted but compelled me to
read an unexpurgated Bible through before
I was fifteen years old. (Rule 12)

In 1907 a librarian defended the book in terms
that Twain himself might have used. In a tongue-in-
cheek article published in The Library Journal, E.
L. Pearson created a mock debate between himself and
a prudish female librarian who expels Huck and Tom
from her shelves on the grounds that they "glorify
mischief." Pearson counters "that literature is
nothing but a record of people doing the things they
should not do" (313).

Though there was a relative lull in the Huck
Finn disputes during the years following the Pearson
article in 1907, a quarter of a century later, in
1931, Harper & Brothers published an expurgated
edition of the novel that was intended to be
acceptable in the classroom (Rule 13). Other new
editions of the novel followed, and by mid-century
many students encountered Huck either straight or
diluted.

The specific battle over Huckleberry Finn as a
book suitable for classroom study began again in
1957 when the New York City schools dropped it from
their list of approved books, largely because of

Name of legal case is underlined in text.

protests about the book's alleged racism. Some
writers assume that the race issue became important
in the <u>Huck Finn</u> conversation only after the Supreme
Court decision of <u>Brown v. Board of Education</u> on
integration in the schools made educators conscious
of the possible harm done to black students by
demeaning racial stereotypes. In fact Twain himself
was very aware that the friendship between Huck and
Jim was a threat to widely accepted ideas about race
at the time the novel was published (Mailloux
110-12). What changed in the more than seventy years
that intervened between the publication in 1884 and
the New York ban in 1957 was the prevailing attitude
about race.

In 1957, however, the civil rights movement was
already beginning to bring an end to the legal
separation of the races, and critics of the novel
ignored Twain's attack on racism and focused instead
on the novel's racial slurs and stereotypes that
would embarrass black students in integrated
classrooms and perpetuate racial prejudice. The <u>New
York Times</u> carried the story for some months. During
the more than thirty years since the New York school
board's action, there have been more banning
incidents in schools. In 1963, the Board of
Education of Philadelphia replaced Twain's <u>Huck</u> with
an adapted version that softens the violence,
simplifies the dialect, and removes all racist

Article title is used when no author is given; no need for page number for one-page article.

passages ("Schools in Philadelphia"). Serious protests about Huck Finn continued: in Washington, Florida, Texas, Pennsylvania, Iowa, and Illinois. A widely publicized case for censorship was made by an administrator at, ironically, the Mark Twain Intermediate School of Fairfax, Virginia, who argued that the novel was "the most grotesque example of racist trash ever written" (Rule 16).

And so the conversation continues. The Fairfax case was in 1982, and others have cropped up regularly. But the condemnations, indictments, and official bans that continue to plague Huck are only half of the story. From the earliest days to the present, Adventures of Huckleberry Finn has also been the object of extravagant praise. Among the early positive reviewers were Brander Mathews, who found in Huck no "waste word"; Thomas Perry, who described the vendetta episode as "a masterpiece"; and Andrew Lang, who declared the whole book "a masterpiece" (Inge 32, 34, 40). The word "masterpiece," once used, set the tone for others to praise Huck with superlatives. William Dean Howells, who as Twain's friend and adviser read the novel four times before publication (Blair 360), wrote in 1901 about having "half a mind to give my whole heart to Huckleberry Finn" (Simpson 3, 104). Others, however, gave all, heart and mind. H. L. Mencken in 1913 declared it "one of the great Masterpieces of

Page numbers are listed in order of reference.

Two quotations from the same source

Medina 10

the world . . . the full equal of <u>Don Quixote</u>" (Inge
69); and V. S. Pritchett in 1941 called it "one of
the funniest books in all literature" and "a comic
masterpiece" (Inge 76, 79).

During the middle decades of the twentieth
century, <u>Huck</u>'s status was rising even higher, as a
number of famous poets, novelists, and critics began
to sing its praises. For T. S. Eliot, the novel was
"the only one of Mark Twain's various books which
can be called a masterpiece," and it is Twain's use
of the Mississippi River that makes a boy's book "a
great book" (Inge 111). F. Scott Fitzgerald
glorified the novel as the first objective insider's
view of America (Simpson 107). Ernest Hemingway
raised the stakes even higher by claiming that "All
American literature comes from one book by Mark
Twain called <u>Huckleberry Finn</u> . . . the best book
we've had" (Blair 7). Respected critics joined the
<u>Huck Finn</u> fan club in the middle of the century: For
the Englishman F. R. Leavis, it was "supremely the
American classic" (Simpson 109), and Lionel Trilling
called it "one of the world's great books and one of
the central documents of American culture" (Inge
82). The importance of these men--and not
surprisingly most if not all champions of this
"boy's book" seem to be men--has resulted in their
opinions being often quoted and used by those who
defend the book as great literature.

Carla's own conclusions; no need for
documentation.

Recent scholars who have defended the novel
against charges of racism have turned their
attention to character and theme in efforts to prove
that Jim is presented as a noble and admirable
figure, that Huck's progress is one that leads him
to understand the evils of slavery, and that the
novel as a whole condemns racism. Far from
submitting to Twain's warning that readers should
avoid searching for a "motive" in the novel, this
new generation of Huck Finn defenders have
deliberately set out to do just that: to find
evidence of what Twain intended to say about race.

In an essay published in 1984, Richard Barksdale
argued that "Twain's literary intention" is to
dramatize how "an authentic black-white friendship"
could develop during pre-Civil War America only away
from society, on a raft, perhaps, in the middle of a
large river. That the partners of this friendship
represent members of social groups that at the time
the book was published had become "inveterate
enemies"--poor whites and recently freed slaves--
suggests that it is social values, not some kind of
inborn racism, that keep people apart (19).
Barksdale concluded then, that Twain's novel, "by
motive and intention, is really an ironic appraisal
of the American racial scene circa 1884" (20).

Like Barksdale, David L. Smith, also in 1984,
defended Huck Finn on grounds that it is a "subtle

Quotations in this paragraph come from
different pages of the same source.

attack on racism" (5). Countering those who denounce
the book because of its stereotyping of Jim, Smith
showed how Jim's behavior actually contradicts the
stereotype and how rather than acting like the
gullible clown that he seems to some, Jim behaves
with "forethought, creativity and shrewdness" (7).
He is "in most ways a better man than the men who
regard him as their inferior" (10).

Three years later, Stephen Railton, who conceded
that Huck Finn is "racist as well as about racism"
(393), argued that Twain ultimately chose to have it
both ways and that the book belongs in the classroom
precisely because of its contradictory attitudes
toward race. While there are passages that expose
"the terrible price people pay for prejudices," the
novel does not finally "overcome Huck's enslavement
to his culture's distorted values" (396-97). It is
true that Huck plays a childish trick; Jim's
response is "as authentically noble as any speech in
Shakespeare" (398); and to Railton, in the whole
first two-thirds of the novel, Huck remains a naive
racist while Jim is "a magnanimous figure"
(399-400). In the ending chapters, Twain shifts,
perhaps to appeal to the racist prejudices of his
readers, and turns Jim into a "comic stereotype"
(407).

The Huck Finn controversy is far from limited
to librarians, scholars, and famous writers. From

Medina 13

time to time, sometimes in response to a particular banning threat, sometimes for no apparent reason, newspapers publish editorials taking a stand on this issue. In August 1982, a writer for the <u>Nation</u> countered the Fairfax County censoring by comparing Huck to Martin Luther King Jr., since both chose to break unjust laws (Hearn 117). The lead editorial of the 1 January 1984 <u>New York Times</u> asked readers to think back to 1884 instead of 1984 and to think about the importance of the freedom to read the documents of the past: "To blot out 1884 by purging or purifying Twain is to rob life, and the passage of time, of all meaning" ("Think Back, Too"). In the fall of 1990, John Head, a columnist for the <u>Atlanta Journal and Constitution</u>, responding to a campaign to ban <u>Huck</u> in Plano, Texas, concurred with some of Twains's earliest defenders that the book is "a masterpiece," and that good teachers can help students understand the novel's context so that they can "learn something valuable from a great writer's portrait of racism's silly and downright ugly face."

The issues debated have altered through the years in response to changing times, but the battles continue. Explaining why they recommended that libraries initiate discussions of censorship, Gerson and Stavely concluded that librarians have a responsibility to create dialogue about controversial books because "only through dialogue

Both authors of this article need to be mentioned if introduced in body of paper.

Carla returns to the paper's thesis in her conclusion.

Medina 14

will those books lined up on our stacks ever stir
and quicken and belong to all of us" (1658).

Whether <u>Adventures of Huckleberry Finn</u> belongs
to all of us is debatable, but no one can deny that
the dialogue goes on, keeping the antics and
language of Huck and Jim alive in the minds of many.
Surely Twain himself intended to stir up such talk
simply by forbidding it:

> Persons attempting to find a motive in
> this narrative will be prosecuted; persons
> attempting to find a moral in it will be
> banished; persons attempting to find a
> plot in it will be shot. (Clemens 2)

This "notice" on the title page of the novel
continues to serve not as a warning, but as a
provocation, as students, scholars, and general
readers argue about what Twain intended, what moral
principles are conveyed by the story, and what harm
or good might be done by those who read it.

Far more important than a discussion about the
novel's literary worth is the debate over social and
cultural values that it incites. Since the values
the novel challenges have altered through the years,
there is reason to think that in a different time,
<u>Adventures of Huckleberry Finn</u> will provoke debate
about still other social concerns.

For an essay in a collection of previously
published works, provide data for earlier
publication, followed by "Rpt. in," title of
collection, and publication data.

Medina 15

Works Cited

Barksdale, Richard K. "History, Slavery, and
    Thematic Irony in <u>Huckleberry Finn</u>." <u>Mark Twain
    Journal</u> 22.2 (1984): 17-20.

Blair, Walter. <u>Mark Twain and Huck Finn</u>. Berkeley: U
    of California P, 1960.

Clemens, Samuel Langhorne. <u>Adventures of Huckleberry
    Finn</u>. Ed. Sculley Bradley, Richmond Croom
    Beatty, E. Hudson Long, and Thomas Cooley. 2nd
    ed. New York: Norton, 1977.

David, Beverly R. "The Pictorial <u>Huck Finn</u>: Mark
    Twain and His Illustrator, E. W. Kemble." Huck
    Finn <u>Among the Critics: A Centennial Selection</u>.
    Ed. M. Thomas Inge. Frederick: University
    Publications of America, 1981. 269-91.

Egan, Michael. <u>Mark Twain's</u> Huckleberry Finn: <u>Race,
    Class and Society</u>. Sussex: Sussex UP, 1977.

Eliot, T. S. Introduction. <u>Adventures of
    Huckleberry Finn</u>. By Samuel Clemens. London:
    Cresset/New York: Chanticleer, 1950. Rpt. in
    Huck Finn <u>Among the Critics: A Centennial
    Selection</u>. Ed. M. Thomas Inge. Frederick:
    University Publications of America, 1981.
    103-11.

Fisher, Victor. "Huck Finn Reviewed: The Reception
    of <u>Huckleberry Finn</u> in the United States, 1885-
    1897." <u>Mark Twain Journal</u> 16.1 (1983): 1-57.

Fitzgerald, F. Scott. <u>Fitzgerald Newsletter</u> 8

When a normally underlined title is part of
an underlined title, the incorporated title is
not underlined.

Medina 16

(Winter 1960). Rpt. as "Viewpoints: F. Scott
    Fitzgerald." <u>Twentieth-Century Interpretations
    of</u> Adventures of Huckleberry Finn. Ed. Claude M.
    Simpson. Englewood Cliffs: Prentice, 1968. 107.
Gerson, Lani, and Keith Stavely. "We Didn't Wait for
    the Censor: Intellectual Freedom at the
    Watertown Public Library." <u>Library Journal</u> 108
    (1983): 1654-58.
Haight, Anne Lyon. <u>Banned Books: 387 B.C. to 1978
    A.D.</u> Updated and enlarged by Chandler B.
    Grannis. New York: Bowker, 1978.
Head, John. "It's Absurd to Accuse Twain of Being
    Racist." <u>Atlanta Journal and Constitution</u> 26
    Nov. 1990, sec. A: 13.
Hearn, Michael Patrick. "Expelling Huck Finn." <u>The
    Nation</u> 7 Aug. 1982: 117.
Howells, William Dean. "Mark Twain: An Inquiry."
    <u>North American Review</u> 172 (1901): 311-15. Rpt.
    as "Viewpoints: William Dean Howells."
    <u>Twentieth-Century Interpretations of</u> Adventures
    of Huckleberry Finn. Ed. Claude M. Simpson.
    Englewood Cliffs: Prentice, 1968. 103-05.
Leavis, F. R. Introduction. <u>Pudd'nhead Wilson</u>. By
    Samuel Clemens. London: Chatto, 1955. Rpt. as
    "Viewpoints: F. R. Leavis." <u>Twentieth-Century
    Interpretations of</u> Adventures of Huckleberry
    Finn. Ed. Claude M. Simpson. Englewood Cliffs:
    Prentice, 1968. 109-11.

Abbreviated publisher's name

Medina 17

Mailloux, Steven. "Reading <u>Huckleberry Finn</u>: The
    Rhetoric of Performed Ideology." <u>New Essays on</u>
    Adventures of Huckleberry Finn. Ed. Louis J.
    Budd. Cambridge: Cambridge UP, 1985. 107-33

Mathews, Brander. Rev. of <u>Adventures of Huckleberry</u>
    <u>Finn</u>, by Samuel Clemens. <u>Saturday Review</u>
    (London) 31 Jan. 1885: 153-54. Rpt. in Huck
    Finn <u>Among the Critics: A Centennial Selection</u>.
    Ed. M. Thomas Inge. Frederick: University
    Publications of America, 1985. 27-32.

Pearson, E. L. "The Children's Librarian Versus
    <u>Huckleberry Finn</u>: A Brief for the Defense." <u>The</u>
    <u>Library Journal</u> 32 (1907): 312-13.

Perry, Thomas Sergeant. Rev. of <u>Adventures of</u>
    <u>Huckleberry Finn</u>, by Samuel Clemens. <u>Century</u>
    <u>Magazine</u> May 1885: 171-72. Rpt. in Huck Finn
    <u>Among the Critics: A Centennial Selection</u>. Ed.
    M. Thomas Inge. Frederick: University
    Publications of America, 1985. 33-35.

Pritchett, V. S. "America's First Truly Indigenous
    Masterpiece." <u>New Statesman and Nation</u> 2 Aug.
    1941: 113. Rpt. in Huck Fin <u>Among the Critics:</u>
    <u>A Centennial Selection</u>. Ed. M. Thomas Inge.
    Frederick: University Publications of America,
    1985. 75-79.

Railton, Stephen. "Jim and Mark Twain: What Do Dey
    Stan' For?" <u>The Virginia Quarterly Review</u> 63
    (1987): 393-408.

If the author's name is unknown, entry is
alphabetized by the first word in the title
other than a definite or indefinite article.

Medina 18

Rule, Henry B. "A Brief History of the Censorship of
the Adventures of Huckleberry Finn." Lamar
Journal of the Humanities 12.1 (1986): 9-18.

"Schools in Philadelphia Edit 'Huckleberry Finn.'"
New York Times 17 Apr. 1963, sec. 1: 44.

Scott, A. L. "The Century Magazine Edits
Huckleberry Finn, 1884-1885." American
Literature 27 (1955): 356-62.

Smith, David L. "Huck, Jim, and American Racial
Discourse." Mark Twain Journal 22 (1984): 4-12.

Stanek, Lou Willett. "Huck Finn: 100 Years of Durn
Fool Problems." School Library Journal 31.6
(1985): 19-22.

"Think Back, Too." Editorial. New York Times 1 Jan.
1984: E12.

Trilling, Lionel. "The Greatness of Huckleberry
Finn." The Liberal Imagination. New York:
Scribner's, 1950. Rpt. in Huck Finn Among the
Critics: A Centennial Selection. Ed. M. Thomas
Inge. Frederick: University Publications of
America, 1985. 81-92.

WRITING RESEARCH PAPERS IN THE SOCIAL SCIENCES USING APA STYLE

13

Approaches to Research in the Social Sciences

The social sciences are primarily concerned with how human beings, and sometimes other animals, relate to each other. There is no absolute agreement about what constitutes a social science, but generally included in the area are anthropology, economics, political science, psychology, and sociology. In some institutions, however, history might be considered one of the social sciences, while certain psychologists consider their work to be part of the biological sciences. There is some overlap in the various social sciences, and some research may be conducted by teams of researchers from various disciplines. There are many topics in the social sciences that are appropriate for college students to research, but most projects that are suitable for the time limitations of an academic term and for the resources of beginning students will involve studying and synthesizing secondary materials. Beginning students in the social sciences mainly work with the written reports of other investigators who are experts in a field they are studying and who have conducted surveys, administered questionnaires, observed behavior, and arrived at conclusions based on studies that may have extended over a period of years.

Anthropology

Students of anthropology tend to specialize in one of two very different areas: physical anthropology, which studies humans as a biological species, and cultural anthropology, which grows from the study of single cultural groups. Each of these two disciplines is subdivided into numerous specialties. In an undergraduate course in physical anthropology, you might want to research the techniques used to examine human fossil remains to determine the diet of primitive peoples or whether they were warlike. As a student of cultural anthropology, you would study the written accounts of anthropologists who have done fieldwork by leaving their own societies behind and immersing themselves in the cultures of relatively simple peoples. You might, for example, want to focus on the work that has been done on a particular group of people, such as the Kung San hunter-gatherers of the Kalahari Desert in southern Africa. Other fields that are sometimes considered part of anthropology are linguistics and archeology.

Economics

The field of economics offers many possibilities for student research: in a course on the history of economic thought, the influence of a particular classical economist—John Stuart Mill, David Ricardo, or Adam Smith; in the study of macroeconomics, one aspect of the complex workings of the Federal Reserve Bank in the contemporary United States; in a course on industrial organization, an analysis of the internal structure of a specific American industry; or in the area of economic development, the strategies for industrialization (or for food distribution) in a less-developed country—Chad, Bolivia, or Turkey.

Political Science

Since the systematic and therefore scientific study of governments and politics dates back to classical Greece, students studying governments and political processes have a vast historical background to explore. If you are taking a course in ancient political theory, you might want to examine how questions of justice or social responsibility are treated by certain classical authors—Aristotle and Plato, perhaps. Students taking a course in contemporary comparative governments might conduct studies of the role of government in education in two different countries, while those studying international relations could explore some aspect of international law (the battle for an international copyright law), of diplomacy (the establishment of diplomatic relations between the United States and China), or international organizations (Eleanor Roosevelt's role in the United Nations).

Sociology

There are many possibilities for pursuing interesting research in the field of sociology. You might explore an historical topic, such as the work of the great social reformers of the nineteenth century, people like Robert Owen, who formed a model industrial community in Scotland and later established a Utopian agricultural community in New Harmony, Indiana, or Charles Fourier, the French social philosopher, whose dreams of social harmony resulted in the establishment of a number of colonies in the United States, including the famous Brook Farm. You might want to investigate the early history of sociology as an academic discipline as reflected in the *American Journal of Sociology,* the first academic journal to publish articles on sociological topics. In a course on that aspect of sociology called social psychology, you might study some aspect of human communication, such as the speech habits of street gangs or some other social unit. Your research in this area might lead you to studies conducted by sociologists, psychologists, and linguists. You may want to focus on some aspect of group life within a single community—an ethnic enclave, a small town, or a hospital for the mentally ill.

Psychology

Like the other social sciences, psychology is rapidly expanding and becoming increasingly complex. Undergraduate students in psychology usually survey the field, taking courses in several areas, such as experimental, developmental, physiological, and abnormal psychology. Students doing research in these areas might study the process by which early investigators—Pavlov and Skinner—discovered the function of rewards in conditioning behavior (experimental), the controversy about attaching psychiatric labels to children (developmental), the role of neural mechanisms in aggressive behavior (physiological), or the theories of the genesis of schizophrenia (abnormal).

Primary Research

As you develop some expertise in a field, you will have more opportunity to do basic or primary research. If you take a course in experimental psychology, for example, you might conduct your own experiment, perhaps using animal subjects like mice or pigeons to investigate the effects of behavior modification techniques. As you advance in a field, you could participate in ongoing research conducted by a team of investigators. Undergraduate students could conceivably conduct primary research by doing one of the following: joining a summer expedition doing fieldwork in cultural anthropology; interviewing people to find out about their political beliefs, voting behavior, or perception of government officials; administering questionnaires to find out about people's drinking habits, sexual behavior, or marriage plans; studying programs conducted in nursing homes, mental health clinics, or birth control clinics and then trying to find out how people value the services they receive; observing children at play in a nursery school or adolescents interacting in a drug rehabilitation center.

Making an APA Reference List for Papers in the Social Sciences

Most undergraduate students doing research projects in the social sciences will find adequate guidance here for making a reference list. Those who need further guidance should consult the *Publication Manual of the American Psychological Association* [APA] (1994). All examples and rules in this chapter are based on the style established by the APA manual.

> ✓ **C H E C K L I S T   2 2**
>
> ### Typing References Using APA Style
>
> 1. The reference list must be double-spaced, and entries should start with a paragraph indent; the following lines should be flush with the left margin.
> 2. Space once after commas, semicolons, the colon following the location of the publisher, and periods.
> 3. Use a solid underline with no break between words of titles and extending under punctuation at the ends of titles.
> 4. Capitalize only the first words and proper names of titles and subtitles of books and articles.

APA STYLE

Books

A Book with One Author

    Coles, R. (1986). <u>The moral life of children.</u> Boston: Atlantic Monthly Press.

A Book with Two Authors

    Colarusso, C. A., & Nemiroff, R. A. (1981). <u>Adult development.</u> New York: Plenum Press.

A Book with a Corporate Author

American Psychological Association. (1994). <u>Publication manual of the American Psychological Association</u> (4th ed.). Washington, DC: Author.

Note: In this citation, the author and the publisher are the same.

A Book with no Author or Editor

<u>Writers' and artists' yearbook.</u> (1980). London: Adam and Charles Black.

An English Translation of a Book

Piaget, J. (1980). <u>Experiments in contradiction</u> (D. Coltman, Trans.). Chicago: University of Chicago Press. (Original work published 1974)

A Book with an Editor

Erikson, E. H. (Ed.). (1978). <u>Adulthood.</u> New York: Norton.

Note: The name of the editor appears first when the whole text is cited rather than a single essay or chapter.

A Revised Edition

Selye, H. (1978). <u>The stress of life</u> (Rev. ed.). New York: McGraw-Hill.

Note: Abbreviate the edition as it is noted on the title page: 2nd ed. for second edition, 3rd ed. for third edition, and rev. ed. for revised edition.

An Encyclopedia or Dictionary

<u>The new encyclopaedia britannica</u> (15th ed., Vols. 1-32). (1991). Chicago: Encyclopaedia Britannica.

A Brochure

Emory University. (1995). <u>Guidelines for 1996-1997 financial aid</u> [Brochure]. Atlanta, GA: Author.

An Article or Chapter in an Edited Book

    Rohlen, T. P. (1978). The promise of adulthood in Japan. In E. H. Erikson (Ed.), <u>Adulthood</u> (pp. 129-140). New York: Norton.

A Chapter in a Volume in a Series

    Taylor, B.E. (1986). Sutton Elber Griggs. In M.J. Bruccoli & C.E.F. Clark Jr. (Series Eds.) & T. Harris (Vol. Ed.), <u>Dictionary of literary biography: Vol. 50 Afro-American writers before the Harlem Renaissance</u> (pp. 140-144). Detroit: Gale.

Note: Begin with the author and name of the chapter, followed by the editors of the series and volume and list the titles in the same order.

An Encyclopedia Entry

    Jones, E. (1981). Sigmund Freud. In <u>Encyclopedia Americana</u> (Vol. 12, pp. 83-87). Danbury, Connecticut: Encyclopedia Americana.

Periodicals

A Journal Article with One Author

    Rogers, C. R. (1964). Toward a modern approach to values. <u>Journal of Abnormal and Social Psychology, 68,</u> 160-167.

A Journal with Two Authors

    Feather, N. T., & Barber, J. G. (1983). Depressive reactions and unemployment. <u>Journal of Abnormal Psychology, 92,</u> 185-195.

A Journal Article with Three to Five Authors

    Abbey, S. E., Kennedy, S. H., Kaplan, A. S., Toner, B. B., & Garfinkel, P. E. (1990). Self-report symptoms that predict major depression in patients with prominent physical symptoms. <u>International Journal of Psychiatry in Medicine, 20,</u> 247-258.

A Journal with Six or more Authors

    Gold, P. W., Gwirtsman, H., Avgerinos, P.C., Nieman, L. K., Gallucci, W. T., Kaye, W., Jimerson, D., Ebert, M., Rittmaster, R., Loriaux, D. L., & Chrousos, G. P. (1986). Abnormal hypothalamic-pituitary-adrenal function in anorexia nervosa: Pathophysiologic mechanisms in underweight and weight-corrected patients. <u>New England Journal of Medicine, 314,</u> 1335-1342.

Note: Cite all authors in the list of references, but in the parenthetical reference in the text, when there are six or more authors, cite the last name of the first author followed by "et al.": (Gold, et al.).

Note: The first letter of the first word of a subtitle is also capitalized.

An Article from a Journal Numbering Pages Continually Throughout a Volume

Grubb, H. J., Sellers, M. I., & Waligroski, K. (1993). Factors related to depression and eating disorders: Self-esteem, body image, and attractiveness. <u>Psychological Reports, 72,</u> 1003-1010.

An Article from a Journal Numbering Pages Separately for Each Issue

Braddock, J. H. (1985). School desegregation and black assimilation. <u>Journal of Social Issues, 41</u> (3), 9-22.

An Article Written in a Language Other Than English

Delgorgue, M., & Engelhart, D. (1985). Style graphique chez l'enfant: Deux recherches sur la discrimination entre dessin d'enfant "normal" et dessin d'enfant "pathologique" [Graphic style among children: Two studies of differences between the drawings of "normal" and "pathological" children]. <u>Bulletin de Psychologie, 38,</u> 303-321.

Note: If the source used is an English translation, cite only the English title, and do not use brackets.

An Article Condensed or Reprinted in a Journal Other Than Its Original Source

Coleman, J. S. (1973). How do the young become adults? <u>The Education Digest, 38,</u> 49-52. (Condensed from <u>Review of Educational Research,</u> 1972, <u>42,</u> 431-439)

A Work Cited in a Secondary Source

Tizard, B. (1984). Problematic aspects of nuclear education. <u>Harvard Educational Review, 54,</u> 271-281.

Note: Cite the secondary source in the reference list, but cite both the original source and the secondary source in the text. For example, Tizard makes a reference to the results of an unpublished paper that you have not read given at a conference in 1984. Cite that study in the text as follows: A study conducted in Sweden by Holmberg and Bergstrom in 1984 . . . (cited in Tizard, 1984, pp. 273–274).

The Entire Issue of a Journal

VandenBos, G. R. (Ed.). (1986). Psychotherapy research [Special issue]. American Psychologist, 41 (2).

Note: If there is no editor for the special issue, cite the title first, alphabetizing it by the first significant word in the title.

An Abstract

Kennedy, S. H., Kaplan, A. S., Garfinkel, P. E., Rockert, W., Toner, B., & Abbey, S. E. (1994). Depression in anorexia nervosa and bulimia nervosa: Discriminating depressive symptoms and episodes [Abstract]. Journal of Psychosomatic Research, 38, 773-782.

Note: If the word *Abstract* appears in the title of the periodical (e.g. *Psychological Abstracts*) do not put it in brackets after the title.

An Abstract from a Secondary Source

Harding, C., & Kristiansen, C. M. (1984). Statistically sophisticated subjects' perceptions of the health risks of smoking. Journal of Social Psychology, 124 (2), 263-264. (From Psychological Abstracts, 1986, 73, Abstract No. 3651)

An Article in a Periodical Published Annually

Kessler, R. C., Price, R. H., & Wortman, C. B. (1985). Social factors in psychopathology: Stress, social support, and coping processes. Annual Review of Psychology, 36, 531-572.

A Magazine Article

Lowe, M. D. (1992, July/August). Reclaiming cities for people. World Watch, 5, 19-25.

A Signed Weekly Newspaper Article

Anderson, J. (1983, July 25). Finding loving homes for hard-to-place children. Christian Science Monitor, p. 16.

Note: APA uses "p." and "pp." in the reference list to indicate pages of newspapers.

An Unsigned Daily Newspaper Article

Women and gun ownership. (1986, February 24). <u>The New York Times,</u> p. 18.

A Newspaper Article with Discontinuous Pages

Pear, R. (1986, February 24). Stiffer rules for nursing homes proposed. <u>The New York Times,</u> pp. 1, 9.

A Signed Newsletter Article

Dandekar, N. (1992, Fall). Becoming Native to a Place. <u>American Nature Writing Newsletter, 4,</u> 7.

An Unsigned Newsletter Article

Effects of cocaine abuse on the unborn. (1986, February 17). <u>Behavior Today, XX,</u> 3.

Other Written Sources

A Report from the Government Printing Office

National Institute on Alcohol Abuse and Alcoholism. (1980). <u>Facts about alcohol and alcoholism</u> (DHHS Publication No. ADM 80-31). Washington, DC: U.S. Government Printing Office.

A Report from an Information or Document Deposit Service

Meyer, J. A. (Ed.). (1982). <u>Meeting human needs, toward a new public philosophy</u> (Report No. ISBN-0-8447-1358-9). Washington, DC: American Enterprise Institute for Public Policy Research. (ERIC Document Reproduction Service No. ED 223 327).

A Report of a Congressional Hearing

Hearing before the House of Representatives Select Committee on Children, Youth, and Families. (1983). <u>Children's fear of war.</u> Washington, DC: U.S. Government Printing Office.

Nonprint and Electronic Sources

A Video Recording

> National Institute of Mental Health. (1980). <u>Drug abuse</u> [Videotape]. Bethesda: Author.

> **Note:** For video recordings of conferences and other public events, give the relevent information that the reader will need to find the recording.

A Cassette Recording

> Shapiro, H. (Speaker). (1971). <u>Future of evolution</u> (Cassette Recording No. 010-13492). Location: Center for Cassette Studies.

A Film

> Frenzini, L. R. (Producer). (1973). <u>Neurotic behavior</u> [Film]. Del Mar, CA: CRM Educational Films.

> **Note:** For films with both director and producer, cite as follows:

> _____ (Producer), & _____ (Director).

Internet Sources

> Long, P. W. (1995). <u>Internet Mental Health.</u> [WWW document]. Retrieved: http://www.mentalhealth.com/p.html

Unsigned Internet Sources

> Eating disorders: New center established. (1994, November 4). <u>Focus.</u> [Gopher menu]. Retrieved: Harvard University Medical Gopher.

Internet Newsletter Article Available in Print

> Serotonin and eating disorders. (1994, October). <u>Medical Sciences Bulletin.</u> [WWW document]. Retrieved: http://pharminfo.com/pubs/msb/seroton.html

Special Cases

You may use sources that cannot be retrieved by people reading your paper. You may acquire information that you want to use in your research from a lecture, a telephone conversation, a mailing list, an e-mail message, a letter, a memo, or even a postcard. You should document such information in parentheses in the text of your paper—not in the reference list—giving the name of the source, the date, and when appropriate, the place that the communication was received. For example: Professor Steve Nowicki, class lecture, Emory University, October 26, 1995. Note how Cherwanda Williams documents an e-mail communication from Dr. Myers on page 4 of her paper (p. 301).

Citing References in the Text

The citations of references within the text of Cherwanda Williams's paper provide models for the most common kinds of references. The following rules will help you cite other references in the text of your paper:

1. Separate references with more than two authors by commas and an ampersand (&) before the last author's name: _____, _____, _____, & _____.
2. List all the names of authors for sources in the reference list. For parenthetical references of sources with three to five authors, cite all of the authors only the first time and in all following references use only the last name of the first author followed by "et al." (a period should follow 'al' but the phrase should not be underlined) and the year for the first citation within the paragraph:

(Abbey, Kennedy, Kaplan, Toner, & Garfinkel, 1990) **[first citation]**
(Abbey et al.) **[subsequent citation in same paragraph does not require date]**
(Abbey et al., 1990) **[subsequent citation in another paragraph]**

For parenthetical references of sources with six or more authors, use the last name of the first author and "et al."

3. Omit initials in textual citations, except when there are two authors with the same last name.
4. Include all references cited in the text in a list of references at the end of the paper, except personal communications (letters, conversations, and some electronic communications, such as an e-mail) that cannot be retrieved by the reader.
5. Write out the full name of corporate authors for the first citation. You may, however, choose to abbreviate for citations after the first citation if the abbreviation is easily understood: American Psychological Association (APA).

6. Cite references that have no author by a shortened version of the title, usually the first two or three words, using quotation marks for articles or parts of books and a solid underline for titles of books.
7. When there is only one citation by a given author in the reference list, give the date in the first reference in each paragraph that the source is used, but not in subsequent references.

If you follow the sample citations here and use the format illustrated in the sample paper in this chapter, your paper will be consistent with the citations in the official APA manual that professional psychologists use for preparing manuscripts for publication. When you take advanced courses in psychology, your professors will want you to adhere strictly to the APA manual as Cherwanda Williams has done in her paper. You will notice that the citations for articles published in journals may vary. Some are printed as a block with no indentation and others use a hanging indent—that is, the second and subsequent lines are indented five spaces. The following examples of citations using the hanging indent are like those in journals published by the APA:

American Psychological Association (1994). <u>Publication manual of the American Association</u> (4th ed.). Washington, DC: Author.

Abbey, S. E., Kennedy, S. H., Kaplan, A. S., Toner, B. B., & Garfinkel, P. E. (1990). Self-report symptoms that predict major depression in patients with prominent physical symptoms. <u>International Journal of Psychiatry in Medicine, 20,</u> 247–258.

Although published articles may use this or other variations of the style, writers of manuscripts follow the APA manual. As a student writing a paper using APA style, you are practicing to write such manuscripts yourself, whether in advanced psychology courses, graduate school, or someday as a professional researcher.

A Sample Paper in the Social Sciences Using APA Style

CHERWANDA WILLIAMS

Cherwanda wrote the paper in this chapter for a course in abnormal psychology. Her search for information that might reveal a correlation between clinical depression and eating disorders uncovered many articles and documents to support her hypothesis that the disorders are related. In her paper she argues that people with eating disorders who are also depressed should be treated for both illnesses.

Steps Leading to Cherwanda's Paper:

1. Studies the table of contents and index of her textbook on abnormal psychology (p. 25)
2. Reads sections on eating disorders and mood disorders, especially the parts on major depressive disorder, anorexia, and bulimia (p. 25)
3. Begins to suspect that her friend Sarah could be depressed and maybe even bulimic (p. 25)
4. Goes to the library and uses NEXIS to find articles that link the two disorders in newspapers and magazines (p. 59)
5. Searches for information on the World Wide Web (p. 92)
6. Consults the library's catalog for books on her topic (p. 93)
7. Asks a reference librarian to recommend indexes that will help her find articles in journals (p. 93)
   - Goes to electronic databases (PsycLit, PsycInfo, and Medline) and finds more than a hundred citations
   - Chooses the articles she wants, finds out which journals are in her library, makes photocopies of them, and begins reading and taking notes
8. Writes a thesis statement setting up her argument (p. 141)
9. Writes a sentence outline and a preliminary draft of her paper (p. 154)
10. Prepares her list of references (p. 197)
    - Revises the paper, checks spelling and punctuation, and prepares the final paper

---

Depression and Eating Disorders 1

The Correlation of Depression and Eating Disorders

Cherwanda R. Williams

Emory University

The page header (at the top right of this title page and every other page) is a short version of the paper's title.

An abstract is a concise summary
of the contents of the paper.

Abstract

A significant number of people are suffering from eating disorders, and the number is on the rise. Also increasing is the number of people suffering from depression. In fact, many people suffering from eating disorders also have been diagnosed with clinical depression. Researchers have found that there is an association between eating disorders, especially anorexia and bulimia, and depression. This correlation seems to be influenced by cultural and/or biochemical factors, but further research is needed to determine causes and effective treatments of these serious disorders.

Notes are at the end of the paper.

Depression and Eating Disorders 3

The Correlation of Depression and Eating Disorders

The number of people suffering from eating disorders has increased significantly in recent years, and there has been a great deal of coverage of this topic in the media.[1] A search through magazine and newspaper indexes of the last ten years calls up literally hundreds of articles that at least mention eating disorders like anorexia and bulimia. Some of these focus on famous people with these disorders or on the tragedy of ordinary people who have died of complications of anorexia. Still others report an increasing amount of medical research that tries to understand the causes of the disorders, the best ways to treat them, and the correlation between them and other psychological problems. A search of the World Wide Web for pages dealing with eating disorders brings up personal testimonials as well as information and advice placed there by medical professionals and public service institutions.

The problem has become so widespread that prestigious universities, such as Harvard, have established Eating Disorder Units in their medical schools. According to an article found on the Harvard University Medical Gopher, more than eight million young women and one million young men suffer from eating disorders in the U.S. The goal of the Harvard Eating Disorders Center is to develop more effective treatments for the disorders and ways to prevent them ("Eating Disorders," November 4, 1994).

The incidence of major depressive disorder is also on the rise (McCarthy, 1990), and a search of popular publications, World Wide Web pages, and psychological and medical indexes shows that many researchers are trying to understand the connection between depression

When a source has no author the first few words used in the reference entry and the year are used for textual citations.

Thesis statement

Use brackets around any material added to a quotation.

Depression and Eating Disorders 4

and eating disorders. Recent research findings reveal a correlation between eating disorders and depression. This correlation is strong enough to suggest that anyone suffering from an eating disorder may also be depressed. Therefore he or she should be tested for depression and treated if depression is found. It is not clear, however, whether depression causes eating disorders or the other way around, but in any case the depression should be treated as soon as it is recognized. Dr. Michael Myers, a practicing physician in California who specializes in eating disorders, believes that "approximately fifty percent of bulimics [in his practice] meet diagnostic criteria for major depression" (personal communication, December 17, 1995). The Diagnostic and Statistical Manual of Mental Disorders, 4th Edition (DSM-IV),[2] published by the American Psychiatric Association (APA), only indicates that anorexia and depression share symptoms and that there is an increased frequency of depressive symptoms among bulimics. What follows is an explanation of the nature of eating disorders and of major depressive disorder; a discussion of selected research findings that have shown a correlation between the two; and an overview of treatment options.

According to the DSM-IV (1994), a classification of anorexia nervosa requires the following symptoms:

A. Refusal to maintain body weight at or above a minimally normal weight for age and height or failure to make expected weight gain during period of growth, leading to body weight less than 85 percent of that expected.

B. Intense fear of gaining weight or becoming fat, even if underweight.

To cite personal communications provide the exact date of the communication. Since readers will not be able to retrieve the communication, there is no need to include it in your reference list.

Sources with a group or corporate author
are cited using the group name, date of
publication, and page numbers.

Depression and Eating Disorders 5

C. Disturbance in the way in which one's body weight or shape is
experienced; undue influence of body weight or shape on self-
evaluation, or denial of the seriousness of the current low body weight.
D. In postmenarcheal females, amenorrhea, the absence of at least
three consecutive menstrual cycles (American Psychiatric Association,
1994, p. 544–545).

The majority of people with anorexia nervosa reduce their weight by
starvation. However, because of their obsession with thinness, it is not
uncommon for anorexics to maintain their low weight by other means,
including vomiting, abusing laxatives or diuretics, or any combination of
these methods. Anorexia nervosa most often appears between the ages of
14 and 18 and strikes nearly one percent of the female population (APA,
1994, p. 540, 543).

A diagnosis of bulimia nervosa, according to DSM-IV (1994), requires
that the following criteria be met:
A. Recurrent episodes of binge eating.
B. Recurrent inappropriate compensatory behavior in order to prevent
weight gain, such as self-induced vomiting; misuse of laxatives,
diuretics, enemas, or other medications; fasting; or excessive exercise.
C. The binge eating and inappropriate compensatory behaviors both
occur, on average, at least twice a week for three months.
D. Self-evaluation is unduly influenced by body shape and weight.
E. The disturbance does not occur exclusively during episodes of
anorexia nervosa (APA, 1994, p. 549–550).
Bulimia nervosa usually occurs in females (90 to 95 percent of the

Example of a group abbreviation
and page number used for a
textual citation.

The list, a quotation from the *DSM-IV*,
is cited at the end of the list.

**Within a paragraph, the first reference
to a study should include the date.**

Depression and Eating Disorders 6

cases), begins in adolescence or young adulthood, and arises after a
period of intense dieting. Because of the increasing number of people
suffering with eating disorders, the organizers of the DSM-IV (1994) have
found it necessary to form a new category for other eating-disordered
behaviors that do not fit into any of the present categories. These disorders
include binge-eating disorder, which is a pattern of binge eating without any
accompanying behaviors to compensate for overeating (APA, 1994, p. 546,
548, 550).

In order to be clinically diagnosed as experiencing a major depressive
A study performed by Lask & Bryant-Waugh (1992) on early-onset
anorexia nervosa and related eating disorders dealt mainly with 8- to 14-
year-olds. Lask & Bryant-Waugh found that in addition to the better-known
eating disorders, anorexia nervosa and bulimia nervosa, there are other
atypical eating disorders of childhood, not mentioned in the DSM, that do
not fulfill the criteria for the more well-known disorders. These include food-
avoidance emotional disorder, pervasive refusal syndrome, selective
eating, food fads, and food refusal. The observation that the absence of
starvation and binge-eating do not make a person free of an eating disorder
is perhaps the most important contribution made by the Lask & Bryant-
Waugh study. A further conclusion of the study was that each of the
atypical eating disorders share depression as a common characteristic.

In order to be clinically diagnosed as experiencing a major depressive
episode, a person must have a depressed mood most of the day, almost
every day for at least two weeks, and have a markedly diminished interest
or pleasure in almost every activity. A diagnosis also requires that at least
five of the following seven symptoms be present: significant weight loss or

**Further references to the study within
this paragraph do not require the date.**

Use author's last name and the date
for textual citations.

Depression and Eating Disorders 7

gain, either insomnia or hypersomnia, either psychomotor agitation or
psychomotor retardation, fatigue or loss of energy, feelings of
worthlessness or guilt, diminished ability to think or concentrate, and
recurrent thoughts of death and suicide or an actual suicidal gesture. These
symptoms should not be caused by drugs or a general medical condition
and should be present nearly every day with the exception of the recurrent
thoughts of death and suicide, which can occur only occasionally. There
are additional types of depressive disorders. One example, major
depressive disorder single episode, can be triggered by a stressful event
such as the death of a loved one or even academic pressures (APA, 1994).
Some researchers conclude that the pressures of dieting can serve as a
stressor and lead to depression (McCarthy, 1990). Others theorize that it is
depression that triggers eating disorders (Goleman, 1995).

A study conducted by Mandy McCarthy concludes that for women the
failure to meet "the cultural ideal of thinness, which is well below the
average weight of women" (1990, p. 205) leads to depression which in turn
leads to atypical eating behaviors. McCarthy uses Seligman's learned
helplessness model of depression to support her conclusions about
depression. According to Seligman (as cited in McCarthy, 1990) the
experience of not having control over something important in one's life and
the expectation of a future inability to gain control is sufficient for the onset
of depression. McCarthy theorizes that the feeling of loss of control
(helplessness) that people experience when they fail at dieting produces
depression. Finally, in an attempt to regain control of their weight, many
women fall victim to eating disorders (McCarthy, 1990). Therefore, the

Because the author's name has been
mentioned, only the date and page
number are given for this quotation.

Indicates that Cherwanda found this
material in a secondary source.

Two or more sources listed within
parentheses are arranged alphabetically
and separated by semicolons.

Depression and Eating Disorders 8

woman who repeatedly diets and fails is at even greater risk for developing

depression and eating disorders than a person who only occasionally diets.

Recent research indicates that changes in brain chemistry may

perpetuate the main symptoms of people with eating disorders. By starving

themselves, anorexics may actually be self-medicating themselves for

depression. Dr. Maurizio Fava, a psychiatrist in the Clinical Pharmacology

Unit at Massachusetts General Hospital in Boston, has found that anorexics

lower their level of norepinephrine when they starve themselves. Extreme

dieting increases the levels of opioids in the system, decreasing the amount

of anxiety and producing a high. Therefore, their extreme dieting is

reinforced by the reduction of anxiety (Goleman, 1989).

Another brain chemical that has been associated with an eating

disorder is serotonin, which has been found in lowered levels in bulimics.

Researchers have found that low levels of serotonin increase hunger,

which could explain binge eating in bulimics. Decreased levels of serotonin

have also been linked to impulsive behaviors, including suicidal thoughts

and ideations (Goleman, 1989, 1995; Rovner, 1985).

Other research has shown associations between depression and each

of the eating disorders individually. Researchers have discovered similar

stress symptoms in depression and anorexia nervosa as well as a

biochemical connection. Gold et al. have found especially high levels of

cortisol in patients with these disorders. Patients with anorexia and patients

with depression both show high levels of the hormone CRH, which leads to

the high levels of cortisol. This suggests a common mechanism involved in

the two disorders. In both cases the abnormality seems to arise in the brain

Sources with more than five authors are
cited in the text with the first author's
last name followed by "et al."

Tables are numbered and placed at the
end of the paper before the notes.

rather than in the endocrine glands. At the same time, these researchers
have found that people suffering from bulimia have normal levels of CRH,
which suggests that bulimia and anorexia may be separate disorders (Gold
et al., 1986).

Further supporting the idea of a biochemical correlation between
depression and eating disorders is the fact that heredity seems to be a
factor contributing to the development of both disorders. As early as 1985
The Washington Post reported that Dr. David Jimerson had discovered a
correlation between family history of depression and eating disorders. Dr.
Jimerson, who was chief of the eating disorders program at the National
Institute of Mental Health (NIMH), indicated that reports from the NIMH
estimate that "up to seventy percent of all eating disorder patients have a
lifetime prevalence of major depression" (as cited in Rovner, 1985). Ten
years later, The New York Times reported on the work of researchers who
had found a higher risk of eating disorders among people who diet and who
have a history of depression or alcoholism in their families (Goleman,
1995).

Depression seems to be more common among people with eating
disorders than among people with certain other illnesses. One study
evaluated and compared the amount of depressive symptoms found in
subjects with four different illnesses: irritable bowel syndrome (IBS), post-
infectious neuromyasthenia (NM), end-stage renal disease (ESRD), and
eating disorders. As shown in Table 1, the majority of the depressed
patients were those with eating disorders (Abbey, Kennedy, Kaplan, Toner,
& Garfinkel, 1990).

Another study conducted by Grubb, Sellers and Waligroski (1993) hypothesized that women suffering from eating disorders experience low self-esteem and high levels of depression and that women with low self-esteem would rate themselves as heavier and less attractive than less depressed individuals. The researchers pointed out previous studies (Eckert, Goldberg, Halmi, Casper, & Davis, 1982) that had reported an association between eating disorders and depression and the decrease in symptoms of depression following treatment of the eating disorders. Results of the study supported the hypothesis by showing that deficits in self-esteem contributed to both eating disorders and depression (Grubb, Sellers, & Waligroski, 1993).

In a study conducted by Vollrath, Koch, and Angst, binge eaters and subjects aged 27–28 with weight concerns were diagnosed as having depression much more often than controls did. The one significant difference observed in the depressive episodes among these two groups, binge eaters and subjects with weight concerns, was that suicidal thoughts were found among the group of binge eaters but not among the subjects with weight concerns. Other depressive symptoms found more prevalently among binge eaters included appetite problems, loss of interest, and feelings of inferiority.

Because of the significant amount of research associating eating disorders with affective disorders, especially depression, psychotropic drugs have been used to treat anorexics and bulimics. These drugs include neuroleptics, tricyclic antidepressants, monoamine oxidase inhibitors, and serotonin-reuptake inhibitors (Pharmaceutical Information Associates, Ltd,

Quotations of more than forty words
are set in a block indented five spaces.

Depression and Eating Disorders 11

1994). Bulimics have been more responsive to drug therapy and cognitive-behavioral therapy than have anorexics. Anorexia is very difficult to treat for a number of reasons, and researchers have not been able to develop a treatment regimen that is generally accepted. In the following statement, Dr. David B. Herzog, who directs the newly established Harvard Eating Disorders Center, explains some of the difficulties clinicians have treating anorexics:

> There are several problems in using drugs to treat anorexia, foremost among them that most people with anorexia don't see themselves as having a problem. In addition, they don't want to take anything that will make them gain weight, and are reluctant to take anything by mouth anyway. On top of that, they are exquisitely sensitive to any side effects (as cited in Goleman, 1989).

The majority of research has indicated support for cognitive-behavioral and drug therapies for the treatment of bulimics. An article in The New York Times indicated recently that there had been several studies using antidepressants, particularly tricyclic medications, to treat bulimia. Between 25 and 40 percent of patients stopped bingeing and purging after drug treatment. The same article also reported that 65 percent of patients with bulimia stopped bingeing and purging after cognitive-behavioral therapy. The best long-term results, however, were observed in patients who were given both cognitive-behavioral and drug therapies (Goleman, 1995).

An earlier issue of the Times reported that 400 bulimics were treated with the drug fluoxetine, which increases serotonin levels. The preliminary

Concluding paragraph summarizes the main
points of the paper and draws conclusions.

Depression and Eating Disorders 12

results of the research indicated that patients taking the drug had a fewer

number of binges and purges than controls did (Goleman, 1989). Similar

results were reported in the Medical Science Bulletin (Pharmaceutical

Information Associates, Ltd, 1994). Clinical trials for treating bulimia with

fluoxetine and fluvoxamine have shown these drugs to be most

successful. Both of these drugs are serotonin-reuptake inhibitors, which

means that they increase the level of serotonin in the brain, and have

been shown to suppress food cravings and to cause weight loss. In

addition, both of the drugs improved symptoms of depression in the

subjects.

Although there has been substantial research on the correlation

between eating disorders and depression, a number of questions remain,

such as whether depression causes eating disorders, whether eating

disorders cause depression, or whether for some people both are true. The

finding of Gold et al. that anorexia and bulimia may be two distinct disorders

suggests that additional research is needed for a better understanding of the

two disorders. Further research could eliminate some of the present

confusion concerning proper treatment of anorexia. Physicians who are

trying to treat anorexia in the same way that they are treating bulimia might

find more effective treatments if future research showed that the two

disorders have different biochemical causes. Much progress, however, has

been made. The knowledge that many people suffering from eating

disorders may also suffer from depression is of major importance. Medical

professionals must now use this information to ensure that patients with

eating disorders and depression receive treatment for both.

The first line of each entry is
indented; subsequent lines
begin at the left margin.

Capitalize the first word of titles and
subtitles for books and articles.

Depression and Eating Disorders 13

References

Abbey, S. E., Kennedy, S. H., Kaplan, A. S., Toner, B. B., & Garfinkel,
P. E. (1990). Self-report symptoms that predict major depression in patients
with prominent physical symptoms. International Journal of Psychiatry in
Medicine, 20, 247–258.

American Psychiatric Association. (1994). Diagnostic and statistical
manual of mental disorders (4th ed.). Washington, DC: Author.

Eating disorders: New center established. (1994, November 4). Focus.
[Gopher menu]. Retrieved: Harvard University Medical Gopher.

Gold, P. W., Gwirtsman, H., Avgerinos, P. C., Nieman, L. K., Gallucci,
W. T., Kaye, W., Jimerson, D., Ebert, M., Rittmaster, R., Loriaux, D. L., &
Chrousos, G. P. (1986). Abnormal hypothalamic-pituitary-adrenal function
in anorexia nervosa: Pathophysiologic mechanisms in underweight and
weight-corrected patients. New England Journal of Medicine, 314,
1335–1342.

Goleman, D. (1989, November 9). New drug treatments may help
some with eating disorders. The New York Times, p. B23.

Goleman, D. (1995, October 4). Eating disorder rates surprise the
experts. The New York Times, p. C12.

Grubb, H. J., Sellers, M. I., & Waligroski, K. (1993). Factors related to
depression and eating disorders: Self-esteem, body image, and
attractiveness. Psychological Reports, 72, 1003–1010.

Hilts, P. J. (1986, May 22). New drug treatments may help some with
eating disorders. The Washington Post, p. A8.

Use "p." or "pp." to indicate page numbers
for newspapers, but not for journal articles.

Capitalize proper nouns.

Depression and Eating Disorders 14

Lask, Bryan, & Bryant-Waugh, Rachel. (1992). Early-onset anorexia nervosa and related eating disorders. Journal of Child Psychology and Psychiatry & Allied Disciplines, 33 (1), 281–300.

McCarthy, M. (1990). The thin ideal, depression and eating disorders in women. Behavior Research and Therapy, 28 (3), 205–215.

Serotonin and eating disorders. (1994, October). Medical Sciences Bulletin. [WWW document]. Retrieved: http://pharminfo.com/pubs/msb/seroton.html

Rovner, S. (1985, December 4). Biological link studied in eating disorders. The Washington Post, Health section, p. 10.

Vollrath, M., Koch, R., & Angst, J. (1992). Binge eating and weight concerns among young adults: Results from the Zurich cohort study. British Journal of Psychiatry, 160, 498–503.

Depression and Eating Disorders 15

Table 1. Distribution of Sample by Diagnosis

N (Row Percent)[a] (Column Percent)[b]	Total Sample	Illness Type			
		IBS	NM	ESRD	Eating Disorder
DIS Diagnosis MDE	69	5 (7.2%) (23.8%)	7 (10.1%) (28.0%)	8 (11.6%) (8.1%)	49 (71.1%) (38.9%)
	(25.5%)				
DIS Diagnosis No MDE	202	16 (7.9%) (76.2%)	18 (8.9%) (72.0%)	91 (45.0%) (91.9%)	77 (38.2%) (61.1%)
	(74.5%)				
TOTAL	271	21	25	99	126

[a]Percent of subjects illness type contributes to DIS diagnosis category.
[b]Percent of subjects within illness type with DIS diagnosis.

Notes that might appear as footnotes in
a published paper are placed on a separate
sheet after the references.

Depression and Eating Disorders 16

Footnotes

[1]My interest in the correlation of depression and eating disorders is a
result of my concern for a friend who I suspect might be suffering from
anorexia and who is also showing signs of depression.

[2]Produced by a team of experts in various fields, the Diagnostic and
Statistical Manual of Mental Disorders, 4th Edition (DSM-IV), is the official
guide for the classification of mental disorders, published by the American
Psychiatric Association.

WRITING RESEARCH PAPERS IN THE NATURAL AND APPLIED SCIENCES USING CBE STYLE

14

Approaches to Research in the Natural and Applied Sciences

The natural sciences are divided into three groups: physical sciences—chemistry, physics, and astronomy; the earth sciences—geology, paleontology, oceanography, and meteorology; and the life sciences—biology and medicine. Each of the individual disciplines is divided into different branches, and a student who does research in one of the sciences would focus on a very narrow aspect of one of the subdisciplines, such as a single chemical reaction.

Students who do research in the sciences might write papers based on one of the following: their own original research projects; a review of the literature in scholarly journals on a particular topic; a study of review articles; or an examination of articles in popular science journals such as *Scientific American.*

In chemistry, senior-level students might do research to develop a method for a particular chemical analysis—toxic wastes, for example—and then write a paper based on the research. Such a paper is divided into three parts. The first is a review of the history of the problem to be studied; the second is a discussion of the methods used, the results obtained, and an interpretation of the results; and the third section is a detailed description of the methods.

Undergraduate students of chemistry may also write research papers based strictly on what other people have done. In a class requiring a research paper, one student might review the literature published in scholarly journals on a topic like the absorption of light by inorganic compounds, bioluminescence (why fireflies light up), or the conversion of coal to oil. Another student might read review articles on a single topic like the synthesis of a chemical compound, while yet another might consult a number of articles in popular-science periodicals to write a paper on pheromones or DNA chemistry.

Undergraduate students majoring in biology will probably write research papers that review the literature on a topic studied in conjunction with a lab project or, as in other sciences, they might review the literature and write a paper on topics that are being discussed in class. The topics that students might research in order to write a review paper range from the effects of acid rain on the growth and development of spruces, firs, and pines to how cell membranes function.

Students of physics, geology, and the remaining natural sciences might write research papers to accompany a laboratory or field project, review the literature on a topic considered in class, or explore the practical application of a natural phenomenon.

The applied sciences include the traditional fields of engineering—mechanical, civil, electrical, architectural, chemical, aeronautical—as well as the rapidly expanding fields of technology related to computer science. Students might research new synthetic building materials, explore the use of computers in diagnosing heart disease, or study and evaluate the achievement of a particularly influential architect.

Making a CBE Reference List for Papers in the Sciences

If you are writing a paper for a science class, your teacher may suggest a particular form to follow. Researchers in the natural sciences typically use either a citation-sequence (number) system or a name/year system similar to the APA style used in chapter 13. This chapter explains how to document a paper using the citation-sequence, or number, system. The examples of bibliographic references listed below and those used at the end of Lisa Lee's paper are consistent with the recommendations of the new style manual published by the Council of Biology Editors (1993), commonly known as the CBE Style Manual. The complete title of the manual is *Scientific Style and Format: The CBE Manual for Authors, Editors, and Publishers,* 6th edition, 1994. The CBE manual is designed to be tailored to particular situations, as it has detailed, comprehensive instructions for documenting papers using both the citation-sequence (number) system and the name-year system. Scientists adapt the recommendations of

LISA LEE

Lisa uses the citation-sequence system recommended by the Council of Biology Editors. Working on a word processor, she first lists her sources alphabetically by author. After composing her paper, indicating sources in parentheses after each use, she then goes back through her paper, numbering the sources in the order they appear in her paper, and then assigning the appropriate number to each reference on her list. She then deletes the parenthetical identification of sources and rearranges the items of her list in numerical order.

the Council of Biology Editors to meet the requirements of specific journals.

Whether you are preparing a paper for a science class or for a composition class, the citation-sequence (number) system of documentation is appropriate and easy to adapt to a class assignment. References are listed in the sequence in which they appear in the paper. Each reference is given

CHECKLIST 23

Typing References Using CBE Style

1. Use periods to separate elements of a reference, such as between author and title.
2. Use commas to separate equivalent items within an element, such as author names, or to add information such as editor or translator.
3. Use a semicolon after the year of publication of a journal or an article.
4. Use a colon before subordinate information such as a subtitle or page numbers following a volume number.
5. Space as follows: one space between surname and initials of author; separate names of multiple authors with a comma and one space; one space after the title of a journal before the year, but no space thereafter, except after commas separating groupings of discontinuous pages.
6. Capitalize only the first word of titles and proper names.
7. Number the citation at the end in a "List of References." Follow the number with a period and one space.

CBE STYLE

a number based on when it is first cited in the text. The first reference is number 1, the second number 2, and so on. Each time information from a source is used, the writer places its number in superscript at the appropriate place in the text.

Students who wish more details for citing unusual sources may consult the *National Library of Medicine Recommended Formats for Bibliographic Citation* (1991) or the style manual of the Council of Biology Editors (1994). The following sample references will be sufficient for the needs of most undergraduate students who choose to use the CBE citation-sequence style.

Books

Note that the format for books is the same as that for booklets or pamphlets.

Book with One Author

1. Wilson, Edward O. The diversity of life. Cambridge: Harvard University Press; 1992. 424 p.

Note: If the whole book is cited, the total number of pages is indicated at the end. It is also appropriate to call attention to particular pages as in citation number 6 of Lisa Lee's paper on page 334.

Book with Two Authors

2. Forsyth A, Miyata K. Tropical nature: life and death in the rain forests of Central and South America. New York: Charles Scribner's Sons; 1984. 242 p.

Book with Three or More Authors

3. Brown LR and others. State of the world 1996: a Worldwatch Institute report on progress toward a sustainable society. New York: W. W. Norton; 1996. 249 p.

Book with Editor or Editors

4. Head S; Heinzman R, editors. Lessons of the rainforest. San Francisco: Sierra Club Books; 1990. 275 p.

Book with Organization as Author

5. Living Earth Foundation. The rainforests: a celebration. San Francisco: Chronicle Books; 1990. 223 p.

Book with a Separate Title That Is One of Two or More Volumes of a Single Work

> 6. Fa JE; Southwick CH, editors. Ecology and behavior of food-enhanced primate groups. Vol. 11, Monographs in primatology. New York: Alan R. Liss; 1988. 355 p.

Parts of Books

Chapter or Part with a Separate Title

> 7. Thomas L. The fragile species. New York: Charles Scribners Sons; 1992. Science and the health of the earth; p. 116-28.

Part with a Different Author and Title

> 8. Boucher DH. Coffee. In: Janzen DH, editor. Costa Rican natural history. Chicago: University of Chicago Press; 1983. p. 86-88.

Journals

Article in Journal Paginated Continually Through the Volume

> 1. Idani G. Seed dispersal by pygmy chimpanzees (Pan paniscus): a preliminary report. Primates 1986;27:441-48.

Article in a Journal Paginated by the Issue

> 2. Jewell JL and others. Microlasers. Scientific American 1991;265(5):86-94.
> 3. Freeth S. Incident at Lake Nyos: Tracking the source of a deadly cloud of gas. The Sciences 1992;May/June:30-36.

Article on Discontinuous Pages

> 4. Davis G. The stormy future of weather forecasting. Popular Science 1991;237(3):78-83, 94, 98.

Article in a Supplement to an Issue

> 5. Fleming TH, Heithaus ER. Frugivorous bats, seed shadows, and the structure of tropical forests. Biotropica Reproductive Botany 1981;13(Suppl.):45-53.

Newspaper Article

> 6. Browne MW. Second greatest toolmaker? a title crows can
>   crow about. New York Times 1996 Jan 30, natl. ed;Sect. B:1
>   (col 4).

Note: The format for newspaper articles is the same as that for journals with the addition of section, page, and column.

Other References

Paper Published as Part of a Volume of Conference Proceedings

> 1. Russell R. Environmental changes through forces independent
>   of man. In: Thomas WL, editor. Man's role in changing the
>   face of the earth. Proceedings of an International
>   Symposium; 1955 June 16-22; Princeton, NJ. Chicago:
>   University of Chicago Press; 1956. p. 453-70.

Audio and Audiovisual Publications and Materials

To write a citation for a nonprint source like an audiocassette or videocassette, adapt the information you have to the following general format: Title [medium]. Authors, editors, narrators, directors, or producers, as appropriate. Producer, if other than publisher. Place of publication: publisher; date of publication. Description of item, indicating number of tapes, format, whether there is sound, color. Accompanying materials, etc.

> 2. Audobon society's videoguide to birds of North America: II
>   songbirds [videocassette]. Godfrey M, author, director,
>   narrator. Audobon Society, producer. New York: MasterVision;
>   1988. 1 videocassette: 80 min., sound, color, 1/2 in.

Electronic Publications

In general, electronic publications will be cited in the same format as their counterparts in print form. For nonprint publications indicate the form you use in brackets after the title of the publications (such as title of encyclopedia, journal, or newspaper). For more details on citing electronically retrieved information, consult the *National Library of Medicine Recommended Formats for Bibliographic Citation.*

A Sample Paper in the Natural and Applied Sciences Using CBE Style

LISA LEE

Lisa's English teacher allowed her to fulfill her research assignment by writing a paper on a scientific topic. As a biology major who intends to study environmental studies or forestry in graduate school, Lisa Lee began her project by reading general works on tropical rain forests. She then consulted her biology teacher for guidance in focusing her topic on some aspect of the ways plants and animals interact. After narrowing her topic again to "the role of animals in seed dispersal in certain tropical forests," she then limited her paper to factors that determine effective seed dispersal. She organizes her paper into parts commonly used in scientific writing. Her headings include an abstract, an introduction, methods, discussion of three main points, and a conclusion.

Steps Leading to Lisa's Paper

1. Develops an existing interest (p. 10)
   - Attends a lecture on rain forests
   - Reads *Tropical Nature*
2. Breaks down a large subject (the environment) using a branching diagram (p. 15)
3. Narrows her topic further by making a list of questions she'd like answered (p. 17)
3. Brainstorms on the subject of rain forests (p. 18)
4. Focuses her subject (pp. 23–24)
   - Gets approval from her instructor to do research on tropical forests
   - Checks out books and begins reading
   - Makes an appointment with her biology teacher, who helps her brainstorm
   - Arrives at a tentative topic
5. Reads an encyclopedia article on the subject of rain forests (p. 33)

6. Identifies other sources (p. 50)
   - Searches the online computer catalog by subject and identifies several books
   - Using a more specific subheading, locates additional sources
7. Writes a letter to Professor Vitousek requesting an interview when he visits her campus (p. 101)
8. Interviews Professor Vitousek (p. 106)
   - Prepares a list of questions for her interview on a computer file
   - Conducts the interview, takes notes, and records answers on a computer file
9. Is careful while writing her paper not to plagiarize inadvertently (p. 135)
10. Discovers that her implied hypothesis is inaccurate and develops a new working hypothesis (p. 140)
11. Writes a thesis statement setting up her argument (p. 144)
12. Organizes her material and constructs an outline on the computer (p. 152)
13. Sorts out unnecessary material in a separate file labeled "Sources not used" (p. 164)
14. Lists her sources alphabetically by author, composes her paper, and numbers her sources (p. 316)
15. Organizes her final paper into parts commonly used in scientific writing (p. 320)

Lisa's title is brief and basic, and clearly
indicates the focus of her paper.

The Fate of Seeds in Tropical Forests:
Determining Factors
Lisa Lee
English 102
University of California, Santa Cruz
February 12, 1995

This abstract indicates the three main points of the paper.

ABSTRACT

Whether a seed will have a chance to grow to a mature tree in a tropical forest depends on features of its parent tree, such as the rate at which it ripens fruit, the size of its fruit crop, and the seasonal timing of its fruiting. The fate of seeds is also determined by the treatment they receive by the digestive processes of animals that ingest them and by the way such animals handle them. Seeds that are favorably treated by primary dispersers and that escape being eaten by seed predators must also have the space and light necessary for germination and growth.

INTRODUCTION

Countless species of trees in tropical rain forests depend on the activities of animals for survival. Animals carry pollen, eat insects that prey on leaves and bark, and transport seeds to locations in the forest where they may have a chance to germinate. Some will grow into saplings; and a few, maybe only one from a solitary tree, will find the space and light necessary to mature and rise to the high canopy of the forest. D. H. Janzen, an eminent scientist committed to understanding the workings of tropical forests, explains that "the progression from adult tree to seed to another adult tree involves many complex interactions with animals"[1].

In the last two decades, tropical scientists have

1

References are numbered in sequence as they are cited.

Punctuation follows the citation number.

steadily published the results of their
investigations into how animals and plants interact
in tropical forests. Some researchers concentrate on
the animals' use of plants, emphasizing the
biological basis of an animal's selection of usable
foods that will supply its nutritional needs[2]. In
1984, most studies of fruit-eating (frugivorous)
primates had focused on feeding behavior for its own
sake rather than its role in seed dispersal[3]. Other
investigators consider the strategies that plants
use to maximize the use of fruit by animals, thus
resulting in maximum scattering of seeds[4].
Increasing numbers of recent studies that focus on
animal feeding behavior from the perspective of
plant survival suggest that most tropical plants
would not survive without the help of animals[5].

While the seeds of some plants high in the canopy
are transported by the wind and others have
explosive pods that eject seeds many meters, a
significant number produce succulent fruits that
attract animals to disperse the seeds[6]. Among the
creatures known to be responsible for scattering
seeds throughout a forest are birds, rodents, crabs,
insects, bats, large mammals, and primates.
Frugivores disperse seeds by carrying the fruit some
distance and discarding the seeds, regurgitating the
seeds after the fruit pulp has been removed, or more
commonly by ingesting the seeds and defecating them

2

This is Lisa's description of the research process.

elsewhere in the forest. Seed predators, those that diet on seeds rather than fruits, often remove the seeds from the dung piles of the dispersers and either eat them or hoard them for later.

METHODS

Based on a selective review of the recent literature on seed dispersal in tropical forests, this study surveys and in the following discussion explains the current scientific understanding of the ways that plants facilitate seed dispersal, the role of animals in that process, and other factors that affect the possibility of germination. Significant published results in this field were identified by searching through <u>Biological Abstracts</u>, both the available CD-ROM as well as bound volumes of the index, using the heading "seed" and the subheading "dispersal." The list of references at the end of key essays identified in this search, such as Colin Chapman's "Primate Seed Dispersal"[7] and Fleming and Williams's "Phenology, Seed Dispersal, and Recruitment"[8], provided other important sources.

D. McKey's "The Ecology of Coevolved Seed Dispersal Systems"[9], given as a paper in 1973 and published in 1975, evaluates the field of seed dispersal studies and offers hypotheses to be tested by future research. A study of selected papers published in Frugivores and Seed Dispersal[10] reveals the progress that has been made since then in

3

Headings for separate parts of paper are
capitalized.

understanding how the interaction of plants and
animals determines how a forest works. The studies
cited in this paper are based on research conducted
in tropical forests of Costa Rica, Mexico, Panama,
and Peru. New world tropical forests are commonly
referred to as neotropical forests.

HOW PLANTS FACILITATE DISPERSAL

Four features of a plant's fruiting behavior
determine how animals are attracted to eat its fruit
and disperse its seeds:

1. Schedule of ripening
2. Influence of disperser's feeding behavior on
ripening
3. Size of fruit crops
4. Availability during periods of scarcity

The amount of available ripe fruit determines the
amount of time dispersers stay in a particular tree
and ultimately affects the likelihood that seeds
will travel to a location where germination and
survival are even possible. In a study of spider
monkeys, one researcher observed that the animals
spent much of a day in the same part of the forest
feeding from trees with abundant ripe fruit. Since
the first seeds from a meal pass through the spider
monkey's gut in about four hours, most of the seeds
would be passed near the parent tree, where they
would have no chance of ultimate survival. When the
same monkeys eat from trees that ripen only a few

4

Lisa lists her main points at the beginning
of each of the three parts.

fruits at a time, they typically eat and move on to another part of the forest, thus increasing the opportunity for some seeds to have a chance to become mature trees[11].

Though very little is known about the effect that feeding animals have on a host plant, at least one plant is known to encourage dispersers by ripening fruit more rapidly when dispersers are abundant. The <u>Hamelia patens</u> tree will ripen remaining fruit faster when almost ripe fruits are removed. By this process the tree makes its fruit more available to highly seasonal, migratory dispersers[12].

While some plants seem to regulate their fruit production and ripening schedules to attract occasional dispersers, others beat the odds by playing all out for a short period of time. By producing a copious crop of fruits that are consumed by numerous dispersers, some trees succeed in the reproductive game by increasing the probability that a few, or even just one, will end up in an opportune spot[13].

Though it may seem that a tree's reproductive future would be insured simply by providing succulent, nutritious fruit that is attractive to a number of dispersers, some trees seem to hedge their bets by fruiting during the dry season when other fruits are scarce. One researcher, who has studied extensively the feeding behavior of five neotropical

5

Lisa uses a word taken from the article just cited.

primates, has determined that during the annual
period of scarcity, these animals feed on a mere
dozen plant species[14]. Of these "keystone" plants,
those with seeds to be dispersed would seem to have a
much better chance of success during the dry season
than during a time of plenty when the competition for
animal attention is fierce.

FACTORS DETERMINING A DISPERSER'S EFFECTIVENESS
Four factors in an animal's physiology and behavior
determine its reliability as a disperser of seeds:

1. The degree to which digested seeds survive
and/or are made more viable by the digestive process

2. The rate of passage through the gut of the
animal that is adequate to allow the animal to move
a sufficient distance from the parent tree to
occasionally deposit seeds in favorable locations

3. The way the animal handles seeds in the
process of eating fruit

4. The frequency with which the animal fails to
retrieve seeds that have been hoarded for later use

What happens to a seed once an animal takes it
into its mouth varies considerably from seed to seed
and animal to animal. Seeds may be destroyed by an
animal's teeth or damaged by digestive juices. Still
others might be rendered more likely to germinate by
mechanical scarring of their hard outer shells or by
chemical action that encourages sprouting. Some
seeds seem to fare better if they are actually

6

Citation in parentheses (8) is the source of information.

changed somehow by the animal, while others survive to grow into seedlings apparently unaltered by their journey[9].

Studies of the fruit-eating and dispersing habits of howler monkeys have demonstrated that, for several plant species, seeds that pass through a monkey's digestive track are more likely to germinate than seeds that do not[3]. The results of this study, however, do not apply to primates in general. Other researchers report a failure to germinate seeds passed through spider monkeys[15] (cited in 8).

Scientists attempting to determine which animals deposit seeds in locations appropriate for germination have reached some tentative conclusions. In general, birds and bats pass seeds rapidly, sometimes in less than thirty minutes. Birds, however, are more likely than bats to defecate seeds under a tree where there would be next to no chance of their germinating and growing to maturity; bats may deposit seeds as they return some distance to their roosts. Since seeds pass much slower through monkeys than through birds and bats, monkeys have more time to move away from the parent tree before depositing a seed[8]. But then, if some monkeys fail to pass viable seeds, it hardly matters that they are deposited in a favorable spot. For some trees in specific habitats, bats may be the most effective

7

Reference is to an article already referred to earlier in the paper.

dispersers, with birds following, and monkeys having little or no effect.

Also of significance are the variable ways that animals handle fruit and seed. While some birds pass most seeds in just a few minutes under or near their source, others handle different seeds in different ways, and thus become better dispersers for some trees than others. Some birds spit or regurgitate seeds under the parent tree, while others defecate seeds at least some of the time away from their source. Horses that feed on fruit from tropical trees will spit some seeds and ingest and pass others in a viable state[16].

Seeds that are too large to be passed unharmed through an animal's digestive system are usually dispersed by animals that hoard food for times of scarcity. Agoutis, large rodents common in low-lying neotropical forests, are dispersers of large seeds. Typically they carry fruit some distance from the parent tree to an open spot, eat the edible material surrounding the seeds, and then bury the remaining seeds. Since agoutis seem to remember the kind of environment where they hide seeds, rather than the exact location, they presumably leave some seeds to germinate and mature[17]. Some agoutis would themselves become victims of predators, an ocelot perhaps, and never have a chance to retrieve their seeds[18].

8

Lisa defines new words or terms *when she introduces them.*

OTHER FACTORS THAT AFFECT THE FATE OF A SEED
1. Presence of seed predators
2. Number of seeds in dung pile
3. Adequate light and space: treefalls

The fact that a seed survives the activities of its disperser and is successfully placed in a place favorable for germination does not insure that it will even sprout, let alone grow to a sapling. Seeds defecated on the forest floor become an attractive meal to animals that feed on seeds. In his work on the fate of guanacaste seeds deposited on the forest floor by horses, D. H. Janzen observed spiny pocket mice foraging at night in horse dung searching for seeds which they store in their underground burrows. Generally the mice eat up to 99 percent of these stored seeds[1]. Chapman found that most of the seeds that primates disperse are eventually destroyed as they are eaten by seed predators, or moved by secondary dispersers, perhaps buried by hoarding rodents. Following the fate of a particular seed once it is traveling in the pouch of a second animal is not easy, and researchers recognize the need for more knowledge about what happens when secondary dispersers move in on a seed[7].

How the number of seeds deposited in a dung pile affects the prospect of one seed growing to maturity is a complicated and poorly understood matter. In cases where there are many effective seed predators

9

preying on a particular pile, the likelihood of a seed surviving would seem greater if there are many seeds. But Janzen has observed that piles with many seeds are more thoroughly mined than are those with just a few, which may be ignored by predators seeking abundance[1]. When there are no seed predators, a large number of seeds in a pile reduces the possibility of any single seed's success since there is such fierce competition for nutrients and space.

Suppose all goes well for a seed: it survives the eating habits and digestive processes of its disperser and is deposited in a spot favorable to germination where it avoids destruction by seed predators. With little competition from neighboring seeds, it sprouts and becomes a seemingly healthy seedling. Unless the overall habitat is amenable to growth, it will ultimately languish and die before fulfilling its potential. The space, light, and nutrients required for a seedling to mature usually are provided by the death of another tree. Treefalls create gaps in otherwise dense, dark forests, and it is in these gaps that young trees flourish.

A lucky seed may be the one that is deposited at random in a very recently formed gap, one that has yet to be filled in by masses of striving plants; perhaps even more fortunate are those that manage to survive in a part of the forest which is opened up later by a treefall, so that its growth is

10

Multiple citation numbers are separated by commas and have no space between them.

stimulated by the added light and nutrients[18]. The most promising spot of all for a seed to germinate may be on the periphery of a gap, since trees on these borders are often unstable and likely to fall, opening up new space, widening the gap, and allowing new seedlings a chance to grow[4,13].

CONCLUSIONS

Though a number of significant scientists are engaged in studying the mechanisms of seed dispersal, much remains to be explored. Study after study concludes by warning that there is much we do not know and that only a small number of fruiting trees and animals have been studied and those for inadequate periods of time. John Terborgh suggests that keystone plant species may determine how groups of animals evolve over time, but he urges that this possibility "be regarded as wide-eyed speculation"[14]. Many scientists would agree with Peter Vitousek that in order to reach effective generalizations, we need "more specific examples of how animals interact with plants"[18].

As scientists continue to explore the interactions within the lower ranges of tropical forests and in the canopy, which Norman Myers has referred to as ''the last, great unexplored frontier of life on Earth"[19], some questions are answered. But with each new answer additional questions are raised.

11

Use only initials (without space or
punctuation between them) for first and
middle names of authors.

LIST OF REFERENCES

1. Janzen DH. Removal of seeds from horse dung by
    tropical rodents: influence of habitat and
    amount of dung. Ecology 1982;63:1887-1900.

2. Rodman PS, Cant JG, editors. Adaptions for
    foraging in nonhuman primates: contributions to
    an organismal biology of prosimians, monkeys,
    and apes. New York: Columbia University Press;
    1984. 351 p.

3. Estrada A, Coates-Estrada R. Fruit eating and
    seed dispersal by howling monkeys (Alouatta
    palliata) in the tropical rain forest of Los
    Tuxtlas, Mexico. American Journal of
    Primatology 1984;6:77-91.

4. Levey DJ. Tropical wet forest treefall gaps and
    distributions of understory birds and plants.
    Ecology 1988;69:1076-89.

5. [Anonymous]. Fruit and seed eaters. In Collins
    M, editor. The last rainforests: a world
    conservation atlas. New York: Oxford University
    Press; 1990. p. 76-79.

6. Longman KA, Jenik J. Tropical forest and its
    environment. 2nd ed. Essex (England): Longman;
    1987. p. 98-99.

7. Chapman C. Primate seed dispersal: The fate of
    dispersed seeds. Biotropica 1989;21:148-54.

8. Fleming TH, Williams CF. Phenology, seed
    dispersal, and recruitment in Cecropia Peltate

12

Capitalize only the first word of title and
subtitle.

(Moraceae) in Costa Rican tropical dry forest. Journal of Tropical Ecology 1990;6:163-78.

9. McKey D. The ecology of coevolved seed dispersal systems. In: Gilbert LE, Raven PH, editors. Coevolution of animals and plants. Austin: University of Texas Press; 1975. p. 159-91.

10. Estrada A, Fleming TH, editors. Frugivores and seed dispersal. Dordrecht (Netherlands): Dr. W. Junk; 1986. 392 p.

11. White F. Census and preliminary observations on the ecology of the black-faced spider monkey. American Journal of Primatology 1986;11:125-32.

12. Levey DJ. Facultative ripening in Hamelia patens (Rubiaceae): effects of fruit removal and rotting. Oecologia 1987;74:203-8.

13. Howe HF. Monkey dispersal and waste of a neotropical fruit. Ecology 1980;61:944-59.

14. Terborgh J. Community aspects of frugivory in tropical forests. In: Estrada A, Fleming TH, editors. Frugivores and seed dispersal. Dordrecht (Netherlands): Dr. W. Junk; 1986. p. 371-84.

15. Vasquez-Yanes C, Orozco-Segovia A. Dispersal of seeds by animals. Effect of light controlled dormancy in Cecropia obtusifolia. In: Estrada A, Fleming TH, editors. Frugivores and seed dispersal. Dordrecht (Netherlands): Dr. W. Junk; 1986. p. 71-77.

13

Name of periodical, date, volume number,
and pages of article.

16. Janzen DH. Guanacaste tree seed-swallowing by
    Costa Rican range horses. Ecology
    1981;62:587-92.

17. Smythe N. Relationships between fruiting
    seasons and seed dispersal methods in a
    neotropical forest. American Naturalist
    1970;104:25-35.

18. Vitousek P. Interview with: Lisa Lee. 1995 Jan
    21.

19. Myers N. The primary source: tropical forests
    and our future. Exp. ed. New York: W. W.
    Norton; 1992. p. 60.

14

Note style for interview with Professor
Vitousek.

Appendix A

DOCUMENTING WITH NOTES

Some instructors may request that you document your papers with both notes and a list of sources, though you may be asked to document a paper with endnotes or footnotes only. Since all the information needed to identify a source is included in a note, notes provide adequate documentation. Footnotes differ from endnotes only in their placement in the text. Footnotes are placed at the bottom of the page—the same page on which the citation is found. Endnotes are consolidated in one list and placed at the end of the paper.

Number notes consecutively throughout your paper, beginning with 1. Place the number at the end of a phrase, sentence, or paragraph, or immediately following any quoted material, even if only a single word. Raise the number slightly above the line; such numbers are called superscripts.

The form used for notes is slightly different from that of a list of sources. For example, an author's first name is given first since notes are not listed alphabetically. There are also variations in punctuation and indentation. Compare the bibliographic citation below with the note that follows.

Bibliographic Citation

    Lash, Joseph P. Eleanor: The Years Alone. New York: Norton,
        1972.

Note Citation

        [1]Joseph P. Lash, Eleanor: The Years Alone (New York:
    Norton, 1972) 220.

Documentary Notes (Endnotes and Footnotes)

The following models are consistent with the form recommended for notes by the *MLA Handbook* (1995). Use them to design documentary endnotes, footnotes, and content notes. For APA and CBE styles see chapters 13 and 14.

Books

A Book with One Author

[2]Stanley Fish, <u>Is There a Text in This Class?</u> (Cambridge: Harvard UP, 1980) 103.

Note: For two or more books by the same author, give the author's complete name in each note.

A Book with Two Authors or Editors

[3]Paul R. Ehrlich and Anne H. Ehrlich, <u>Healing the Planet</u> (Reading: Addison, 1991) 171.

[4]Marjorie Pryse and Hortense J. Spillers, eds., <u>Conjuring: Black Women, Fiction, and the Literary Tradition</u> (Bloomington: Indiana UP, 1985) 133.

A Book with Three Authors

[5]Herman Kahn, William Brown, and Leon Martel, <u>The Next 200 Years</u> (New York: Morrow, 1976) 84.

A Book with More Than Three Authors

[6]Bernard Bailyn et al., <u>The Great Republic: A History of the American People</u> (Lexington: Heath, 1977) 959.

Note: The abbreviation "et al." stands for "and others."

A Book with a Corporate Author

[7]U.S. Department of Energy, <u>An Assessment of Thermal Insulation Materials</u> (Washington: GPO, 1978) 57.

Note: GPO is an abbreviation for Government Printing Office.

A Book with an Anonymous Author

> [8]<u>Writers' and Artists' Yearbook, 1980</u> (London: Adam and Charles Black, 1980) 93.

A Book with an Author Who Uses a Pseudonym (a Fictitious Name)

> [9]Michael Innes [J. I. M. Stewart], <u>Going It Alone</u> (New York: Dodd, 1980) 23.

Note: The author's real name may be supplied in brackets.

A Scholarly Edition

> [10]Charles Dickens, <u>Oliver Twist</u>, ed. Kathleen Tillotson, The Clarendon Dickens (Oxford: Clarendon, 1966) 211.

Note: If the work of the editor is being discussed or cited, the editor's name comes first:

> [11]Kathleen Tillotson, ed., <u>Oliver Twist</u>, by Charles Dickens, The Clarendon Dickens (Oxford: Clarendon, 1966) 211.

A Work in a Series

> [12]Donald H. Reiman, <u>Shelley's "The Triumph of Life": A Critical Study</u>, Illinois Studies in Lang. and Lit. 55 (Urbana: U of Illinois P, 1965) 34.

A Single Work Published in More Than One Volume (with Continuous Pagination)

> [13]Edgar Johnson, <u>Sir Walter Scott: The Great Unknown</u>, 2 vols. (London: Hamilton, 1970) 117.

A Multivolume Work Cited in its Entirety

> [14]Arthur Conan Doyle, <u>The Annotated Sherlock Holmes</u>, ed. William S. Baring-Gould, 2 vols. (New York: C. N. Potter, 1967).

A Multivolume Work Cited in its Entirety Published over a Period of Time

> [15]Gordon S. Haight, ed., <u>The George Eliot Letters</u>, 9 vols. (New Haven: Yale UP, 1954-78).

A Book That Is Part of a Multivolume Work with a Single Title

[16]Arnold Kettle, <u>An Introduction to the English Novel</u>, vol. 2 (London: Hutchinson U Library, 1953) 74.

A Book That Is Part of a Multivolume Work by One Author When Each Volume Has a Separate Title

[17]Robert Coles, <u>Privileged Ones</u>, vol. 5 of <u>Children of Crisis</u> (Boston: Little, 1977) 506.

A Book That Is Part of a Multivolume Work When Each Volume Has a Separate Title and Author

[18]J. I. M. Stewart, <u>Eight Modern Writers</u> (Oxford: Oxford UP, 1963) 519, vol. 12 of <u>Oxford History of English Literature</u>, ed. John Baxton and Norman Davis, 1945-86.

A Book with Different Authors for Each Chapter and a Single Editor

[19]Daniel Hoffman, ed., <u>Harvard Guide to Contemporary American Writing</u> (Cambridge: Harvard UP, 1979) iv.

A Republished Book

[20]Ernest J. Gaines, <u>The Autobiography of Miss Jane Pittman</u> (1971; New York: Bantam, 1972) 64-74.

A Republished Book with New Material

[21]Zora Neale Hurston, <u>Their Eyes Were Watching God</u>, foreword, Sherley Anne Williams (1937; Urbana: U of Illinois P, 1978) 24.

A Republished Book with Original Publisher Cited

[22]Doris Lessing, <u>The Golden Notebook</u> (1962; New York: Simon & Schuster; New York: Bantam, 1973) 25.

A Paperback Reprint of a Hardback Edition

[23]Jill Ker Conway, <u>The Road from Coorain</u> (1989; New York: Vintage, 1990) 58-60.

A Second, Subsequent, or Revised Edition

[24]Richard Ellmann, <u>James Joyce</u>, 2nd ed. (New York: Oxford UP, 1982) 395.

A Revised Version of a Work of Literature

> ²⁵John Fowles, The Magus, rev. version (Boston: Little, 1977) 245.

A Translation

> ²⁶Homer, The Iliad, trans. Richmond Lattimore (Chicago: U of Chicago P, 1951) 142.

Note: If the work of the translator is being discussed, this should be cited as follows:

> ²⁷Richmond Lattimore, trans., The Iliad, by Homer (Chicago: U of Chicago P, 1951) 142.

Sacred Writings

Citations from the Bible and other sacred writings are usually documented within parentheses in the text of the paper: (Gen. 20: 1–17). Sacred writings referred to in a note are neither underlined nor placed in quotation marks.

Parts of Books

An Article, Essay, Chapter, or Other Part of a Book with a Single Author

> ¹Doris Lessing, "The Temptation of Jack Orkney," Stories (New York: Knopf, 1978) 564.

An Introduction, Afterword, Preface, or Foreword to a Book Written by Someone Other Than the Book's Author

> ²Alice Walker, afterword, I Love Myself: A Zora Neale Hurston Reader, ed. Alice Walker (Old Westbury: Feminist Press, 1979) 297.

A Previously Published Essay or Article from a Collection of Writings by Different Authors

> ³Edward W. Said, "An Ideology of Difference," Critical Inquiry 12 (1985): 89-107, rpt. in "Race," Writing, and Difference, ed. Henry Louis Gates Jr. (Chicago: U of Chicago P, 1986) 41.

An Essay or Article from a Collection of Works Not Previously Published

    [4]Dennis Brutus, "English and the Dynamics of South African Creative Writing," <u>English Literature: Opening Up the Canon</u>, Selected Papers from the English Institute, 1979, ed. Leslie A. Fiedler and Houston Baker Jr. (Baltimore: Johns Hopkins UP, 1981) 1-14.

A Short Story, Poem, or Essay from an Anthology

    [5]George Herbert, "The Flower," <u>Seventeenth-Century Prose and Poetics</u>, ed. Alexander M. Witherspoon and Frank J. Warnke, 2nd ed. (New York: Harcourt, 1963) 857.
    [6]Alexander Pope, "The Rape of the Lock," <u>The Norton Anthology of World Masterpieces</u>, ed. Maynard Mack et al., 6th ed., vol. 2 (New York: Norton, 1992) 306-26.

A Novel or Play from an Anthology

    [7]Toni Morrison, <u>Sula</u>, <u>The Norton Introduction to the Short Novel</u>, ed. Jerome Beaty, 2nd ed. (New York: Norton, 1982) 581.

Afterword, Preface, Introduction, or Other Editorial Comment on Individual Pieces in a Collection

    [8]Jerome Beaty, afterword to <u>Sula</u>, <u>The Norton Introduction to the Short Novel</u>, ed. Jerome Beaty, 2nd ed. (New York: Norton, 1982) 661.

An Unsigned Article in a Widely Known Reference Work

    [9]"Solar Energy," <u>The New Columbia Encyclopedia</u>, 4th ed. (1975) 2556.

A Signed Article in a Widely Known Reference Work

    [10]Howard Suber, "Motion Picture," <u>Encyclopedia Americana</u>, 1981 ed.

An Article in a Specialized, Less Familiar Reference Work

    [11]D. H. Monro, "William Godwin," <u>The Encyclopedia of Philosophy</u>, ed. Paul Edwards, 8 vols. (New York: Macmillan, 1967) 3: 358.

¹²John W. Roberts, "James Baldwin," <u>Dictionary of Literary Biography</u>, ed. Thadious M. Davis and Trudier Harris, 134 vols. (Ann Arbor: Gale, 1984) 33: 14.

Periodicals

A Signed Article from a Daily Newspaper Divided into Sections Paginated Separately

¹Milton R. Benjamin, "U.S. Is Allowing Argentina to Buy Critical A-System," <u>Washington Post</u> 19 July 1982: A1+.

Note: Use "+" for an article that begins in one part of a periodical and continues elsewhere.

A Signed Article from a Daily Newspaper Paginated Continuously

²Peter Passell, "Czechs Tread Minefield on the Way to Capitalism," <u>New York Times</u> 18 Apr. 1992, natl. ed.: 17+.

Note: Some newspapers are published in more than one edition, and the pagination varies from one to another. Indicate the edition if it is specified on the masthead.

An Unsigned Article from a Daily Newspaper

³"Soviet Group Presses for Broader Arms 'Dialog,' " <u>New York Times</u> 5 Sept. 1982, sec. 1: 16.

A Signed Article from a Weekly Magazine or Newspaper

⁴Bruno Bettelheim, "Reflections: Freud and the Soul," <u>New Yorker</u> 1 Mar. 1982: 52+.

⁵James Lewis, "Jobless Reality Fails to Impress Thatcher's Cabinet," <u>Manchester Guardian Weekly</u> 5 Sept. 1982: 3.

An Unsigned Article from a Weekly Publication

⁶"Computers," <u>Time</u> 2 Aug. 1982: 72.

A Serialized Article

⁷William J. Broad, "Science Showmanship: A Deep 'Star Wars' Rift," <u>New York Times</u> 16 Dec. 1985: 1+, pt. 2 of a series begun on 15 Dec. 1985.

A Signed Editorial

    [8]Gerard Smith, "Toward Arms Control," editorial, <u>New York Times</u> 29 June 1982: A23.

An Unsigned Editorial

    [9]"Tuition Subsidies Are Not Benign," editorial, <u>New York Times</u> 3 July 1982: 20.

An Article from a Monthly Magazine

    [10]William Greider, "The Education of David Stockman," <u>Atlantic</u> Dec. 1981: 27.

An Article in a Journal with Pages Numbered Continuously Through Each Yearly Volume

    [11]Blanche H. Gelfant, "Mingling and Sharing in American Literature: Teaching Ethnic Fiction," <u>College English</u> 43 (1981): 763.

Note: The numbers after the title of the journal refer to the volume number, the date, and the pages of the article cited.

An Article in a Journal That Numbers Pages Separately for Each Issue

    [12]Peter Biskind, "Rebel Without a Cause: Nicholas Ray in the Fifties," <u>Film Quarterly</u> 28.5 (1974): 32.

Note: The numbers following the journal title refer to the volume (28) and issue (5).

    [13]Claire Sprague, "Dialectic and Counter-Dialectic in the Martha Quest Novels," <u>Journal of Commonwealth Literature</u> 14 (1979): 39.

Note: Where there is no volume number, treat the issue number as though it were a volume number.

A Signed Review with a Title

    [14]Peter L. Berger, "A Woman of This Century," rev. of <u>Hannah Arendt: For Love of the World</u>, by Elizabeth Young Bruehl, <u>New York Times Book Review</u> 25 Apr. 1982: 1, 20-21.

A Signed, Untitled Review

[15]John F. C. Harrison, rev. of <u>The Age of Capital,</u> <u>1848-1875</u>, by E. G. Hobsbawm, <u>Victorian Studies</u> 20 (1977): 423.

An Unsigned, Untitled Review

[16]Rev. of <u>The French Lieutenant's Woman</u>, by John Fowles, <u>Times Literary Supplement</u> 12 June 1969: 629.

A Letter to the Editor

[17]R. W. Flint, letter, <u>New Republic</u> 18 Feb. 1957: 23.

A Response to a Letter or Letters

[18]Nicholas Lemann, reply to letters of Roger Williams and Virginia K. Williams, <u>Atlantic</u> Dec. 1984: 14.

A Speech or Address for a Special Occasion Printed in a Periodical

[19]Toni Morrison, "Address to the American Writers Congress," 9 Oct. 1981, in <u>Nation</u> 24 Oct. 1981: 396.

An Article from Dissertation Abstracts *or* Dissertation Abstracts International

[20]John Bryan Webb, "Utopian Fantasy and Social Change," <u>DA</u> 43 (1982): 8214250 (State U of New York at Buffalo).

An Article from a Volume of Abstracts

[21]John W. C. Johnstone, "Who Controls the News," <u>American Journal of Sociology</u> 87 (1982): 1174-81, abstract from <u>America: History and Life</u> 20.A (1983): 2120.

An Article from a Newsletter

[22]Douglas Cliggott, "Proposed Tax Reform Will Have Negative Effect on Capital Investment," <u>Business Executive Expectations</u> Third Quarter 1985: 2.

Note: Newsletters may not include volume and issue numbers, dates, or even pagination. In cases where a publication does employ the usual conventions needed for a citation, adapt what information you have to a form as close as possible to that of a conventional periodical citation, making sure that you provide enough information for readers to find the source.

Other Written Sources

The Published Proceedings of a Conference

[1]Conserving the Historical and Cultural Landscape, proc. of the Conference of the National Trust for Historic Preservation, Western Region, 2-3 May 1975, Denver (Washington: Preservation Press, 1975) 54.

A Government Publication

[2]United States, Senate, Committee on Appropriations, Subcommittee on Departments of Labor, Health and Human Services, Education, and Related Agencies, Impact of Proposed Budget on Health Research, 99th Cong., 2nd Sess. S. Hrg. 99-678 (Washington: GPO, 1986) 10-15.

[3]John S. Lewis, Final Report, National Aeronautics and Space Administration, Planetary Atmospheres Program on a Program of Research on the Origin and Evolution of Planetary Atmospheres (Washington: National Aeronautics and Space Administration, 1992) 4-8.

A Legal Reference

[4]Brown v. Board of Education of Topeka, 347 US 483 (US Supr. Ct., 1954).

A Pamphlet

[5]Jules Saltman, Teenagers and Alcohol: Patterns and Dangers (New York: Public Affairs Comm., 1983) 3.

A Letter Printed in a Volume of Collected Letters

[6]Edmund Wilson, "To William Faulkner," 25 Sept. 1956, Letters on Literature and Politics, 1912-1972, ed. Elena Wilson (New York: Farrar, 1977) 540.

An Unpublished Letter from a Collection

[7]Adlai E. Stevenson, letter to Ralph McGill, 11 May 1954, Ralph McGill Papers, Emory University, Atlanta.

A Personal Letter

   [8]Grace Paley, letter to the author, 30 July 1981.

A Dissertation, Unpublished

   [9]Donald Joseph Gray, "Victorian Verse Humor," diss., Ohio
State U, 1956, 29.

A Document from an Information Service

   [10]Paul V. Delker, <u>Adult Education--1980 and Beyond</u>,
Occasional Paper No. 59 (Columbus: Ohio State U, 1979) 19 (ERIC
ED 189 309).

A Manuscript or Typescript

   [11]Hart Crane, <u>The Bridge</u>, ms., Hart Crane Collection,
Columbia U, New York.

Nonprint and Electronic Sources

A Lecture or Publicly Delivered Paper

   [1]George Levine, "George Eliot's Scientific Ideal: The
Hypothesis of Reality," The English Institute, Cambridge, MA, 1
Sept. 1979.

A Radio or Television Program

   [2]<u>The Doomsayers</u>, prod. Brian Capener, PBS Special, 8 Sept.
1982.
   [3]"Maya Angelou," narr. Bill Moyers, <u>Creativity</u>, PBS
Special, WPBA, Atlanta, 8 Jan. 1982.

Note: When you want to refer to a particular individual (producer, director, narrator, or actor), cite that person's name first:

   [4]Bill Moyers, narr., "Maya Angelou," <u>Creativity</u>, PBS
Special, WPBA, Atlanta, 8 Jan. 1982.

A Performance of Music, Dance, or Drama

   [5]Giacomo Puccini, <u>La Bohème</u>, cond. James Levine, with
Teresa Stratas, Metropolitan Opera, Metropolitan Opera House,
New York, 13 Jan. 1982.

Note: When you want to refer to a particular individual (conductor, director, choreographer), cite that person's name first:

> [6]James Levine, cond., <u>La Bohème</u>, by Giacomo Puccini, with Teresa Stratas, Metropolitan Opera, Metropolitan Opera House, New York, 13 Jan. 1982.

A Film

> [7]<u>Vietnam: An American Journey</u>, Films Inc., 1979.
> [8]<u>Rebel Without a Cause</u>, dir. Nicholas Ray, with James Dean, Sal Mineo, and Natalie Wood, Warner Brothers, 1955.

Note: When you want to refer to a particular individual, cite that person's name first:

> [9]Nicholas Ray, dir., <u>Rebel Without a Cause</u>, with James Dean, Sal Mineo, and Natalie Wood, Warner Brothers, 1955.

A Face-to-Face Interview

> [10]Peter Vitousek, Professor of Biology, Stanford University, personal interview, 21 Jan. 1995.

A Telephone Interview

> [11]Coretta Scott King, telephone interview, 1 Nov. 1982.

A Work of Art

> [12]Paul Cézanne, <u>A Modern Olympia</u>, Louvre, Paris.

A Work of Art with a Cited Illustration

> [13]Pierre Bonnard, <u>The Open Window</u>, The Phillips Collection, illus. in <u>Master Paintings from the Phillips Collection</u>, by Eleanor Green et al. (New York: Penghurst, 1981) 71.

A Musical Composition

> [14]George Frideric Handel, <u>Messiah</u>, ed. Watkins Shaw, Novello Handel Edition (Sevenoaks, Eng.: Novello, n.d.).

Note: Use "n.d." (no date) for any undated material.

An Audio Recording

> [15]Hammer, <u>Too Legit to Quit</u>, Capitol Records, 1991.

An Audio Recording from Which a Particular Song Is Referred to or Quoted

> [16]The Beatles, "Revolution," <u>The Beatles/1967–1970</u>, Capitol, 1973.

An Audio Recording When the Work of the Performer or Performers Is Discussed

> [17]Marilyn Horne, <u>Orfeo ed Euridice</u>, by Christoph Willibald Gluck, cond. by George Solti, Orchestra and Chorus of the Royal Opera House, Covent Garden, London, 1970.

A Videotape or Videorecording

> [18]<u>The Nuclear Dilemma</u>, videorecording, BBC-TV, New York: Time Life Multimedia, 1974.

A Computer Program on Tape or Disk

> [19]Richard J. Ward, <u>The Executive Game</u>, computer software, Bowling Green State U, Hewlett-Packard, A880-2232A.

Note: Computer programs vary considerably. For this reason you will have to adapt a citation to the information you have. When possible, you should include an author, title, place of production, company or organization that produces the program, identifying number, and date.

A Source From a Database Published Periodically on CD-ROM

> [20]Judith Havermann, "White House Holding the Line on Medicaid," <u>Washington Post</u> 10 Dec. 1995: A4, <u>Newspaper Abstracts</u>, CD-ROM, UMI, 1995.

A Text Other Than a Periodical Published on CD-ROM

> [21]Mary Weston Fordham, "Atlanta Exposition Ode," <u>Database of African-American Poetry, 1760-1900</u>, CD-ROM (Alexandria: Chadwyck-Healy; Electronic Book Technologies, Inc., 1995).

A Publication on Diskette

> [22]Tau Rho Alpha, <u>The Northridge, California, Earthquake of January 1994</u>, diskette (Menlo Park, CA: US Dept. of the Interior, 1994).

A Publication on Magnetic Tape

  [23]United States, Internal Revenue Service, <u>Form 941,</u>
<u>Employers Quarterly Federal Tax Return</u>, magnetic tape
(Washington: Dept. of the Treasury, Internal Revenue Service),
1985.

Material from an Online Full Text Database

Sources with Print Versions

  Author. Title. Date of print publication. <u>Database</u>. Online.
Name of computer service. Date of access.
  [24]"Addiction Is a Family Problem, Too." <u>New York Times</u> 20
March 1988, late ed., sec. 1:50. <u>Nexis</u>. Online. 18 Dec. 1995.

Note: Cite sources without print versions as follows:

  Author. "Title of the Material Accessed." Date of the
material. <u>Title of the Database</u>. Online. Name of Computer
Service. Date of access.

*Material (Electronic Journals, Newsletters, and Conferences) from a Computer
Network*

  Author. "Title of the article or document." <u>Title of</u>
<u>Journal, Newsletter, or Conference</u>. Volume, issue, or other
numbers (year or date of publication): number of pages or
paragraphs or n. pag. Online. Name of computer network. Address
Date of Access.

Note: Because punctuation is an important part of Internet addresses,
do not add punctuation between an address and the date of retrieval.

  [25]Beerman, Dave. "Galapagos: An Adventure in Nature." <u>A</u>
<u>Sense of Place</u> 5.1 (1994): 7 pars. Online. Retrieved Dartmouth
Home Page. World Wide Web. http://www.dartmouth.edu/ (8 Jan.
1996).

An Electronic Personal Communication (E-Mail)

  Author of the letter. "Title" or description of the letter.
Date.
  [26]Cattier, Alan. "The World Wide Web." E-mail to Melissa
Walker. 4 Dec. 1995.

Material from an Electronic Text Retrieved from the Internet

> Author. <u>Title of text</u>. Place of publication: publisher, date of publication. Online. Place where the text is held. Name of computer network. Date of access.
> [27]Twain, Mark. <u>Adventures of Huckleberry Finn</u>. New York: Harper & Bros., 1886. Online. Literature and Publications Gopher. Internet. 4 Jan. 1996.
> [28]Swift, Jonathan. <u>An Argument Against the Abolishing of Christianity</u>. Online. English and Literature Gopher. U of Pennsylvania Literature and Publications Gopher. Internet. 4 Jan. 1996.
> [29]Clinton, William Jefferson. <u>Inaugural Presidential Address</u>. 20 Jan. 1993. Online. Literature and Publications Gopher. Internet. 14 Dec. 1995.

Note: Include information about the printed source when it is provided.

Mailing List (Newsgroup or Listserve)

> [30]Sierra Club. "Reach Out for Earth Day!" Online. Retrieved e-mail: Sf.moderator@sfsierra.sierra (1 April 1996).

FTP Sites

> [31]Newscorp Project. "Newscorp FTP file on Curtis B. Dall." ftp://ftp.almanac.bc.ca/pub/fascism/dossier/dall (4 January 1996).

Telnet Sites

> [32]University of North Carolina. <u>Grants and Funding Index</u>. Internet. telnet://info.acs.unc.edu (Retrieved April 1996).

USENET Newsgroup

> [33]Litt. J. "Indian Wars." Discussion. Internet. Retrieved e-mail: USENET Newsgroup: alt.revisionism (11 April 1996).

World Wide Web Site

> [34]Rainforest Action Network. "Global Rates of Destruction." http://www.ran.org/info_center/rates.html (Retrieved 12 April 1996).

Subsequent Citations in Notes

If you are using documentary notes—as in the sample paper in this appendix—you should fully identify each source in the first citation, including, when appropriate, author, title, place of publication, publisher, date, and page. For each note after the first, indicate the source as briefly as possible and give the page for that reference. Follow these guidelines for references to a source after the first full citation note:

When Only One Work by an Author Is Listed, Cite the Author's Last Name and the Page Number

> [1]Hareven 307.

When There Is More Than One Work by an Author, Use the Author's Last Name, a Shortened Title, and the Page

> [2]Lash, <u>Love</u> 213.
> [3]Lash, <u>E&F</u> 201.

For Citations Without an Author, Use an Abbreviated Title and the Page

> [4]"Reflections" 52.

Selected Pages from a Sample Paper with Endnotes

The paper that Michael Gold turned in to his professor (see p. 236) was documented with the MLA style of parenthetical references in the text and a bibliography, or "Works Cited" list, at the end. Some teachers ask students to use endnotes (or footnotes) while others may require both notes and a bibliography. What follows are the last two pages of Michael's paper as they would look if the paper were documented with endnotes—as well as complete endnotes for the paper.

would insist today that James Dean lives, <u>Rebel
Without a Cause</u> is still alive in the minds of
people who study the history of film. In recent
years, scholars have tried to judge the film as a
whole, rather than as a showcase for the magic
that Dean created. They are studying its values,
its art, and its place in American film history.
Peter Biskind, writing in <u>Film Quarterly</u>, sees
<u>Rebel</u> as a reflection of the conservative values
of mid-fifties America. He argues that the young
characters condemn their parents' weaknesses, but
that in the end the film affirms traditional
family values and remains "a profoundly
conservative film."[30] David Cook, on the other
hand, in his <u>History of Narrative Film</u>, sees the
film as "a definitive statement of the psychic
and emotional ills that beset America during the
period."[31] Douglas McVay considers <u>Rebel</u> to be
Nicholas Ray's masterpiece and one of the four
best films of the fifties.[32] David Thomson, who
thinks of <u>Rebel</u> as the work of a director who was
both a serious social critic and a "great
romantic" producing great art,[33] warns of the
difficulty of ever recreating that initial
response:

> So <u>Rebel</u> is vibrant with yearning
> aspirations, and Ray's beautiful and
> brave venturing with space, decor, and

Gold 11

faces lost in a night wilderness of
screen. We can never regain the view we
had of the film in 1955, when its rueful
passion swept so many of us away.[34]

Even though almost thirty years have passed
since audiences first settled down to watch Rebel
Without a Cause, evaluating its place both in
film history and in American society is still not
easy. A profoundly conservative film, a tragedy
in the classical sense, a high romance, or
scathing social comment--which is the appropriate
category for this still controversial film? When
we consider the many different people who
contributed to its creation, we may conclude that
it is all of these. It is certainly not
surprising to discover that the film that has
what Kreidl calls "a disparate smattering of
different vocabularies from different sources"
should evoke such varied responses.[35]

Rebel Without a Cause was generated through
conflict; it was finally realized when the
community of people who wanted to bring it about
discovered ways to compromise and cooperate. But
the conflict that created Rebel is still alive in
the minds of people who interpret it. A film more
than a book exists in the minds of its viewers.
Although some may have a videotape of the film,
which they can study at their leisure, most

Gold 12

people must rely on memory.[36] The community of
interpreters--those who remember, study, and talk
and write about <u>Rebel</u>--will probably always be
fraught with conflict both because memories are
highly personal and because the struggle between
generations that <u>Rebel</u> explores is constantly
being renewed.

Gold 13

Notes

[1]Jack Lusk, president, Swank Motion Pictures, letter to the author, 28 Feb. 1995.

[2]Ezra Goodman, "Delirium over Dead Star," <u>Life</u> 24 Sept. 1956: 75.

[3]Sam Astrachan, "The New Lost Generation," <u>New Republic</u> 4 Feb. 1957: 17–18.

[4]Herbert Mitgang, "The Strange James Dean Death Cult," <u>Films and Filming</u> 23.2 (1979): 114.

[5]Goodman 78.

[6]"Fan," "Talk of the Town," <u>New Yorker</u> 2 Aug. 1969: 22.

[7]Lusk.

[8]Mayberry, George, "Alternatives to the Novel," <u>New Republic</u> 24 July 1944: 108.

[9]Edwin J. Lukas, rev. of <u>Rebel Without a Cause . . . The Hypnoanalysis of a Criminal Psychopath</u>, by Robert M. Lindner, <u>The Annals of the American Academy of Political and Social Science</u> 236 (1944): 216.

[10]John Francis Kreidl, <u>Nicholas Ray</u>, Twayne's Theatrical Arts Ser. (Boston: Twayne, 1981) 91.

[11]Nicholas Ray, "Story into Script," <u>Sight and Sound</u> 26 (1956): 70.

[12]Kreidl 94.

[13]Ray 71–72.

[14]David Dalton, <u>James Dean: The Mutant King</u> (San Francisco: Straight Arrow, 1974) 225.

Gold 14

[15]Ray 73.

[16]Ray 73.

[17]Kreidl 93.

[18]Kreidl 86.

[19]Dalton 236.

[20]Dalton 232.

[21]Dalton 236, 253.

[22]Penelope Houston and John Gillett, "Conversations with Nicholas Ray and Joseph Losey," <u>Sight and Sound</u> 3 (1961): 184.

[23]Kreidl 208.

[24]Dalton 230.

[25]David Thomson, "Rebel Without a Cause," <u>Take One</u> Mar. 1979: 15.

[26]Kreidl 77.

[27]Ray 74.

[28]Kreidl 82.

[29]Dalton 227.

[30]Peter Biskind, "Rebel Without a Cause: Nicholas Ray in the Fifties," <u>Film Quarterly</u> 28.5 (1974): 37.

[31]David A. Cook, <u>A History of Narrative Film</u>, 2nd ed. (New York: Norton, 1991) 500.

[32]Douglas McVay, "Rebel Without a Cause," <u>Films and Filming</u> 23.2 (1979): 24.

[33]Thomson 15.

[34]Thomson 16.

[35]Kreidl 86.

Gold 15

[36]The availability of videotape makes it
possible to study films the way scholars study
written works of literature. Future responses to
<u>Rebel</u> may be based more on careful critical
analysis than on emotional response.

Appendix B

AN ANNOTATED LIST OF SELECTED REFERENCE WORKS

The following list of reference works represents only a small percentage of books available in the reference sections of even small libraries. By consulting this list, however, you should get a good idea about where to start researching almost any topic. If you find one reference work in a discipline, others will be shelved nearby.

It will be helpful if you understand the specialized vocabulary used to describe reference books. The word **bibliography** refers to lists of books or other material about a subject. There are very broad bibliographies that cover a whole field of studies (the humanities, for example), more limited ones that cover a discipline (psychology), and ones that list material on a very specific topic (the novels of William Faulkner). **Abstracts** are brief summaries of books, articles, research reports, dissertations, or speeches. **Indexes** are used to retrieve pieces of information from larger units—periodicals, parts of books, microform collections, or nonprint materials. Some indexes include abstracts of the entries. Most **dictionaries** provide information about words, proper names, and phrases. **Encyclopedias** provide more detailed information, background, and explanations of people, places, things, events, and ideas. There is, however, often some overlap, since dictionaries may give more than definitions, and some encyclopedias include definitions of many specialized words.

Before you use a reference work, you should study the format and instructions for users. If you read the introduction or other explanation about how to use a given work, you should soon be able to use it successfully. If you have trouble, however, consult the reference librarian for assistance.

The works listed below are cited as they are usually referred to by researchers and librarians: those usually identified by the name of the author are listed with the author's name first; titles are noted first for works primarily identified by title, as in the case of encyclopedias and most other multivolume works.

Many reference works are now produced both in book form and in computer databases (online), and the number of sources available online is increasing rapidly. If you are planning to do a computer search, you may want to ask your computer librarian whether those reference works appropriate to your topic are available online.

General Reference Works

Bibliographies

Bibliographic Index. New York: Wilson, 1938–.
   This extensive listing by subject includes bibliographies that appear in books, pamphlets, and periodical articles. It also lists bibliographies published as individual books and pamphlets.

Books in Print. New York: Bowker, 1948–.
   See page 57. Available in electronic format.

Cumulative Book Index. New York: Wilson, 1898–.
   Lists books published in English by author, subject, and title.

Katz, Bill, and Linda Sternberger Katz. *Magazines for Libraries.* 8th ed. New York: Bowker, 1995.
   Useful for students looking for information about the purpose, scope, and audience of a periodical. In some cases you can find out about a periodical's bias or value judgments.

Biographical Sources

Contemporary Authors. Detroit: Gale, 1962–.
   An up-to-date source of information on living authors of fiction and nonfiction in many fields. A good place to look for material on authors who are not well known.

Current Biography. New York: Wilson, 1940–.
   Attempting to cover all important living people in all fields, this is a good source of information for popular figures such as entertainers.

Dictionary of American Biography (DAB). 21 vols. New York: Scribner's, 1927, with supplements.

Covers only people not living and provides authoritative signed articles on important Americans. Also cites further sources of information.

Dictionary of American Negro Biography. Ed. Rayford W. Logan and Michael R. Winston. New York: Norton, 1982.
Spanning some three centuries, this is an invaluable source of information about more than seven hundred black Americans in all fields. Covers only those who died before 1970.

Dictionary of Canadian Biography. Toronto: U of Toronto P, 1966, with supplements.
Includes native Canadians as well as people from other countries who have contributed to Canadian life. As with DAB and DNB, no living people are included.

Dictionary of National Biography (DNB). 22 vols. London: Oxford UP, 1908–1909, with supplements.
Provides substantial biographical material for notable individuals no longer living. Covers Great Britain and colonial countries.

The McGraw-Hill Encyclopedia of World Biography. New York: McGraw, 1973.
Includes information on the living and the dead. A good place to go for biographies of women and members of minority groups less represented in more traditional sources.

Who's Who. New York: St. Martin's, 1849–.
Begun in 1849 as a list of titled British aristocracy and still primarily a British source, since 1897 these annual volumes have provided biographical information and current addresses (and for authors, a list of works) for prominent people in many fields. A reliable source for information about the living. *Who Was Who* is a compilation of biographies of people no longer living selected from *Who's Who* 1897–1970.

Who's Who in America. Chicago: Marquis, 1899–.
Up-to-date biographical information about living Americans. The standards for selection are high, as people must be well-known for significant and reputable achievements. *Who Was Who in America* is a selection from previous volumes of people now deceased. *Note:* There are many specialized biographical sources that include *Who's Who* as part of their title. Some are published by Marquis Press of Chicago, and some are from other publishing houses. You may find one of these helpful when more general biographical sources fail. Available online as *Marquis Who's Who.*

Dictionaries

American Heritage Dictionary of the English Language. 2nd college ed. Boston: Houghton, 1982.
  A good desk dictionary that includes new words used in business, science, and technology. It also contains valuable material on the history of the English language as well as guides to punctuation, grammar, and usage.

Oxford English Dictionary (OED). 20 vols. 2nd ed. London: Oxford UP, 1989.
  Traces the historical development of English words. Dated quotations listed in chronological order illustrate the ways each word has been used, detailing how its meaning has changed. This is a fascinating work and an invaluable resource for finding out much of what is known about the history of words. Available in electronic format.

Random House Dictionary of the English Language. 2nd ed. New York: Random, 1987.
  This unabridged dictionary is comprehensive, up-to-date, and fun to use.

Webster's New Collegiate Dictionary. 10th ed. Springfield: Merriam, 1985.
  An authoritative desk dictionary for help in understanding the English language as it is actually spoken and written today. It includes both specialized terminology and new words.

Webster's Third New International Dictionary of the English Language. Springfield: Merriam, 1981.
  An unabridged dictionary, this work gives brief definitions of words from both standard and spoken English. There are also quotations from contemporary sources.

Encyclopedias

Academic American Encyclopedia, Collier's Encyclopedia, Encyclopaedia Britannica, the *Encyclopedia Americana,* and the *New Columbia Encyclopedia* are discussed on pages 33–36.

Random House Encyclopedia. New York: Random, 1990.
  A good, easy-to-use, readable reference work for a wide range of general topics. Comparable to the *New Columbia Encyclopedia.*

Geographical Sources

Columbia Lippincott Gazetteer of the World. Ed. Leon E. Seltzer, with the co-operation of the American Geographical Society. New York: Columbia UP, 1952. Supplement 1961.

Lists places of the world alphabetically, including countries, parts of countries, cities, and towns, as well as major geographical features such as bodies of water, mountains, etc. It also gives information about industry, agriculture, size, and other details.

The Times Atlas of the World. 9th ed. New York: Times Books, 1992.
Detailed maps and listings of most of the places of the world. Each item listed is coded so that you can easily find it on a map.

The Times Atlas of the World. Multivolume, Comprehensive (9th) ed. London: The Times, 1994.
These outstanding volumes are known for the beauty and accuracy of their maps. Some of the material could already be out-of-date, and you might want to supplement it with more recent atlases. Concise ed., 1995.

The Times Index-Gazetteer of the World. London: The Times, 1965.
Lists almost three times as many communities and geographical features as *Columbia Lippincott.* It provides latitude and longitude along with map locations, but it does not include descriptions.

Webster's New Geographical Dictionary. Springfield: Merriam, 1988.
Provides brief, basic information such as location, size, population, history, and economy for many places. Not as extensive as *Columbia Lippincott,* but more up-to-date.

Indexes

Biography Index. New York: Wilson, 1946–.
You will often save time searching for biographical material by beginning with this index, as it will lead you to particular volumes or editions of reference books as well as to book-length biographies and biographical information in periodicals. It also contains a listing by profession or occupation of all the people included, so that a student looking for names of important people in various fields—animal trainers, criminologists, hermits, midwives, pacifists—can easily find them.

Biography and Genealogy Master Index. Ed. Miranda C. Herbert and Barbara McNeil. Detroit: Gale, 1980–.
A consolidated index to more than 450,000 biographical sketches in over 80 dictionaries of biography. Does not cover book-length biographies or biographical material in periodicals. A good place to go when you want basic information about people's lives: birth date, dates of

major accomplishments, or educational background. Available in electronic format.

Book Review Digest. New York: Wilson, 1906–.

Cites selected reviews of works of literature and nonfiction books in all fields. The citations are alphabetized by the author of the book reviewed, and each includes a brief description of the book, quotations from selected reviews, and references to other reviews.

Book Review Index. Detroit: Gale, 1965–.

Covers more than three times as many periodicals as *Book Review Digest,* but does not provide excerpts or summaries. Publication was suspended from 1969 to 1977. Available in electronic format.

Essay and General Literature Index. New York: Wilson, 1900–.

Published three times a year, this index emphasizes material in the humanities and social sciences. Indexed by author, subject, and some titles, this work will lead you to individual essays and portions of books on topics that you would not be able to find in card catalogs or standard periodical indexes. For example, a general work on twentieth-century British novelists may have an important chapter on D. H. Lawrence; such a chapter would be indicated here, but not in a card catalog.

InfoTrac. Foster City, CA: Information Access Co., 1986.

Provides access to several indexes to newspapers, general periodicals, and some journals. *Infotrac* is useful for researching current topics as most of the databases go back only a few years.

Monthly Catalog of United States Government Publications. Washington: GPO, 1895–.

The most comprehensive index to government-generated materials. Indexed by author, subject, key words, title, and other categories. Before you use this index, find out—ask a librarian—if there are more specialized indexes to government publications treating your subject. Available in electronic format.

The New York Times Index. New York: The New York Times, 1913–.

See page 41. Volumes covering the years from 1851 through 1912 have been published in ten volumes as *The New York Times Index, Prior Series.*

Periodical Abstracts. Ann Arbor: UMI, 1992.

An index to article abstracts from over 1,600 periodicals, including the most recent six months of the *New York Times* and the *Wall Street Jour-*

nal. Five large subject areas are included: social sciences, humanities, business, general science, and general interest. The index is updated monthly and is also available in electronic format.

Personal Name Index to the New York Times Index. 22 vols. Succasunna: Roxbury, 1976–1983.
  Consolidated index to name entries appearing in *The New York Times Index* from 1851 to 1974. An excellent index for finding articles on individual people. Includes obituaries.

Readers' Guide to Periodical Literature. New York: Wilson, 1900–.
  See pages 39–40. Also available in electronic format.

Yearbooks

Facts on File: A Weekly World News Digest. New York: Facts on File, 30 October 1940–.
  A good source for a brief overview of events and information reported in newspapers. You could start here for the basic facts about an international crisis, the highlights of sports events, or a list of the bestsellers. The cumulative five-year index can be very useful for identifying the dates when long-term news events were covered. Available online.

Whitaker's Almanac. London: Whitaker, 1868–.
  Contains valuable statistical information on government, finance, population, commerce, and general statistics of countries all over the world, with special emphasis on the British Commonwealth. A good place to go if you want information on a wide range of topics from the activities of the royal family to the winners of the London Film Festival.

The World Almanac and Book of Facts. New York: Newspaper Enterprise, 1868–.
  A good source for factual material in many fields. Valuable both for current and for historical topics.

Humanities

General

Directory of American Scholars. 8th ed. New York: Bowker, 1982.
  An excellent source for information about American scholars in the hu-

manities who are currently active in teaching, research, and publishing. The directory is arranged in four subject volumes—History (I), English, Speech, and Drama (II), Foreign Languages, Linguistics, and Philology (III), and Philosophy, Religion, and Law (IV). Turn here to find out about the education and professional history of important figures in these fields.

Humanities Index. New York: Wilson, 1974–. (Formerly *International Index,* 1907–65; *Social Sciences and Humanities Index,* 1965–74.)
Indexes articles in periodicals by author and subject in the following fields: archeological and classical studies, area studies, folklore, history, language and literature, literary and political criticism, performing arts, philosophy, and religion and theology. A separate book-review section is organized by author of the book reviewed. Available in electronic format.

Art

Art Index. New York: Wilson, 1929–.
An excellent index to periodicals that publish articles on archeology, architecture, art history, fine arts, crafts, and related fields. There are subject and author entries, and there is a separate section of book reviews alphabetized by the author reviewed. Available in electronic format.

McGraw-Hill Dictionary of Art. 5 vols. London: McGraw, 1969.
An encyclopedia despite its title, this is a useful source for basic information about artistic movements, schools of art, periods, and individual artists. The articles are signed and include bibliographies.

Film

Film Literature Index. Albany: Filmdex, 1973–.
Indexes selected articles about films in some three hundred various periodicals, not all chiefly concerned with film. There is also an index of reviews of books about films.

Halliwell's Filmgoer and Video Companion. 11th ed. By Leslie Halliwell. New York: Harper Perennial, 1995.
Emphasis is on details about actors and movies rather than serious critical evaluations. Intended for the general reader rather than the student, this book is mainly useful for quickly finding the date, director, and actors of a given film or for identifying the names of films in which

particular actors have played. The index is invaluable for identifying even the most obscure person associated with a film.

International Index to Film Periodicals. New York: Bowker, 1972–.
Indexes some sixty periodicals devoted exclusively to film. The best index for serious studies of films.

The New York Times Film Reviews, 1913–1968. 5 vols. New York: The New York Times and Arno, 1970. (Subsequent volumes update the collection.)
Reproduces film reviews in chronological order exactly as they first appeared in the *Times,* including photographs. These volumes provide critical discussion of thousands of movies, and they also serve as a fascinating history of film.

History

America: History and Life. Santa Barbara: Clio, 1964–.
Cites articles in over two thousand periodicals. Volumes published from 1974 on include a brief abstract of each article. As with other complex indexes, you should study the format before you begin to use it, but you may find this one more cumbersome than others. Available in electronic format.

An Encyclopedia of World History. Ed. William L. Langer. Boston: Houghton, 1972.
A chronological listing of world events from the time of the first historical records through 1970. The *New Illustrated Encyclopedia of World History* is the same work except for the correction of a few errors and the addition of illustrations.

Harvard Guide to American History. 2 vols. Ed. Frank Freidel. Cambridge: Harvard UP, 1974.
An invaluable bibliography covering all periods of American history. The first volume also includes an introduction to the methods and materials of historical research.

Historical Abstracts. Santa Barbara: Clio, 1955–. Brief summaries of periodical essays on the history of the world from 1450 to the present; 1955–72 cover 1775 to present; 1973 on covers 1450 to present. After 1964 *Historical Abstracts* excluded the history of the United States and Canada, which has since been treated in the companion, *America: History and Life.* Available in electronic format.

Morris, Richard, et al. *Encyclopedia of American History.* New York: Harper, 1982.

This valuable single-volume work is divided into three parts: a narrative of events from the founding of the colonies through the 1970s, a section treating various topics in American history, and an alphabetical listing of brief biographies of five hundred notable Americans in several different fields. The second section is useful for students who want a chronological overview of a broad subject such as American music or developments in medicine.

New Cambridge Modern History. 14 vols. Cambridge: Cambridge UP, 1957–.
Authoritative discussion of world history from the Renaissance through the mid-twentieth century. The first twelve volumes are arranged chronologically, with chapters—each written by a renowned authority—focusing on nations and geographical regions and with subheadings treating political, religious, economic, and cultural events. Volume 13 consists of twelve essays—each written by an expert—on broad subjects such as industry, revolution, or warfare, providing a good historical overview. Volume 14 is an historical atlas.

Shepherd, William. *Historical Atlas.* New York: Barnes, 1967.
Provides maps for world history from 1450 B.C. to the early 1960s. A useful supplement to the study of many historical topics such as the territorial expansion of the Roman Empire, the countries that remained neutral during World War II, or the original members of the United Nations.

Literature

Altick, Richard, and Andrew Wright. *Selective Bibliography for the Study of English and American Literature.* 6th ed. New York: Macmillan, 1979.
A highly selective, up-to-date list of the best materials available to students of English and American literature. Students doing research on almost any topic in these fields will find valuable help here. Many of the 636 items are books in related fields—philosophy, history, religion—that are important to the study of literature.

Articles on American Literature, 1900–1950. Comp. by Lewis Leary. Durham: Duke UP, 1954. (Separate volumes for 1950–67 and 1968–75.)
These three volumes include an extensive—though admittedly incomplete—listing of articles on major and minor American authors.

Cambridge Bibliography of English Literature. 5 vols. Ed. F. W. Bateson. Cambridge: Cambridge UP, 1940–57.
Covers significant literary works from the Old English through the modern periods. Arranged both by genre (poetry, drama, novel) and chronology. Cites books and articles that treat each work listed.

Kolb, Harold. *A Field Guide to the Study of American Literature.* Charlottesville: U of Virginia P, 1976.

A useful introduction to selected works on American literature. The annotations indicate the content and value of each citation. This is a good book to consult if you want to do research on some aspect of American literature or culture.

Literary History of the United States. 2 vols. Ed. Robert E. Spiller et al. New York: Macmillan, 1972 and 1974.

Volume 1 is a comprehensive history of American literature presented chronologically. Separate essays feature major writers, individual genres (poetry, fiction, drama, folklore, etc.), and various literary phenomena and types. Also includes a selected list of books. Volume 2 is a cumulative bibliography of books and articles organized by type, period, topic, and author.

The MLA International Bibliography of Books and Articles on the Modern Languages and Literatures. (Formerly *American Bibliography,* 1921–55, *Annual Bibliography,* 1956–62.) New York: MLA, 1963–.

Divided by national literatures and subdivided by literary periods, this index is comprehensive and thorough. Since the index has gradually expanded to include more periodicals, it is important that you study the table of contents and the format of each volume that you use. An indispensable index for topics that focus on a given author. Available in electronic format.

The New Cambridge Bibliography of English Literature. 5 vols. Ed. George Watson. Cambridge: Cambridge UP, 1969–77.

An updated version of the original *Cambridge Bibliography.* Along with the original, this work provides a comprehensive overview of English literature and indicates the scope of materials available on each literary figure.

Oxford History of English Literature. 12 vols. Ed. F. P. Wilson and Bonamy Dobrée. Oxford: Oxford UP, 1945–.

A continuous history of English literature from the earliest times to the modern period, aimed at both the scholar and the general reader. Includes treatment of other fields—the arts, philosophy, science—where they relate to literature. Bibliographies accompany each volume.

Patterson, Margaret. *Literary Research Guide.* 2nd ed. New York: MLA, 1983.

A very helpful guide for all areas.

Year's Work in English Studies. London: Murray, 1919/20–.

Articles and books on a selective survey of English literature. There is a brief description and usually a critical evaluation of each work cited. A good source to use to learn what kind of studies were published on authors during specific years. If you are studying an author's changing reputation, for example, you will find a record of that change here. Each volume published since 1954 contains a chapter on American literature.

Music

New Harvard Dictionary of Music. Rev. ed. By Willi Apel and Don Michael Randel. Cambridge: Harvard UP, 1986.
A storehouse of valuable information on all aspects of music, this is a classic work of music literature. Here you can learn about instruments, composers, types of music, and specific compositions, as well as definitions of musical terms. Many items are placed historically. You will find, for example, a brief history of the cello and the guitar.

Music Index. Detroit: Information Coordinators, 1949–.
Indexes periodicals that specialize in music and articles on musical topics published in more general publications. There are citations to articles on all kinds of music, including popular, jazz, opera, dance, and many others.

The New College Encyclopedia of Music. By J. A. Westrup and F. Ll. Harrison, rev. by Conrad Wilson. New York: Norton, 1976.
This useful work contains six thousand entries on musical terms, composers, compositions, instruments, and so on. Beginning students should find the many brief bibliographies particularly helpful.

The New Grove Dictionary of Music and Musicians. 20 vols. Ed. Stanley Sadie. London: Macmillan, 1980; Reprinted with minor corrections, 1995.
An excellent source of authoritative information on all aspects of music. There are substantial signed articles on topics ranging from music in ancient times to the contemporary world. Most include bibliographies.

Philosophy and Religion

A Dictionary of Comparative Religion. Ed. S. G. F. Brandon. New York: Scribner's, 1970.
This one-volume work includes short informational entries and twenty-eight longer, more comprehensive articles on world religions. Good bibliographies and a helpful system of cross-references make this an ex-

cellent place to begin research, especially for quick identification of key figures and concepts.

Encyclopedia of Bioethics. Rev. ed. vols. Ed. Warren T. Reich. 1995. New York: Macmillan, 1995.
A comprehensive, detailed, and easy-to-use encyclopedia that covers all aspects of a new and exciting field. Written by a large team of experts from many traditions, this work is useful both for an overview and for detailed investigation. Includes bibliographies and an index.

Encyclopedia of Philosophy. 8 vols. Ed. Paul Edwards. New York: Macmillan, 1967. (Reprinted 8 vols. in 4 vols., New York: Macmillan, 1972.)
This is the most authoritative and comprehensive reference work on philosophy available in English. Each signed article has its own bibliography. There are articles on concepts and systems in philosophy, historical essays, and over nine hundred articles on individual thinkers.

Encyclopedic Dictionary of Religion. 3 vols. Ed. Paul Kevin Meagher et al. Washington: Corpus, 1979.
This is the most up-to-date and comprehensive work of its kind available in English. Signed entries by experts in the field cover a wide range of facts, events, persons, issues, and concepts. Focuses on Western religions, but includes Eastern religions as well. Especially good on important figures in religious thought and history. Includes a bibliography and cross references for each entry.

The Philosopher's Guide to Sources, Research Tools, Professional Life, and Related Fields. Ed. Richard T. DeGeorge. Lawrence: Regents Press of Kansas, 1980. (Replaces DeGeorge's *Guide to Philosophical Bibliography and Research.*)
This well-organized companion to philosophical research should also be helpful to students in religion, social science, the fine arts, literature, and other allied fields. In twenty-two chapters, it lists thousands of guides, handbooks, indexes, overviews, summaries, biographies, and so on. Turn here for a guide to the standard works in philosophical research.

The Philosopher's Index. Bowling Green: Philosophy Documentation Center, Bowling Green State U, 1967–.
This comprehensive index to periodicals and books in philosophy and closely related fields consists of a subject index, an author index with abstracts of articles and books, and a book-review index. If you are looking for a work in philosophy, it's here. Available in electronic format.

A Reader's Guide to the Great Religions. Ed. Charles J. Adams. New York: Free Press, 1977.

A rich and authoritative guide to the best materials on the history and traditions of the world's major religions. Each chapter, written by an expert, provides a good introduction to a particular religion and discusses the usefulness and value of the works cited.

Religion Index I: Periodicals. Ed. G. Fay Dickerson. Chicago: American Theological Library Association, 1977–. (Formerly *Index to Religious Periodical Literature,* 1949–77.)

This major and indispensable index for religious periodicals provides a cumulative guide to over three hundred major journals. It contains a subject index with extensive cross-references and an author index with abstracts of most articles. Thus it not only locates material, but also saves time in that it allows you to judge whether an article seems appropriate for a given research topic. (*Religion Index II* covers multivolume works not generally useful to the beginning student.)

Social Sciences

General

American Men and Women of Science: Social and Behavioral Sciences. 13th ed. Ed. Jaques Cattell Press. New York: Bowker, 1978.

Excellent source for information about people currently active in the social sciences.

Encyclopaedia of the Social Sciences. 15 vols. Ed. Edwin R. A. Seligman. New York: Macmillan, 1930–35.

An invaluable work, particularly useful for learning how the social sciences were understood in the 1930s. Want to know what the established view of Freud was in the 1930s? It is here. About half the articles are biographical. Provides excellent historical information on many topics such as abortion, adoption, segregation, and unemployment.

International Encyclopedia of the Social Sciences. 19 vols. Ed. David L. Sills. New York: Macmillan, 1991.

Intended to complement rather than replace the *Encyclopaedia of the Social Sciences.* The articles, which are signed and include bibliographies, are mainly analytical and comparative, rather than historical and descriptive.

PAIS International in Print. New York: Public Affairs Information Service, 1991–. (Formerly *Public Affairs Information Service Bulletin* [PAIS]. New York: Public Affairs Information Service, 1915–1990.)

An outstanding general index, *PAIS* covers all aspects of public affairs: copyright laws, interest rates, taxes, international affairs, education, social movements, political issues, and much more. Excellent for finding information and sources on current events and issues of current concern such as nuclear nonproliferation. Available in electronic format as PAIS International.

Social Sciences Index. New York: Wilson, 1974–. (Formerly *International Index,* 1907–65; *Social Sciences and Humanities Index,* 1965–74.)

Indexes articles and periodicals by author and subject for all the social sciences. A separate book-review section is organized by author of the book reviewed.

Webb, William, and Carl M. White. *Sources and Information in the Social Sciences.* 3rd ed. Chicago: American Library Association, 1985.

An excellent introduction to reference materials for all areas of social science, including economics, sociology, anthropology, psychology, and political science. Disciplines that overlap with these subjects—education, business administration, geography, and history—are also included. Much more than a descriptive list of sources, each chapter serves as an introduction to the discipline. Any student would do well to browse through this valuable book both to learn how information in the social sciences is organized and to discover reference tools for specific research topics.

Anthropology, Psychology, and Sociology

Frantz, Charles. *The Student Anthropologist's Handbook.* Cambridge: Schenkman, 1972.

An interesting overview of the discipline, including a discussion of the training required to become an anthropologist, the kinds of activities professional anthropologists engage in, and an introduction to research materials and institutions.

Kottak, Conrad Phillip. *Researching American Culture: A Guide for Student Anthropologists.* Ann Arbor: U of Michigan P, 1982.

This interesting work focuses on anthropological studies in the United States.

McInnis, Raymond G. *Research Guide for Psychology.* Westport: Greenwood, 1982.

A guide to some 1,200 information sources in psychology, including general works, handbooks, encyclopedias, etc.

Psychological Abstracts. Washington: American Psychological Association, 1927–.

Covering more than those subjects strictly considered part of psychology, this work provides brief summaries (abstracts) of articles from journals and chapters from books in all the social sciences. This important index is not as easy to use as the *Social Science Index,* but it is more specialized and provides more information about each reference. To find material in the volumes from 1973 to the present, consult the *Sources of Psychological Index Terms.* As with any reference work, you should study the introductory material (instructions for the user) of the volume actually used since the format for citations may vary. Available in electronic format.

Sociological Abstracts. New York: Sociological Abstracts, 1953–.

Like *Psychological Abstracts,* this work is useful for many disciplines within the social sciences. To use it, however, you will find it necessary to study the table of contents and the indexing system. If you find a source cited in this or other abstract volumes, you can study the abstract to decide whether you want to look for the original. The latest studies on child care, alcohol abuse, and sexism are among the thousands of sociological topics indexed here on *Sociofile,* available in electronic format as *Sociofile.*

Business and Economics

Business Index. Menlo Park: Information Access, 1979–.

Available on microform, this index is especially useful for finding very current material on business topics in general magazines, business periodicals, and newspapers (including the *Wall Street Journal*). Since the listings are cumulative, you will be able to locate material on many business topics efficiently and easily. This index is constantly updated, and older material is dropped as new listings are added. Available in electronic format.

Business Periodicals Index. New York: Wilson, 1958–.

Indexes articles in the following fields: accounting, advertising, automation, banking, communications, economics, finance and investments, insurance, labor, management, marketing, taxes, etc. An overview of articles in the significant journals. Book reviews are in a separate section. Available in electronic format.

Daniels, Lorna M. *Business Information Sources.* 3rd ed. Berkeley: U of California P, 1993.

The best guide to sources in all aspects of business and economics. Any student interested in studying a topic related to these fields should consult this book first to learn about the available sources.

Encyclopedia of Management. 3rd ed. Ed. Carl Heyel. New York: Van Nostrand, 1982.
A very good encyclopedic dictionary on a variety of topics such as consumer protection, data communications, motivation, and trade shows. Substantial articles on these and many other topics include references that direct the reader to important texts and articles on the subject.

McGraw-Hill Dictionary of Modern Economics: A Handbook of Terms and Organizations. 3rd ed. New York: McGraw, 1983.
A very useful dictionary; each entry includes a definition as well as at least one other source that provides more information.

MIT Dictionary of Modern Economics. 4th ed. Cambridge: MIT Press, 1992. Students interested in economics will enjoy browsing through this valuable source of information.

Moody's Manuals. New York: Moody's Investors Service.
Moody's Manuals provide comprehensive financial information in seven annual publications, six devoted to U.S. companies, one to leading foreign companies. If you want financial information about a particular company, begin with *Moody's Complete Corporate Index,* which will lead you to the appropriate manual. Students doing substantial research on business topics should be familiar with all Moody's publications. *Moody's Corporate Profiles* is available online; it provides access to information in other Moody's publications.

Standard and Poor's Corporation Records. New York: Standard and Poor's. A widely used reference for information on more than 10,000 U.S. companies. Basic information on companies is revised regularly and latest developments are reported in daily updates. If you are looking for particular topics, begin with the topical index. Students doing substantial research on business topics should be familiar with all *Standard and Poor's* publications. *Standard and Poor's Corporation Records Online* provides access to current and historical business information.

Value Line Investment Survey. New York: A. Bernhard.
Provides objective, authoritative information on some 1,700 companies. Excellent source for investment information.

Education

Current Index to Journals in Education (CIJE). Phoenix: Oryx, 1969–.
An index to almost eight hundred educational and education-related
materials. The place to turn for a thorough review of the literature on
a topic. Produced by the Educational Resources Information Center
(ERIC), CIJE uses the same subject headings (descriptors) as *Resources in
Education,* described below. Available in electronic format as *ERIC.*

Education Index. New York: Wilson, 1929–.
Includes fewer periodicals than *CIJE,* but covers a much longer period
of time. You may prefer to use this more selective index, since you will
not find many of the periodicals indexed in *CIJE* in small or even
medium-sized libraries. Available in electronic format.

The International Encyclopedia of Education: Research and Studies. New York:
Pergamon, 1985 (Supplement, 1988).
Excellent up-to-date overview of scholarship on educational systems
throughout the world.

Resources in Education (RIE). [Known as *ERIC*] Washington: GPO, 1975.
Formerly *Research in Education,* 1966–74.
An index to many documents not published in journals. Contains an
order form for obtaining copies of documents. These documents are
stored on microform in many libraries. Copies can usually be made with
a microform reader-printer. Like *CIJE, RIE* is produced by the Educational Resources Information Center; this index and the collection of
documents it catalogs are often referred to by librarians and researchers
as *ERIC.* Available in electronic format as *ERIC.*

World of Learning. London: Europa, 1947–.
Gives basic information about a variety of educational institutions
throughout the world, including libraries, research institutes, colleges,
and universities, as well as learned societies and museums. This is a
good place to find the address, telephone number, and purpose of an
institution. You will also find general information on when and how
an institution was founded; the number of students; and for large or
prestigious schools, the names of chief officers.

Political Science and Government

The Almanac of American Politics. By Michael Barone and Grant Ujifusa.
Washington: Barone, 1972–.
The subtitle of this delightful book tells you what you will find in it: al-

most anything you ever wanted to know—and then some—about "The President, the Senators, the Representatives, the Governors: Their Records and Election Results, Their States and Districts."

Brock, Clifton. *The Literature of Political Science.* New York: Bowker, 1969. An introduction to library materials and research methods in political science. It includes descriptions of various indexes and abstracts to help you find material in periodicals. An excellent introduction to government publications and the many publications of public organizations.

Congressional Quarterly Almanac. Washington: Congressional Quarterly, 1945–. Summarizes congressional activity every year. Here you will find concise information about committee hearings, voting records, investigations, texts of presidential addresses, and lobbying efforts, as well as details of major legislations.

Congressional Quarterly's Guide to Congress. 4th ed. Eds. Robert A. Diamond and Patricia Ann O'Connor. Washington: Congressional Quarterly, 1991. Periodically revised, this comprehensive overview of the workings of Congress is placed in a large historical context; it explains the powers, procedures, and structures of Congress; and it discusses the relationship of Congress to the society at large.

Congressional Quarterly's Politics in America. Washington: Congressional Quarterly, 1989–. Similar to the *Almanac of American Politics,* this work provides information about Congressional Committees, election districts, and election manuals and handbooks.

Congressional Quarterly Weekly Report. Washington: Congressional Quarterly, 1943–. Gives a comprehensive summary of congressional activity for each week. If you are researching a specific legislative act—the Civil Rights Act of 1964, for instance—you may want to go to the *Weekly* for a summary of all the activities and debate leading to its passage.

Holler, Frederick L. *Information Sources of Political Science.* 4th ed. Santa Barbara: Clio, 1986. More up-to-date and comprehensive than *The Literature of Political Science* (see above), this work describes the important reference works in related fields such as psychology and philosophy. A pleasure to read, this guide will be very useful to students doing research on topics concerning the public aspects of social science.

The United States Government Manual. Washington: GPO, 1935–.
An up-to-date source of information on all aspects of the organization of the federal government. Published every year, it includes names, addresses, and telephone numbers of public officials in all branches of government; explanations of the function of all government departments; and basic information about domestic and international organizations that are allied to the United States. Want to know the names of the Supreme Court justices, how to obtain information from the Environmental Protection Agency, or how the Department of Health and Human Services is organized? To answer these and many other questions, check the *Government Manual.*

York, Henry E. *Political Science: A Guide to Reference and Information Sources.* Englewood: Libraries Unlimited, 1990.
This up-to-date research guide includes bibliographical references and indexes.

Natural and Applied Sciences

General

American Men and Women of Science: Physical and Biological Sciences. 7 vols. 17th ed. Ed. Jaques Cattell Press. New York: Bowker, 1989.
The best source for information about living scientists who are currently active. Available in electronic format.

Dictionary of Scientific Biography. 18 vols. New York: Scribner's, 1970–81 (Supplement, 1977; Index, 1981).
A valuable source for the history of science. The articles provide reliable information on the professional lives of thousands of scientists from classical antiquity to modern times. The twentieth-century figures have all been dead for some years, and all achieved considerable distinction.

General Science Index. New York: Wilson, 1978–.
This cumulative subject index to general science periodicals is commonly found in public libraries. It is a good source for beginning science students to use. Available in electronic format.

McGraw-Hill Encyclopedia of Science and Technology. 20 vols. 7th ed. New York: McGraw, 1992.
This high-quality, up-to-date work provides excellent background reading in almost all scientific and technological topics. It is appropriate for

the sophisticated student of science as well as for the beginning researcher who is investigating a scientific topic.

McGraw-Hill Yearbook of Science and Technology. New York: McGraw. Published annually.
Updates the latest edition of the *Encyclopedia.* A good source for a summary of scientific development in recent years.

Science Citation Index. Ed. Eugene Garfield. Philadelphia: Institute for Scientific Information, 1982.
An interdisciplinary index to scholarly journals in the sciences and to books since 1977. It links each publication listed with all others that cite it. Once you learn to use the *Science Citation Index,* you will find that it provides a relatively easy way to find the important information on a given topic. Available in electronic format as *Scisearch.*

Astronomy

The Cambridge Encyclopaedia of Astronomy. Ed. Simon Milton. Cambridge: Institute of Astronomy, 1977.
A well-illustrated, topically arranged survey of astronomy, this work provides an authoritative introduction to many aspects of the field.

Biology, Medicine, and Nursing

Biological Abstracts. Philadelphia: BioSciences Information Service of Biological Abstracts, 1926–.
The basic research tool for research in biology and biomedicine. Excellent abstracts give you a summary of each citation. Available in electronic format as *Biosis.*

Cumulative Index to Nursing and Allied Health Literature. Glendale: Glendale Adventist Medical Center, 1977–. (Formerly *Cumulative Index to Nursing Literature,* 1956–1976.) Available on CD-ROM as *CINAHL.* Organized by both subject and author, this comprehensive index will lead you to articles on all aspects of nursing and allied health sciences.

The Encyclopedia of the Biological Sciences. 2nd ed. Ed. Peter Gray. New York: Van Nostrand, 1970.
This single-volume work provides accurate information on biological topics for nonexperts.

Grzimek's Animal Life Encyclopedia. 13 vols. Ed. Bernhard Grzimek. New York: Van Nostrand, 1972–75.

This is an informative and fascinating reference work. Each volume treats its subject—fishes, birds, mammals, reptiles, and so on—with authority and style. Generous use of color plates and photographs enhances the readable text. International in scope, this is a good place to turn for an overview of the animal kingdom. Each volume has a good index and a list of suggested readings.

Index Medicus. U.S. Department of Health and Human Services. N.I.H. Publications. Washington: National Library of Medicine, 1960– (monthly). This is the authoritative index to periodical literature in medicine and related fields. Biological literature is well represented. Although many of the articles cited are technical and intended for experts, you may find this index helpful if you are researching general topics in medicine or biology. Available in electronic format as *Medline.*

Chemistry and Physics

The Condensed Chemical Dictionary. 10th ed. New York: Van Nostrand, 1981. In addition to providing definitions of chemical terms, this is a useful source for concise information about commercial and trade market products and for pharmaceuticals and drugs.

The Encyclopedia of Physics. Eds. Rita G. Lerner and George L. Trigg. Reading: Addison, 1981. This single-volume work is an authoritative source for background information and for an overview of the major principles and problems of physics. More than this, it contains speculative articles on controversial developments, written by experts engaged in current research. Extensive bibliographies and clear charts and diagrams make this a useful and usable source.

Handbook of Chemistry and Physics. 58th ed. Cleveland: Chemical Rubber, 1913–. This is the most useful single-volume reference work available to the undergraduate and graduate student in chemistry and physics. It is divided into six parts with a good index and constitutes, as its subtitle indicates, "A Ready Reference Book of Chemical and Physical Data." Turn here for the facts, and go to the sources listed above for the explanations.

Computer Science

Computer and Control Abstracts. Piscataway: Institute of Electric Engineers with The Institute of Electrical and Electronic Engineers, 1969–.

Part C of the three-part *Science Abstracts*. Published twice monthly, this excellent index provides sources for information on all aspects of computer science, including computer languages, equipment, software, hardware, new terminology, and latest developments in the field. Available in electronic format as *Inspec*.

The Directory of On-line Databases. Cuadra Associates, 1980–.
Updated quarterly, this excellent directory provides accurate, concise, and useful information about databases in all fields.

Gale Directory of Databases. 2 vols. Detroit: Gale Research, 1995.
Comprehensive coverage of the electronic database industry.

Information Industry Directory. 2 vols. 16th ed. Detroit: Gale Research, 1996.
International guide to organizations, systems, and services involved in the production and distribution of information in electronic form.

Engineering

Applied Science and Technology Index. Ed. Rose Manofsky. New York: Wilson, 1958–.
A multidisciplinary subject index covering a wide range of topics including several kinds of engineering, as well as the applied aspects of chemistry, geology, and physics. If you are researching general science topics, you will want to browse through this index to get an idea of the scope of its coverage.

Engineering Index. New York: Engineering Index, 1906–.
Worldwide coverage of the journal literature, publications of engineering societies and organizations, and selected government books. Available in electronic format as *Compendex*.

Environmental Science

Allaby, Michael. *Dictionary of the Environment.* 3rd ed. New York: New York UP, 1989.
Provides definitions of extensive list of terms related to environmental concerns. Here is a place to get brief definitions of chlorofluorocarbons, the greenhouse effect, or desertification.

Burke, John Gordon. *Guide to Ecology Information and Organizations.* New York: Wilson, 1976.
For research on environmental issues before 1976 this work is a useful source, but it would be out-of-date for recent topics.

Burton, John A. *The Atlas of Endangered Species.* New York: Macmillan, 1991.

An overview of selected species threatened by extinction. A good general discussion of factors that have caused the crisis. Excellent photographs and a good index.

Grzimek's Encyclopedia of Ecology. Ed. Bernhard Grzimek. New York: Van Nostrand, 1976.

A comprehensive approach to the study of ecology. Beautifully illustrated and a pleasure to read, this work is a valuable source of general and detailed information on ecological topics.

McGraw-Hill Encyclopedia of Environmental Science. 2nd ed. Ed. Sybil P. Parker. New York: McGraw, 1980.

Concerned with the complex interaction between living things and environmental phenomena, this specialized encyclopedia focuses on many aspects of the earth and the ways it has been used.

PERMISSIONS
ACKNOWLEDGMENTS

P. 185: "China's Baby Budget" by Jodi L. Jacobson, from *The Worldwatch Reader on Global Environmental Issues* by Lester Brown, et al. Copyright © 1991 by Worldwatch Institute. Reprinted by permission of W. W. Norton & Company, Inc.

P. 312: Table from Abbey et al. study. © 1990 by Baywood Publishing Co., Inc. Reprinted by permission of Susan Abbey, M.D.

INDEX